American Civil War
Biographies

10/01

American Civil War Biographies

Kevin Hillstrom
and
Laurie Collier
Hillstrom

Lawrence W. Baker, Editor

U·X·L®

AN IMPRINT OF THE GALE GROUP

DETROIT · SAN FRANCISCO · LONDON
BOSTON · WOODBRIDGE, CT

American Civil War: Biographies

Kevin Hillstrom and Laurie Collier Hillstrom

Staff

Lawrence W. Baker, *U•X•L Senior Editor*
Carol DeKane Nagel, *U•X•L Managing Editor*
Tom Romig, *U•X•L Publisher*

Rita Wimberley, *Senior Buyer*
Evi Seoud, *Assistant Production Manager*
Dorothy Maki, *Manufacturing Manager*
Mary Beth Trimper, *Production Director*

Michelle DiMercurio, *Art Director*
Cynthia Baldwin, *Product Design Manager*

Shalice Shah-Caldwell, *Permissions Specialist*
Pamela Reed, *Imaging Coordinator*
Leitha Etheridge-Sims, *Cataloger*
Robert Duncan, *Senior Imaging Specialist*
Michael Logusz, *Imaging Specialist*
Randy A. Bassett, *Image Database Supervisor*
Barbara J. Yarrow, *Imaging and Multimedia Content Manager*

Marco Di Vita, Graphix Group, *Typesetting*

Library of Congress Cataloging-in-Publication Data

Hillstrom, Kevin, 1963–
    American Civil War. Biographies / Kevin Hillstrom and Laurie Collier
Hillstrom ; Lawrence W. Baker, editor.
    p. cm.
    ISBN 0-7876-3820-X — ISBN 0-7876-3821-8 (v. 1) — ISBN 0-7876-3822-6 (v. 2)
        1. United States—History—Civil War, 1861–1865—Biography. 2. United
States—History—Civil War, 1861–1865—Biography—Miscellanea. I. Hillstrom,
Laurie Collier, 1965– II. Baker, Lawrence W. III. Title.

E467.H656 1999
973.7′092′2—dc21
[B]
                                                                    99-046920

Cover photographs of John Wilkes Booth and Jefferson Davis are reproduced courtesy of the National Archives and Records Administration; Sojourner Truth, courtesy of the Library of Congress; and Martin R. Delany, reproduced by permission of Archive Photos, Inc.

Printed in the United States of America

10 9 8 7 6 5 4 3

Contents

Advisory Board

S pecial thanks are due to U•X•L's Civil War Reference Library advisors for their invaluable comments and suggestions:

- Deborah Hammer, Former Librarian, Queens Borough Public Library, Jamaica, New York
- Ann Marie LaPrise, Librarian, Detroit Public Library, Elmwood Park Branch, Detroit, Michigan
- Susan Richards, Media Specialist, Northwest Junior High School, Coralville, Iowa

Reader's Guide

American Civil War: Biographies presents biographies of sixty men and women who participated in or were affected by the Civil War. These two volumes profile a diverse mix of personalities from both the North and the South, including military leaders, politicians, abolitionists, artists, spies, and escaped slaves. Detailed biographies of major Civil War figures (such as Abraham Lincoln, Jefferson Davis, Ulysses S. Grant, Frederick Douglass, Robert E. Lee, Stonewall Jackson) are included. But *American Civil War: Biographies* also provides biographical information on lesser-known but nonetheless important and fascinating men and women of that era. Examples include Thaddeus Lowe, the daring commander of the Union's manned balloon corps; Mathew Brady, the famed Civil War photographer; and Rose O'Neal Greenhow, a Confederate spy who drowned during an attempt to smuggle gold into the South in the hoops of her dress.

American Civil War: Biographies also features sidebars containing interesting facts, excerpts from diaries and speeches, and short biographies of people who are in some way connected with the leading figures of the era. Within each full-length biography, boldfaced cross-references direct readers to other individuals profiled in the two-volume set. Finally, each volume includes photographs and illustrations, an "American Civil War Timeline" that lists significant dates and events of the Civil War era, and a cumulative subject index.

American Civil War Reference Library

American Civil War: Biographies is only one component of a three-part American Civil War Reference Library. The other two titles in this multivolume set are:

- *American Civil War: Almanac:* This work presents a comprehensive overview of the Civil War. The volume's fourteen chapters cover all aspects of the conflict, from the prewar issues and events that divided the nation to the war itself—an epic struggle from 1861 to 1865 that changed the political and social landscape of America forever. The chapters are arranged chronologically and explore such topics as the events leading up to the war, slavery, Europe's view of the war, the secession of Southern states, various Civil War battles, and Reconstruction. Also included are two chapters that cover two unique groups during the Civil War: women and blacks. The *Almanac* also contains over ninety photographs and maps, "Words to Know" and "People to Know" sections, a timeline, and an index.

- *American Civil War: Primary Sources:* This title presents fourteen full or excerpted speeches and written works from the Civil War. The volume includes an excerpt from Harriet Beecher Stowe's *Uncle Tom's Cabin,* President Abraham Lincoln's Emancipation Proclamation and Gettysburg Address, and the letters between Union general William T. Sherman and Atlanta, Georgia, city leaders. Each entry includes an introduction, things to remember while reading the excerpt, information on what happened after the work was published or event took place, and other interesting facts. Photographs, source information, and an index supplement the work.

- A cumulative index of all three titles in the American Civil War Reference Library is also available.

Acknowledgments

The authors extend thanks to Larry Baker and Tom Romig at U•X•L for their assistance throughout the production of this series. Thanks, too, to Christine Alexanian for her quick and thorough copyediting and Amy Marcaccio Keyzer for lending her considerable editorial talents in the form of proofreading. The editor wishes to thank Marco Di Vita at Graphix Group for always working with common sense, flexibility, speed, and, above all, quality. Admiration, love, and a warm hug go to Beth Baker for her year of bravery. And, finally, a very special hello goes to Charlie and Dane, whose decision to move up their pub date made the Summer of '99 so very interesting.

Comments and suggestions

We welcome your comments on *American Civil War: Biographies* and suggestions for other topics in history to consider. Please write: Editors, *American Civil War: Biographies*, U•X•L, 27500 Drake Rd., Farmington Hills, Michigan 48331-3535; call toll-free: 800-877-4253; fax to 248-414-5043; or send e-mail via http://www.galegroup.com.

American Civil War Timeline

1775 Philadelphia Quakers organize America's first antislavery society.

1776–83 English colonies' War for Independence against Great Britain ends with the formation of the United States.

1788 The U.S. Constitution is ratified, providing legal protection to slaveowners.

1793 Eli Whitney invents the cotton gin, which will dramatically increase Southern cotton production.

1803 President Thomas Jefferson purchases the Louisiana Territory from France.

1775
"Yankee Doodle" is written.

1789
George Washington takes office as the first U.S. president.

1800
The Library of Congress is established.

| 1775 | 1789 | 1800 |

1816 The American Colonization Society is formed with the idea of settling free blacks back in Africa.

1820 Congress passes the Missouri Compromise, which maintains the balance between slave and free states in the Union.

1828 Congress passes the so-called "Tariff of Abominations" over the objections of Southern states.

1831 Slave Nat Turner leads a violent slave rebellion in Virginia.

1832–33 The "Nullification Crisis" in South Carolina ends after tariffs on foreign goods are lowered.

1833 The Female Anti-Slavery Society and the American Anti-Slavery Society are founded.

1837 Abolitionist Elijah P. Lovejoy is murdered by a proslavery mob in Illinois.

1838 **Frederick Douglass** escapes from slavery and joins the abolitionist movement.

1839 New York governor **William Henry Seward** refuses to return three escaped slaves to Virginia.

1839 Abolitionist **Theodore Dwight Weld** publishes *American Slavery as It Is.*

1841 **Horace Greeley** launches the *New York Tribune,* which becomes a leading abolitionist newspaper.

1845 Texas is annexed by the United States over the objections of Mexico, which regards it as part of its country.

1846 **Dred Scott** files his famous lawsuit in an effort to win his freedom.

1818
Congress adopts
a U.S. flag.

1825
The New York
Stock Exchange
opens.

1844
Samuel F. B. Morse
transmits the first
telegraph message.

1818   1825   1844

1848   The Mexican War ends with the United States acquiring five hundred thousand square miles of additional land in western North America.

1849   **Harriet Tubman** escapes from slavery.

1850   *The Narrative of **Sojourner Truth*** is published.

1850   **Harriet Tubman** makes the first of her nineteen trips to the South to lead slaves to freedom via the Underground Railroad.

1850   The Compromise of 1850, including the controversial Fugitive Slave Act, becomes law.

1852   **Harriet Beecher Stowe**'s novel *Uncle Tom's Cabin* is published, increasing support for the abolitionist movement in the North.

1854   The Kansas-Nebraska Act is passed, returning decisions about allowing slavery back to individual states.

1856   South Carolina congressman Preston Brooks attacks Massachusetts senator **Charles Sumner** in the Senate chambers over an abolitionist speech.

1856   **John Brown** and his followers attack and kill five proslavery men in Kansas.

1857   The U.S. Supreme Court issues its famous ***Dred Scott*** decision, which increases Northern fears about the spread of slavery.

1858   New York senator **William Henry Seward** warns of an approaching "irrepressible conflict" between the South and the North.

1858   Illinois senate candidates **Abraham Lincoln** and Stephen Douglas meet in their famous debates over slavery and its future place in America.

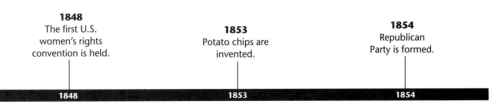

1848
The first U.S. women's rights convention is held.

1853
Potato chips are invented.

1854
Republican Party is formed.

1848   1853   1854

1859 Abolitionist **John Brown** leads a raid on Harpers Ferry, Virginia, in an unsuccessful effort to start a slave revolt across the South.

5/18/1860 The Republican Party nominates **Abraham Lincoln** as its candidate for president.

11/6/1860 Abraham Lincoln is elected president of the United States.

12/20/1860 South Carolina secedes from the Union.

1/9/1861 Mississippi secedes from the Union.

1/10/1861 Florida secedes from the Union.

1/11/1861 Alabama secedes from the Union.

1/19/1861 Georgia secedes from the Union.

1/26/1861 Louisiana secedes from the Union.

1/28/61 Pierre G. T. Beauregard is fired as superintendent of the U.S. Military Academy at West Point for supporting secession.

1/29/1861 Kansas is admitted into the Union as the thirty-fourth state.

2/1/1861 Texas secedes from the Union.

2/8/1861 The Confederate Constitution is adopted in Montgomery, Alabama.

2/9/1861 Jefferson Davis is elected provisional president of the Confederacy.

2/18/1861 Jefferson Davis is inaugurated as the president of the Confederacy.

3/4/1861 Abraham Lincoln is inaugurated as the sixteenth president of the United States.

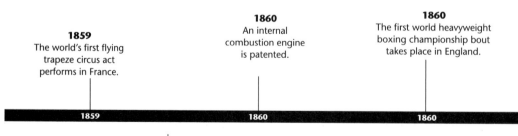

1859
The world's first flying trapeze circus act performs in France.

1860
An internal combustion engine is patented.

1860
The first world heavyweight boxing championship bout takes place in England.

1859   1860   1860

3/6/1861 The Confederacy calls for one hundred thousand volunteers to join its military.

4/1861 **Edward Pollard** publishes *Letters of a Southern Spy,* harshly criticizing **Abraham Lincoln** and all Northerners.

4/12/1861 South Carolina troops open fire on Fort Sumter, marking the beginning of the American Civil War.

4/13/1861 Major Robert Anderson surrenders Fort Sumter to the Confederates.

4/15/1861 President **Abraham Lincoln** calls for seventy-five thousand volunteers to join the Union army.

4/19/1861 President **Abraham Lincoln** orders a blockade of Southern ports.

4/20/1861 **Thaddeus Lowe** makes a successful balloon flight from Cincinnati, Ohio, to Unionville, South Carolina.

5/1/1861 **Winfield Scott** develops his "Anaconda Plan."

5/6/1861 Arkansas secedes from the Union.

5/7/1861 Tennessee forms an alliance with the Confederacy that makes it a Confederate state for all practical purposes.

5/13/1861 Queen Victoria proclaims British neutrality in the conflict between America's Northern and Southern sections.

5/14/1861 **Emma Edmonds** disguises herself as a man and joins the Union army.

5/20/1861 North Carolina secedes from the Union.

5/23/1861 Virginia secedes from the Union.

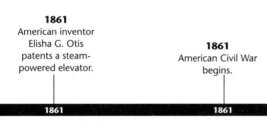

1861
American inventor
Elisha G. Otis
patents a steam-
powered elevator.

1861
American Civil War
begins.

1861

1861

6/3/1861 Stephen A. Douglas dies in Chicago, Illinois.

6/10/1861 Napoleon III declares French neutrality in the American Civil War.

6/11/1861 Counties in western Virginia resist Virginia's vote to secede and set up their own government, which is loyal to the Union.

7/20/1861 Confederate Congress convenes at the Confederate capital of Richmond, Virginia.

7/21/1861 Confederate forces win the First Battle of Bull Run, the war's first major battle.

7/22/1861 **Julia Ward Howe** writes the words to "Battle Hymn of the Republic" in her hotel room.

7/25/1861 U.S. Congress passes the Crittenden Resolution, which states that the North's war aim is to preserve the Union, not end slavery.

7/27/1861 General **George B. McClellan** assumes command of Federal forces in Washington.

8/30/1861 Union general **John C. Frémont** proclaims martial law in Missouri, which is torn by violence between pro-Union and pro-Confederate forces.

11/1861 **John Bell Hood**'s Texas Brigade is organized.

11/6/1861 **Jefferson Davis** is elected to a six-year term as president of the Confederacy.

11/8/1861 Union Captain Charles Wilkes seizes two Confederate officials traveling on the *Trent,* a British vessel. The incident triggers deep outrage in England.

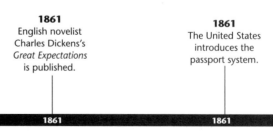

1861
English novelist
Charles Dickens's
Great Expectations
is published.

1861
The United States
introduces the
passport system.

1861   1861

11/20/1861 The Union organizes the Joint Committee on the Conduct of the War in order to review the actions and qualifications of the North's military leadership.

11/27/1861 Confederate officials seized from the *Trent* are released from custody with apologies.

2/6/1862 Union general **Ulysses S. Grant** captures Fort Henry on the Tennessee River.

2/16/1862 **Ulysses S. Grant** captures Fort Donelson on the Cumberland River.

2/22/1862 **Jefferson Davis** is inaugurated as president of the Confederacy.

2/25/1862 Confederates abandon Nashville, Tennessee, to oncoming Union forces.

3/1862 **Emma Edmonds** makes her first trip behind Confederate lines as a Union spy.

3/9/1862 The Union ship *Monitor* battles the Confederate ship *Virginia* to a draw at Hampton Roads, Virginia.

4/6–7/1862 Union and Confederate forces fight in the inconclusive Battle of Shiloh in Tennessee.

4/16/1862 The Confederate Congress passes a conscription act requiring most able-bodied men between the ages of eighteen and thirty-five to sign up for military service.

4/25/1862 The Union fleet under the command of Admiral **David R. Farragut** captures New Orleans.

5/13/1862 Slave **Robert Smalls** leads a group of slaves who steal the Confederate ship *Planter* and turn it over to the Union Navy.

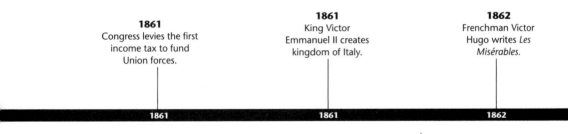

1861
Congress levies the first income tax to fund Union forces.

1861
King Victor Emmanuel II creates kingdom of Italy.

1862
Frenchman Victor Hugo writes *Les Misérables*.

1861   1861   1862

6/1/1862 General **Robert E. Lee** assumes command of Confederate forces defending Richmond, Virginia.

6/6/1862 Union forces take control of Memphis, Tennessee.

6/17/1862 Confederate forces led by **Thomas "Stonewall" Jackson** leave the Shenandoah Valley after a successful military campaign.

6/25/1862 The Seven Days' Battles begin between **George B. McClellan**'s Army of the Potomac and **Robert E. Lee**'s Army of Northern Virginia.

7/2/1862 President **Abraham Lincoln** calls for three hundred thousand enlistments for three-year periods in order to further strengthen the Union army.

7/17/1862 U.S. Congress passes laws allowing blacks to serve as soldiers in Union army.

7/29/1862 Confederate commerce raider *Alabama* leaves England and starts attacking Northern trading vessels.

8/29–30/1862 The Second Battle of Bull Run ends in a disastrous defeat for the Union.

9/5/1862 General **Robert E. Lee** leads the Army of Northern Virginia into Northern territory for the first time, as his force enters Maryland.

9/15/1862 **Thomas "Stonewall" Jackson**'s army captures twelve thousand Union troops at Harpers Ferry, Virginia.

9/17/1862 **George B. McClellan**'s Army of the Potomac and **Robert E. Lee**'s Army of Northern Virginia fight at Antietam in the bloodiest single day of the war. Neither side registers a conclusive victory, but the draw convinces Lee to return to Virginia.

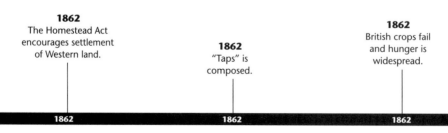

1862
The Homestead Act encourages settlement of Western land.

1862
"Taps" is composed.

1862
British crops fail and hunger is widespread.

1862   1862   1862

9/22/1862 President **Abraham Lincoln** issues his preliminary Emancipation Proclamation, which will free slaves in Confederate territory.

10/8/1862 Confederate invasion of Kentucky ends after the Battle of Perryville.

10/12/1862 **Jeb Stuart**'s Confederate cavalry completes ride around **George B. McClellan**'s Union army after raid on Chambersburg, Pennsylvania.

11/7/1862 President **Abraham Lincoln** removes General **George B. McClellan** from command of the Army of the Potomac, replacing him with General **Ambrose Burnside**.

12/13/1862 General **Robert E. Lee**'s Confederate forces hand the Union a decisive defeat at the Battle of Fredericksburg.

1/1/1863 President **Abraham Lincoln** issues the Emancipation Proclamation, which frees all slaves in Confederate territory.

1/1/1863 **John Singleton Mosby** is named captain of the Confederate guerrilla rangers.

1/2/1863 Union victory at the Battle of Stones River stops Confederate plans to invade middle Tennessee.

1/23/1863 General **Ambrose Burnside**'s new offensive against **Robert E. Lee**'s Army of Northern Virginia sputters to a halt in bad weather. Burnside's "Mud March" convinces President **Abraham Lincoln** to replace him with General Joseph Hooker.

3/3/1863 U.S. Congress passes a conscription act requiring most able-bodied Northern men to sign up for military service.

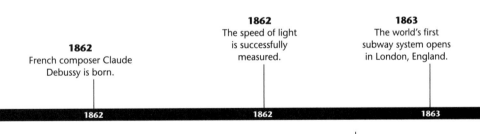

1862
French composer Claude Debussy is born.

1862
The speed of light is successfully measured.

1863
The world's first subway system opens in London, England.

1862   1862   1863

4/2/1863 Bread riots erupt in Richmond, Virginia, as hungry civilians resort to violence to feed their families.

5/1863 Union spy **Pauline Cushman** is captured and sentenced to death by Confederate general **Braxton Bragg**, but she is rescued near Shelbyville, Tennessee.

5/2/1863 General **Robert E. Lee** and the Confederates claim a big victory at Chancellorsville, but **Thomas "Stonewall" Jackson** is killed during the battle.

5/22/1863 General **Ulysses S. Grant** begins the siege of Vicksburg, Mississippi, after attempts to take the Confederate stronghold by force are turned back.

5/26/1863 Ohio congressman **Clement L. Vallandigham** is exiled to Confederate territory for criticizing President **Abraham Lincoln** and encouraging Union soldiers to desert.

6/9/1863 The largest cavalry battle of the Civil War ends in a draw at Brandy Station, Virginia.

6/20/1863 West Virginia is admitted into the Union as the thirty-fifth state.

7/1–3/1863 The famous Battle of Gettysburg takes place in Pennsylvania. Union general **George G. Meade** and the Army of the Potomac successfully turn back General **Robert E. Lee**'s attempted invasion of the North, doing terrible damage to Lee's Army of Northern Virginia in the process.

7/4/1863 Vicksburg surrenders to General **Ulysses S. Grant** and his Union force after a six-week siege of the city.

7/9/1863 Union troops take control of Port Hudson, Louisiana. The victory gives the North control of the Mississippi River.

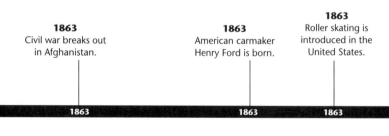

1863
Civil war breaks out in Afghanistan.

1863
American carmaker Henry Ford is born.

1863
Roller skating is introduced in the United States.

1863   1863   1863

7/13/1863 Antidraft mobs begin four days of rioting in New York City.

7/18/1863 Black troops of the Fifty-Fourth Massachusetts regiment make a valiant but unsuccessful attempt to seize Fort Wagner in South Carolina from the Confederates.

8/21/1863 Confederate raiders led by William C. Quantrill murder 150 antislavery settlers and burn large sections of Lawrence, Kansas.

9/2/1863 Union troops take control of Knoxville, Tennessee.

9/9/1863 Union forces take control of Chattanooga, Tennessee, after the city is abandoned by General **Braxton Bragg**'s army.

9/20/1863 The two-day Battle of Chickamauga ends in a major defeat for the Union.

9/23/1863 General **Braxton Bragg** begins the Confederate siege of Chattanooga.

10/17/1863 General **Ulysses S. Grant** is named supreme commander of Union forces in the west.

11/19/1863 President **Abraham Lincoln** delivers his famous Gettysburg Address at a ceremony dedicating a cemetery for soldiers who died at the Battle of Gettysburg in Pennsylvania.

11/25/1863 The three-day Battle of Chattanooga results in a major victory for the North, as Union troops led by General **George Henry Thomas** scatter General **Braxton Bragg**'s Confederate army.

12/8/1863 President **Abraham Lincoln** proposes his Ten Percent Plan, which says that seceded states can return to the Union provided that one-tenth of the

1863
President Abraham Lincoln proclaims the first national Thanksgiving Day.

1863
The Capitol dome in Washington, D.C., is capped.

1863

1863

1860 voters agree to form a state government that is loyal to the Union.

12/27/1863 General **Joseph E. Johnston** takes command of the Confederate Army of Tennessee.

3/12/1864 General **Ulysses S. Grant** is promoted to leadership of all of the Union armies.

3/18/1864 General **William T. Sherman** is named to lead Union armies in the west.

4/12/1864 Confederate troops led by **Nathan Bedford Forrest** capture Fort Pillow, Tennessee, and are accused of murdering black Union soldiers stationed there.

4/17/1864 General **Ulysses S. Grant** calls a halt to prisoner exchanges between North and South, further increasing the Confederacy's manpower problems.

5/5/1864 General **Robert E. Lee**'s Army of Northern Virginia and General **Ulysses S. Grant**'s Army of the Potomac battle in the Wilderness campaign.

5/9–12/1864 General **Robert E. Lee** stops the Union advance on Richmond at the brutal Battle of Spotsylvania.

5/11/1864 **Jeb Stuart** is mortally wounded in a battle with **Philip H. Sheridan**'s cavalry at Brandy Station, Virginia.

6/1864 U.S. Congress passes a law providing for equal pay for black and white soldiers.

6/3/1864 The Union's Army of the Potomac suffers heavy losses in a failed assault on **Robert E. Lee**'s army at Cold Harbor, Virginia.

6/18/1864 General **Ulysses S. Grant** begins the Union siege of Petersburg, which is defended by **Robert E. Lee**'s Army of Northern Virginia.

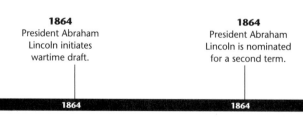

1864
President Abraham Lincoln initiates wartime draft.

1864
President Abraham Lincoln is nominated for a second term.

1864

1864

6/23/1864 Confederate forces led by Jubal Early begin a campaign in the Shenandoah Valley.

7/11/1864 Confederate troops commanded by Jubal Early reach outskirts of Washington, D.C., before being forced to return to the Shenandoah Valley.

7/17/1864 General **John Bell Hood** takes command of the Confederate Army of Tennessee.

7/30/1864 Union general **Ambrose Burnside** makes a disastrous attack in the Battle of the Crater.

8/5/1864 Admiral **David G. Farragut** leads the Union Navy to a major victory in the Battle of Mobile Bay, which closes off one of the Confederacy's last remaining ports.

8/29/1864 The Democratic Party nominates General **George B. McClellan** as its candidate for president of the United States and pushes a campaign promising an end to the war.

9/1/1864 General **William T. Sherman** captures Atlanta, Georgia, after a long campaign.

9/4/1864 General **William T. Sherman** orders all civilians to leave Atlanta, Georgia, as a way to hurt Southern morale.

9/19–22/1864 Union troops led by **Philip H. Sheridan** defeat Jubal Early's Confederate army in the Shenandoah Valley.

10/1/1864 **Rose O'Neal Greenhow** drowns in the Atlantic Ocean while trying to smuggle gold into the Confederacy in the hoops of her dress.

10/6/1864 **Philip H. Sheridan**'s Union troops begin a campaign of destruction in the Shenandoah Valley in

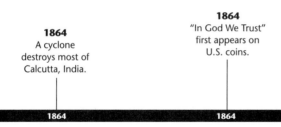

1864
A cyclone destroys most of Calcutta, India.

1864
"In God We Trust" first appears on U.S. coins.

1864   1864

order to wipe out Confederate sympathizers and sources of supplies.

10/19/1864 **Philip H. Sheridan**'s army drives Jubal Early's Confederate force out of the Shenandoah Valley.

10/31/1864 Nevada is admitted into the Union as the thirty-sixth state.

11/8/1864 **Abraham Lincoln** is reelected to the presidency of the United States by a comfortable margin.

11/15/1864 General **William T. Sherman** begins his famous March to the Sea, in which his Union army destroys a large area of Georgia on its way to the port city of Savannah.

12/16/1864 Union forces under the command of General **George Henry Thomas** crush **John Bell Hood**'s Army of Tennessee at the Battle of Nashville.

12/21/1864 **William T. Sherman**'s Union army completes its March to the Sea by taking control of Savannah, Georgia.

1/31/1865 The U.S. Congress submits the Thirteenth Amendment, which abolishes slavery, to the individual states for passage.

2/17/1865 General **William T. Sherman**'s army occupies the South Carolina capital of Columbia.

2/18/1865 Union forces seize control of Charleston, South Carolina.

2/22/1865 Confederate president **Jefferson Davis** returns command of the Army of Tennessee to General **Joseph E. Johnston** in a desperate attempt to stop **William T. Sherman**'s advance into North Carolina.

1864
Pasteurization is invented.

1864
American novelist Nathaniel Hawthorne dies.

1865
Lewis Carroll writes *Alice's Adventures in Wonderland.*

1864   1864   1865

2/27/1865 **Martin Delany** is commissioned as a major in the Union army, becoming the first black soldier to hold a field command in U.S. military history.

3/2/1865 Remaining Confederate troops in Shenandoah Valley go down to defeat at the hands of **Philip H. Sheridan.**

3/4/1865 President **Abraham Lincoln** is inaugurated for a second term of office.

3/13/1865 The Confederate Congress authorizes the use of slaves as Confederate combat soldiers.

4/1–2/1865 **Ulysses S. Grant**'s Army of the Potomac successfully breaks through Confederate defenses at Petersburg, forcing **Robert E. Lee**'s Army of Northern Virginia to evacuate the city and give up its defense of Richmond, Virginia.

4/3/1865 Union troops take control of Richmond, Virginia, and prepare for a visit from President **Abraham Lincoln** a day later.

4/9/1865 Trapped by pursuing Federal troops, General **Robert E. Lee** surrenders to General **Ulysses S. Grant** at Appomattox in Virginia.

4/14/1865 President **Abraham Lincoln** is shot by **John Wilkes Booth** while attending a play at Ford's Theatre in Washington, D.C.

4/15/1865 Vice president **Andrew Johnson** becomes president after **Abraham Lincoln** dies.

4/18/1865 Confederate General **Joseph E. Johnston** surrenders his Army of Tennessee to **William T. Sherman** near Raleigh, North Carolina.

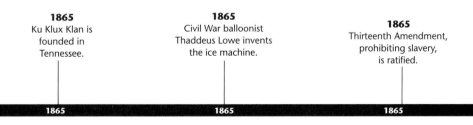

1865
Ku Klux Klan is founded in Tennessee.

1865
Civil War balloonist Thaddeus Lowe invents the ice machine.

1865
Thirteenth Amendment, prohibiting slavery, is ratified.

1865   1865   1865

4/26/1865 **John Wilkes Booth** is killed by Federal soldiers in a barn near Bowling Green, Virginia.

5/10/1865 Confederate president **Jefferson Davis** is taken prisoner by Federal troops at Irwinsville, Georgia.

5/26/1865 The very last Confederate troops put down their weapons, as a rebel army west of the Mississippi River led by Kirby Smith surrenders to Union officials.

6/6/1865 William Quantrill dies in federal prison.

11/10/1865 **Henry Wirz** becomes the only Confederate official to be executed for war crimes committed during the Civil War.

1866 **Ambrose Burnside** is elected governor of Rhode Island.

1866 **David R. Farragut** becomes the first admiral in U.S. naval history.

1866 The Republican Congress passes a Civil Rights Act over President **Andrew Johnson**'s veto. The Act gives citizenship and other rights to black people.

1866 Race riots between blacks and whites erupt during the summer in Memphis, Tennessee, and New Orleans, Louisiana.

1866 Tennessee is readmitted into the Union by Congress.

1866 George M. Maddox of Quantrill's Raiders is acquitted of murder charges from massacre at Lawrence, Kansas.

1867 Congress passes the Military Reconstruction Act over President **Andrew Johnson**'s veto.

1866
The first U.S. oil pipeline
is completed.

1866
Alfred Nobel
invents dynamite.

1866

1866

1867   The Ku Klux Klan adopts a formal constitution and selects former Confederate general **Nathan Bedford Forrest** as its first leader.

1867   Former Confederate president **Jefferson Davis** is released from a Virginia jail after two years of imprisonment.

1867   Former slave and Union war hero **Robert Smalls** is elected to the South Carolina state legislature.

1868   Political disagreements between Congress and President **Andrew Johnson** become so great that the president is impeached. He avoids being removed from office by one vote in his Senate impeachment trial.

1868   Congress passes the Fifteenth Amendment, which extends voting rights to blacks, and sends the bill along to individual states for ratification.

1868   Alabama, Arkansas, Florida, Louisiana, North Carolina, and South Carolina are readmitted into the Union by Congress.

1868   Republican **Ulysses S. Grant** is elected the eighteenth president of the United States.

1868   Georgia expels black representatives, saying they are not eligible to hold political office. U.S. Congress responds by refusing to recognize Georgia representatives.

1868   Federal government sends troops back into Georgia to reestablish military law.

1870   The Fifteenth Amendment, guaranteeing voting rights for blacks, is ratified by the states and becomes law.

1867
The United States purchases Alaska from Russia.

1868
Louisa May Alcott writes *Little Women*.

1869
The first intercollegiate football game is played.

1867   1868   1869

1870   Congress passes the Enforcement Act of 1870 in an effort to protect the voting rights of all citizens—especially blacks—in the South.

1870   Georgia, Mississippi, Virginia, and Texas are readmitted into the Union by Congress.

1870   The Fifteenth Amendment guaranteeing voting rights for blacks is ratified by the states and becomes law.

1871   Congress passes the Ku Klux Klan Act, which outlaws conspiracies, use of disguises, and other practices of the white supremacist group.

1872   **Ulysses S. Grant** is reelected president of the United States.

1874   **Robert Smalls** is elected to the U.S. Congress.

1875   Congress passes a Civil Rights Act barring discrimination in hotels, theaters, railroads, and other public places.

1876   Republican Rutherford B. Hayes and Democrat Samuel J. Tilden run a very close race for the presidency of the United States. Tilden wins the popular vote, but neither candidate receives enough electoral votes for election. The two political parties eventually agree to a compromise in which Hayes becomes president in exchange for a guarantee that he remove federal troops from South Carolina, Florida, and Louisiana.

1877   President Rutherford B. Hayes removes Federal troops from the South. This withdrawal increases the vulnerability of blacks to Southern racism and marks the end of the Reconstruction period in American history.

1881   **Clara Barton** founds the American Red Cross.

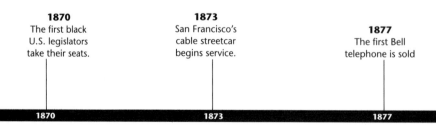

1870
The first black
U.S. legislators
take their seats.

1873
San Francisco's
cable streetcar
begins service.

1877
The first Bell
telephone is sold

1870   1873   1877

1891   **Ambrose Bierce** publishes *Tales of Soldiers and Civilians,* a collection of stories about the Civil War that includes his famous story "An Occurrence at Owl Creek Bridge."

1895   **Thomas Nast** completes his famous painting of **Robert E. Lee**'s surrender to **Ulysses S. Grant.**

1981   Southern writer **Mary Boykin Chesnut**'s diary of her Civil War experiences is published in its original form—over one hundred years after it was written—as *Mary Chesnut's Civil War* and wins the Pulitzer Prize.

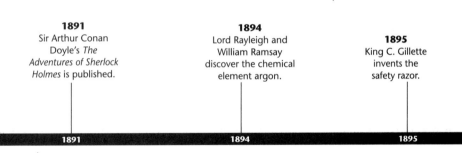

1891
Sir Arthur Conan Doyle's *The Adventures of Sherlock Holmes* is published.

1894
Lord Rayleigh and William Ramsay discover the chemical element argon.

1895
King C. Gillette invents the safety razor.

1891   1894   1895

A map of the United States east of the Mississippi River shows the key battles and events of the Civil War. *(Illustration by XNR Productions. Reproduced by permission of The Gale Group.)*

Clara Barton

Born December 25, 1821
Oxford, Massachusetts
Died April 12, 1912
Glen Echo, New York

Union nurse known as the "angel of the battlefield" for treating wounded Union soldiers
Founded the American Red Cross

Clara Barton is one of the most remarkable women in American history. A former schoolteacher, she never received any formal training in nursing. But she became a famous figure on Civil War battlefields, where she tended to thousands of sick and wounded soldiers and delivered huge quantities of medicine, food, and other provisions to Union troops. She also remained in the public spotlight after the war concluded. In 1881 she founded the American Red Cross, and in her later years she emerged as a leader in the fight to gain women's suffrage (right to vote).

An early taste of nursing

Clarissa Harlowe Barton was born in Oxford, Massachusetts, on Christmas Day 1821. She grew up on a large farm with her parents, Stephen and Sarah Stone Barton, and four older brothers and sisters. Clara was ten years younger than any of the other children. This situation, she later admitted, sometimes made it seem like she had "six fathers and mothers. . . . All took charge of me, all educated me, each according to personal taste."

"When there is no longer a soldier's arm to raise the Stars and Stripes above our Capital, may God give strength to mine."

Clara Barton. *(Courtesy of the National Archives and Records Administration.)*

In many ways, Clara had a very good childhood. The family farm was quite successful, and she received lots of attention from her parents and her older siblings. But she had few playmates, and Barton's childhood interests were not always shared by her older brothers and sisters. This sometimes made her feel isolated from others, and she became a shy and sensitive youngster.

When Barton was eleven years old, her brother David was injured in a construction accident. "I was distressed beyond measure at his condition," Barton recalled. "From the first days and nights of illness, I remained near his side." Eventually, she learned to give David his medications and "to administer them like a genuine nurse." As Barton cared for her older brother over the next several months, she felt more useful than ever before.

When David finally recovered from his injuries, Clara decided to continue caring for the sick and injured. Following her father's example, she began to take on charity work in the area. After a while, she became a tutor to poor children. She even provided nursing assistance to area families when a deadly smallpox epidemic washed over the region. Barton eventually caught smallpox herself. But even though her recovery was long and difficult, she never regretted the assistance that she had provided.

A talented teacher

In 1838, Barton became a schoolteacher in the Oxford area. Teaching was one of the few career paths that were open to women during that period, and Barton was determined to make the most of her talents. The seventeen-year-old excelled as a teacher, and within a few months of starting classes, she received many teaching offers from other area communities. She spent the next decade teaching children throughout the region while also continuing with her charitable work. But as time passed she grew restless and dissatisfied with her life and began to look for other challenges.

In 1850 Barton abruptly left teaching behind to continue her own education at the Clinton Liberal Institute in New York. She spent a year at the school, deeply absorbing herself in mathematics, science, and other subjects that women rarely had an opportunity to study. In 1852, Barton returned to teaching, accepting a position in Bordentown, New Jersey.

At the time that Barton arrived in Bordentown, the community's only school was one that charged students a fee to take classes. Since this situation often made it impossible for children from poor families to go to school, Barton approached the town's leaders with an intriguing offer: if they would provide her with a bigger building and allow all children to attend school for free, then she would give up her salary for three months.

On the first day that Barton's school opened, only six students showed up. But as time passed, more and more parents heard about the free classes and the community's dynamic new teacher. Within a year or so, the school's enrollment increased to more than two hundred students, with four hundred more on a waiting list. As Barton hired other teachers to help with the swelling student population, she expressed great satisfaction with the school's amazing success.

Bordentown's leaders recognized the popularity of Barton's school, too. They established generous salaries for Barton and the other teachers, and helped pass a local bill that set aside $4,000 for the construction of a brand new school that would provide rooms and school equipment for all six hundred children who wanted to attend. But when the new school opened in the fall of 1853, Barton discovered that prejudice against women holding positions of authority remained strong. The community's school board selected a man to serve as the school's principal, even though she was the one who was responsible for its very existence. Frustrated and disappointed, Barton resigned from the school and left Bordentown.

Rumblings of war

Over the next several years, Barton divided her time between the national capital of Washington, where she worked as a government clerk, and her old hometown of Oxford, Massachusetts. Then, as the 1850s drew to a close, Bar-

ton found herself increasingly drawn into the political tur-
moil (confusion) that was sweeping across the nation.

For years, America's Northern and Southern states had
been arguing over several issues. One of these issues was slavery. Many Northerners believed that slavery was wrong and
wanted to abolish it. But the economy of the South had been
built on slavery, and Southerners resented Northern efforts to
halt or contain the practice.

By early 1861, hostilities between the North and
South had become so fierce that a number of Southern states
voted to secede from (leave) the United States and form a new
country that allowed slavery, called the Confederate States of
America (a total of eleven states seceded by the end of the
year). The U.S. government declared that those states had no
right to secede and that it was willing to use force to make
them return to the Union. In the spring of 1861, the two
sides finally went to war over their differences.

Treating the wounded

When the Civil War began, Barton was a strong supporter of the North's position. She thought that slavery was a
terrible practice, and she expressed patriotic outrage at the
South's decision to secede. "When there is no longer a soldier's arm to raise the Stars and Stripes above our Capital, may
God give strength to mine," she said in one letter to a friend.

Barton proved her willingness to support the Union
cause from the very start. In April 1861, the Union Army's
Sixth Massachusetts Regiment was traveling to Washington
when it was attacked by a pro-South mob in Baltimore, Maryland. When the soldiers who had been wounded in the assault finally reached Washington, Barton sprang into action.
She immediately went to help care for the wounded, and she
organized a drive to provide the troops with supplies that
they had lost in Baltimore.

A few months later, Washington received far greater
numbers of Union wounded in the aftermath of the First Battle of Bull Run (also known as the First Battle of Manassas).
More than three thousand Federal troops were killed, wounded, or missing from this battle, which was the first major

Florence Nightingale

Clara Barton struggled throughout the Civil War to convince people that women could make major contributions in the effort to help save wounded young soldiers. She often encountered resistance, but her efforts were made a little easier by the example of Florence Nightingale.

Florence Nightingale (1820–1910) is regarded as the founder of modern nursing. An English woman from an upper-class background, she became involved in caring for sick and wounded people in the mid-1850s, when the Crimean War (1853–56) engulfed several nations. The Crimean War pitted Russia against Turkey, which wanted to rule itself without interference from Russia. England and France took part in the war on Turkey's side.

When Nightingale heard about the horrible hospital conditions in which wounded soldiers were treated, she decided to do something about it. Ignoring critics who argued that women had no business being in the midst of rough soldiers and dirty conditions, she organized a group of thirty-eight women nurses and traveled to army hospitals throughout the war zone. Led by Nightingale, these women nurses treated thousands of wounded soldiers and made great improvements in hospital conditions and organization. "The very first requirement in a hospital," Nightingale declared, "must be that it should do the sick no harm." Within a matter of months, Nightingale and her nurses had helped

Florence Nightingale. *(Reproduced by permission of Archive Photos, Inc.)*

lower the death rate in military hospitals from more than 40 percent to about 2 percent.

By the time the Crimean War ended in 1856, Nightingale had become a legendary figure around the world. In 1860 her fame increased when she opened the world's first nursing school in St. Thomas's Hospital in London, England. The establishment of this school further increased the reputation of nursing as a legitimate career for women. A year later, when the American Civil War broke out, Nightingale's activities inspired an entire generation of Northern and Southern women. Using Nightingale's bravery and dedication as an example, hundreds of American women volunteered as nurses during the Civil War.

clash of the war. When the injured Union soldiers reached Washington, the city was completely unprepared to care for them. Once again, Barton devoted her energies to helping the wounded. Working night and day, she gathered clothing, food, and other supplies for the soldiers.

Over the next several months, Barton became a constant presence in Washington-area hospitals. She continued to gather supplies for the soldiers, and she spent long hours sitting by their bedsides, reading or talking to them. Some of her conversations with the soldiers distressed her deeply. They told her that medical supplies often lagged far behind the army. They also admitted that many seriously wounded soldiers out in the field had to wait for long periods of time before they received any medical attention because the Union Army had so few doctors. Some soldiers had to endure long wagon rides to Washington or other Northern cities before they received any attention at all. Some of these soldiers died before they reached their destination, bleeding to death or dying from infections.

As Barton listened to these alarming stories, she recognized that the Union troops needed to receive medical attention much more quickly. She then requested permission from the Union authorities to provide aid to wounded soldiers out in the field rather than wait until they were transported all the way to Washington. At first, the officials turned her down because they did not believe that a woman could handle the sight of battlefield gore and misery. But Barton refused to give up on the idea. Instead, she spent months lobbying (attempting to influence) various politicians and army officials. In the spring of 1862, she finally received permission to treat soldiers out on the battlefield.

Angel of the battlefield

As soon as Barton received official permission to work in the field, she made arrangements to carry needed medical supplies and food with her. "People talk like children about 'transporting supplies' as if it were the easiest thing imaginable to transport supplies by wagon thirty miles across a country scouted by guerrilla bands [groups of Confederate raiders]," she wrote.

Barton's first opportunity to provide aid to wounded soldiers out in the field came in August 1862, after a big battle at Cedar Mountain, near Culpepper, Virginia. When Barton heard about the battle, she rushed to the scene and immediately began tending wounded Union soldiers. "At the time when we were entirely out of dressings of every kind, she supplied us with everything," said one Union surgeon at Cedar Mountain. "And while the shells were bursting in every direction . . . she [stayed] dealing out shirts . . . and preparing soup and seeing it prepared in all the [field] hospitals. . . . I thought that night if heaven ever sent out a homely angel, she must be one [since] her assistance was so timely."

One month later, Barton traveled to a region near Antietam Creek in northern Maryland, where a clash between Union and Confederate forces produced the single highest casualty toll of any single day of the Civil War. All day long Barton worked tirelessly to bandage and feed the wounded, even as the sights and sounds of the terrible battle swirled all around her. At one point, she recalled, she bent down to give a wounded soldier a drink of water. "Just at this moment a bullet sped its free and easy way between us, tearing a hole between us, tearing a hole in my sleeve and [finding] its way into his body," she remembered. "He fell back dead. There was no more to be done for him and I left him to rest. I have never mended that hole in my sleeve."

By the time the Battle of Antietam was over, Barton's tireless efforts on behalf of wounded soldiers had made her a beloved figure throughout the Union Army. "Here [at Antietam] her work was truly heroic," wrote Cathy East Dubowski in *Clara Barton: Healing the Wounds,* "and here she won the admiration of the common soldiers and of many surgeons. She had proved her courage and ability beyond a doubt—to the army and to herself. She had marched with the soldiers, gone without food and rest, slept under the stars, and stood her ground under fire, even when others ran."

Barton continued to work as a field nurse for most of the rest of the war, traveling from battlefield to battlefield. In recognition of her efforts on behalf of wounded Union soldiers, people started calling her the "angel of the battlefield." But although Barton appreciated the recognition she received, the war was an emotionally draining experience for her. She sometimes quarreled with other people and organizations who were trying to provide medical supplies to Union troops. In addition, the endless exposure to torn and bleeding bodies sometimes made it hard for her to go on. After one battle, she admitted, "I looked at myself, shoeless, gloveless, ragged, and bloodstained, [and] a new sense of desolation and pity and sympathy and weariness, all blended, swept over me with irresistible force. . . . I sank down . . . and wept." At one point of the war, these pressures combined to push her into a brief emotional breakdown. After several months of rest, however, she was able to return to her nursing work.

International Red Cross

In April 1865, the North finally defeated the South to bring the Civil War to a close. Over the next several months, Barton continued to work on behalf of Union soldiers and families. She helped people find out what happened to missing family members who had fought in the war, and she gave a series of lectures on her wartime experiences.

In 1869, Barton traveled to Europe, where she hoped that a long period of rest might help her deal with growing depression and nagging health problems. Soon after her arrival, she learned about an organization known as the International Convention of Geneva, or International Red Cross. This organization, founded in 1864, was dedicated to providing medical aid and other assistance to people wounded in wartime.

In 1870 a war broke out between Germany and France. This war, known as the Franco-Prussian War (1870–71), gave Barton an opportunity to see how the International Red Cross operated. The organization refused to take sides in the war; instead, it devoted all of its energies to treating soldiers and civilians (people not involved in the war, including women and children) who were injured or made homeless in the conflict. As the Red Cross went into action, Barton marveled at the organization's operation. "The Red Cross societies in the field [accomplished] in four months under this systematic organization what we failed to accomplish in four years without it—no mistakes, no needless suffering, no starving, no lack of care, no waste, no confusion, but order, plenty, cleanliness, and comfort whenever that little [Red Cross] flag made its way."

Founding the American Red Cross

Barton spent the next few years helping the International Red Cross provide food and shelter to European refugees. In 1873, she returned to the United States, where she began working to create an American branch of the international aid organization.

Over the next several years Barton worked tirelessly to see her dream of an American Red Cross become a reality. She published pamphlets that discussed the organization's philosophy and goals and talked with influential congressmen and administration officials in order to gain their support. Finally, in 1881, Barton's crusade paid off, when the American Association of the Red Cross was formally founded. One year later, the U.S. Senate ratified (officially approved) a treaty that made the nation an official member of the International Red Cross.

Over the next two decades, Barton devoted her life to building the American Red Cross into a great relief organization. She served as the organization's president from 1882 to 1904, guiding it as it provided food, shelter, and medical supplies to victims of wars and natural disasters alike. But as the years passed, criticism of Barton's leadership became quite strong. People said that she never listened to anyone else, and that she did a terrible job of recordkeeping and managing the organization's funds. These criticisms seemed to be supported by dwindling public support for the group. By 1902, dissatisfaction with Barton's domineering style and sloppy bookkeeping became so great that a group of Red Cross members made an unsuccessful attempt to remove her from office.

In 1904, continued questions about Barton's handling of the organization's finances led to a Senate investigation. The Senate cleared her of any intentional wrongdoing, but public confidence in the organization continued to decline. Weary and bitter about the whole controversy, Barton finally resigned as president of the American Red Cross on May 14, 1904. The Red Cross reorganized itself after her departure and eventually established itself as one of America's most respected relief organizations.

Barton, meanwhile, adopted a quiet lifestyle. Settling in Glen Echo, New York, she spent her days reading or working in her garden. She died on April 12, 1912.

Where to Learn More

Burton, David H. *Clara Barton: In the Service of Humanity.* Westwood, CT: Greenwood Press, 1995.

Dubowski, Cathy East. *Clara Barton: Healing the Wounds.* Englewood Cliffs, NJ: Silver Burdett Press, 1991.

Hamilton, Leni. *Clara Barton.* New York: Chelsea House, 1987.

National Park Service. *Clara Barton National Historic Site.* [Online] http://www.nps.gov/clba/ (accessed on October 8, 1999).

Oates, Stephen B. *A Woman of Valor: Clara Barton and the Civil War.* New York: Free Press, 1994.

Rose, Mary Catherine. *Clara Barton: Soldier of Mercy.* Champaign, IL: Garrard Press, 1960. Reprint, New York: Chelsea Juniors, 1991.

Stevenson, Augusta. *Clara Barton, Founder of the American Red Cross.* New York: Macmillan, 1982.

Pierre G. T. Beauregard

Born May 28, 1818
St. Bernard Parish, Louisiana
Died February 20, 1893
New Orleans, Louisiana

Confederate general
Southern hero of Fort Sumter and First Bull Run

Pierre G. T. Beauregard was a key figure in many of the South's early Civil War victories. He led the conquest of Fort Sumter that actually started the war, and he helped guide the Confederacy to victory in the first major battle of the conflict in July 1861, the First Battle of Bull Run (also known as the First Battle of Manassas). But his war record ended up being a controversial one. For example, some critics believe that his decisions at the Battle of Shiloh (April 1862) prevented the South from gaining a major victory. In addition, Beauregard's arrogance and political scheming made him very unpopular with Confederate president **Jefferson Davis** (1808–1889; see entry) and some other Southern military and political leaders.

Raised in a Creole household

Pierre Gustave Toutant Beauregard was born on May 28, 1818, on his family's plantation just south of New Orleans, Louisiana. His family, the Toutant-Beauregards, were Creoles—persons descended from or culturally related to original French settlers of Louisiana. Beauregard was thus raised

Pierre G. T. Beauregard was "full of talent and of much military experience."

Confederate president Jefferson Davis

Pierre G. T. Beauregard.

11

in a household that continued to honor the customs and language of France, even though the country was an ocean away. Beauregard even grew up speaking French. In fact, it is believed that he did not learn to speak English until he was at least twelve years old. This environment led Beauregard to develop a deep fascination with Napoléon Bonaparte (1769–1821), a famous French general and emperor.

As Beauregard grew older, he decided that he wanted to follow in Napoléon's footsteps and make his mark as a professional soldier. When Beauregard was sixteen years old, he convinced his father to arrange his enrollment in the prestigious U.S. Military Academy at West Point in New York state. Once he arrived at the school, though, the young Creole cadet became very self-conscious about his French name and background. He quietly dropped the hyphen from his last name, though he kept *Toutant* as an extra middle name. He also abandoned his French-sounding first name and began signing his name as *G. T. Beauregard*.

A top engineering officer

Beauregard was a very good student, especially in the field of engineering (a discipline that uses mathematical and scientific principles in the design, construction, and operation of equipment, systems, and structures). When he graduated from West Point in 1838, he ranked second in a class of forty-five students. One of his classmates was Irvin McDowell (1818–1885), who Beauregard would later defeat at the First Battle of Bull Run. He received a lieutenant's commission in the army's Corps of Engineers, and spent the next several years helping build harbors and defensive fortifications along the eastern coast of Florida and the Gulf of Mexico. Beauregard also started a family around this time. In 1841, he married Marie Laure Villere, the daughter of a wealthy Louisiana planter.

In the late 1840s, Beauregard served in the Mexican War (1846–48), a conflict between Mexico and the United States over possession of territories in the West. By the time the war ended in 1848, American military victories had forced Mexico to cede (give up) its claims on Texas, California, New Mexico, and other lands in the West. Beauregard performed very well in the war with Mexico. Wounded twice, he earned two awards for gallantry (heroic courage) and impressed U.S. general **Winfield Scott** (1786–1866; see entry) with his scouting abilities and strategic suggestions. But Beauregard became bitter about his Mexican War experiences when his superior officers did not single him out for special praise.

After the war ended, Beauregard returned to Louisiana and resumed his work engineering fortifications and drainage systems along America's Southern coastline. In 1850, his wife died in childbirth. A few years later he married Caroline Deslonde, another woman from a wealthy Louisiana family.

By the late 1850s, Beauregard had built himself a reputation as an excellent army engineer. But his anger at the army over the Mexican War never really went away. He began to think of career possibilities outside the military. In 1858, he even launched a campaign to become the mayor of New Orleans, but he was defeated. Beauregard continued his engineering work until 1860, when he used his political connections to get himself appointed as the new superintendent of West Point.

A short stay at West Point

Beauregard officially became superintendent of West Point on January 23, 1861. The position of superintendent was a prestigious one. After all, West Point had provided almost all of the nation's leading military figures with their educations, and the cadets who welcomed Beauregard to the academy were regarded as America's military leaders of the future. As it turned out, however, Beauregard held the position for only five days before being fired.

By the time that Beauregard took over at West Point, long-standing disagreements between America's Northern and Southern regions threatened to spill over into violence at any time. The two sides had become angry with one another over a wide range of issues, from the balance of Federal and state authority to the economy. But the issue that most divided the two sides was slavery. Many Northerners believed slavery was wrong and wanted to abolish (put an end to) it. But the economy and culture of the South were closely linked to slavery, and Southerners resented Northern efforts to end the practice.

When Beauregard arrived at West Point, several Southern states had already announced their intention to secede from (leave) the United States and form their own country that allowed slavery, called the Confederate States of America. Beauregard announced his support for the secessionist cause. He also let it be known that if Louisiana seceded from the Union, he would immediately return to his native state and defend it against Federal troops. Beauregard's remarks infuriated his superiors, and on January 28 he was dismissed from his post at West Point.

Assault on Fort Sumter

On January 26, 1861, Louisiana legislators voted to leave the United States and join the Confederacy. Beauregard resigned from the Federal Army a few weeks later and returned to Louisiana, where he hoped to command that state's forces. When that appointment went to General **Braxton Bragg** (1817–1876; see entry), Beauregard viewed the choice as a great "injustice." He remained angry until February 27, when Confederate president Jefferson Davis named him a brigadier general and gave him command of South Carolina rebel (Confederate) forces at Charleston Harbor.

By March 1861, Charleston Harbor had become one of the best known places in America. A Federal military outpost called Fort Sumter was located in the middle of the harbor. This fort continued to be controlled by U.S. troops, even though the Confederacy had taken control of most other Federal military outposts and offices in the South. By the time that Beauregard arrived in Charleston, the continued occupation of Fort Sumter by Federal troops had become a source of great anger to the people of South Carolina and the rest of the Confederacy. They viewed the garrison (troops) at Fort Sumter as a foreign military presence that should not be permitted to operate in their territory, especially since it was located right in the middle of one of the Confederacy's most important harbors.

Beauregard made several attempts to convince Major Robert Anderson (1805–1871), the commander of Fort Sumter, to give up control of the outpost. At the same time, Confederate officials warned President **Abraham Lincoln** (1809–1865; see entry) to relinquish (give up) the fort. But Lincoln believed that if the Federal government surrendered Fort Sumter, Northern morale would suffer, and Southern confidence in the Confederacy's ability to break away from the Union permanently would increase. Lincoln thus ordered Anderson to stay put.

When it became clear that Anderson did not intend to withdraw his troops from the fort, Beauregard opened fire on the fortress with artillery guns that lined the harbor's shores. This attack, which was launched on the morning of April 12, is regarded as the beginning of the American Civil War. Anderson and his men resisted Beauregard's assault for thirty-four hours, but they finally surrendered on April 13. The capture of Fort Sumter transformed Beauregard into the first war hero of the Confederacy.

First Battle of Bull Run

In June 1861, Beauregard assumed command of Confederate forces around Manassas Junction, Virginia. This rebel encampment along the shores of the Bull Run River was an important one because it blocked the rebel capital of Richmond from Union attacks. In July, though, a Union army led by General Irvin McDowell marched into the region. The Union hoped that McDowell could smash Beauregard's force and seize control of Richmond, thus putting an end to the Confederate rebellion before it really got rolling.

McDowell attacked Beauregard's army on July 21, and at first it appeared that his offensive might succeed. But Beaure-

 Beauregard's Opinion of Lincoln

When Pierre G. T. Beauregard took command of the Confederate army guarding Manassas, Virginia, in mid-1861, he immediately took steps to rally local citizens to his side. One way in which he did this was to make false and insulting statements about the Union and its army. Such statements, while unfair and misleading, were often issued by both sides in the war in efforts to increase public support for their actions. In the following proclamation, released on June 1, 1861, Beauregard characterizes U.S. president Abraham Lincoln as a terrible dictator and Northern soldiers as a pack of murderers, thieves, and rapists:

> A reckless and unprincipled tyrant has invaded your soil. Abraham Lincoln, regardless of all moral, legal, and constitutional restraints [controls], has thrown his Abolitionist hosts among you, who are murdering and imprisoning your citizens, confiscating [seizing] and destroying your property, and committing other acts of violence and outrage, too shocking and revolting to humanity to be enumerated [described].
>
> All rules of civilized warfare are abandoned, and they proclaim by their acts, if not on their banners, that their war-cry is "BEAUTY AND BOUNTY." All that is dear to man—your honor and that of your wives and daughters—your fortunes and your lives, are involved in this momentous contest.

gard received vital reinforcements from Confederate general **Joseph E. Johnston** (1807–1891; see entry) in the middle of the clash, known as the First Battle of Bull Run (First Battle of Manassas). Boosted by these additional troops, Beauregard defeated McDowell's army in one of the most sloppy and disorganized battles of the entire war.

Beauregard's victory at Manassas made him even more popular in cities and farmhouses all across the Confederacy. It also convinced Jefferson Davis to give him even more authority. Davis promoted him to full generalship, describing the Creole officer as "full of talent and of much military experience." But Beauregard's relationship with Davis turned sour when the general started complaining about the Confederate president's leadership to Southern legislators and newspaper editors.

Union major general Irvin McDowell (above) met Confederate general Pierre G. T. Beauregard at the First Battle of Bull Run. They were former West Point classmates. (Courtesy of the Library of Congress.)

Battle of Shiloh

In early 1862, Beauregard's lack of respect for his leaders and constant political scheming led Davis to ship the troublesome general out to the war's western theater (the region of the South west of the Appalachian Mountains). He became second in command to General Albert Sidney Johnston (1803–1862), commander of the South's Army of Mississippi. Soon after his arrival, Beauregard helped plan a major assault on a large Union army led by General **Ulysses S. Grant** (1822–1885; see entry).

Grant's troops were camped at Pittsburg Landing in Tennessee, near a small church called Shiloh. Over the previous few weeks, they had achieved major victories in the region, battering Johnston's army in the process. But Johnston and Beauregard believed that if they attacked Grant before he received additional reinforcements, they might be able to hand the Union a major defeat. They decided to launch a surprise attack on the camp and push the Federal soldiers back into the nearby Tennessee River.

On the morning of April 6, Confederate troops charged out of the woods surrounding Shiloh. Just as Johnston and Beauregard had hoped, the Yankee (Northern) soldiers were completely unprepared for the assault. But Grant rallied his troops, and the clash became a bitter struggle for survival. As the battle progressed, Johnston was killed, and Beauregard assumed command of the Confederate troops.

Beauregard nearly succeeded in driving Grant's army into the river. But as nighttime approached, he decided to break off the attack and resume the battle the next day. This decision remains a very controversial one. Many of his officers felt that if they had continued the fight on April 6, the South might have been able to finish off Grant's forces. But the rebel troops were desperately weary. Beauregard decided that if he gave them a break from the brutal fighting, they might be able to claim victory the next day.

During the night, however, Grant received thirty-five thousand fresh reinforcements and organized his army for a dawn assault on Beauregard's position. In the early morning hours of April 7, Grant led a ferocious strike against the rebel army. This assault took a fearsome toll on the Confederates. Beauregard was finally forced to order a retreat all the way back to Corinth, Mississippi. A few days later, the threat of an approaching Union army forced Beauregard to flee from Corinth as well.

Stripped of command

Beauregard's defeat at the Battle of Shiloh tarnished his reputation, but the general's self-confidence never wavered. A few months later, he traveled to Mobile, Alabama, in hopes of receiving treatment for a nagging throat ailment. He left General Braxton Bragg in temporary command of the army, believing that he would soon return. But Beauregard had made these decisions without receiving authorization from Jefferson Davis or anyone else. When Davis learned about the general's actions, he permanently stripped Beauregard of his command and ordered him to take over the defense of the Atlantic coastlines of Georgia and South Carolina.

Defending the Confederate coastline was an important responsibility, but everyone knew that Beauregard's new assignment was a demotion (moving down to a lower rank). Beauregard's dislike for Davis thus became even greater. In fact, the two men remained hostile toward one another for the remainder of the war.

Beauregard reluctantly reported to his new command on September 15, 1862. Over the next eighteen months he successfully fended off repeated Union assaults against the South Carolina and Georgia coasts. But despite his skillful direction of the South's coastal defenses, Davis refused to give him another opportunity to command a Confederate army in the field. Beauregard's vanity and egotism, meanwhile, prevented him from accepting offers to serve under the command of other Confederate field generals.

Serves under Lee

In April 1864, Beauregard finally left his coastal command. He was reassigned to Virginia, where he took command of a rebel force that was responsible for defending Richmond against attacks from the North. Beauregard performed well in his new responsibilities, defending both Richmond and neighboring Petersburg from Union attacks in May and June. He then settled in to help Confederate general **Robert E. Lee** (1807–1870; see entry) in his defense of Petersburg, even as he traded insults with Davis and other political enemies.

In October 1864, Beauregard was assigned to command a new department called the Military Division of the West. But his new job turned out to be an advisory position with very little direct authority over Confederate armies. Around this same period, Union general **William T. Sherman** (1820–1891; see entry) and his army smashed its way through the Southern heartland with little resistance from Beauregard or anyone else. This "March to the Sea," as it became known, demoralized Confederate citizens and soldiers alike because it proved that the South could no longer defend itself.

In April 1865, the Confederacy finally admitted defeat, as the remnants of the various Southern armies surrendered to pursuing Union armies. Beauregard spent the final days of the war as second in command to Joseph E. Johnston in North Carolina. When Johnston surrendered his army to Sherman on April 26, Beauregard's involvement in the war came to an end.

Postwar career

After the Civil War concluded, Beauregard returned home to Louisiana. Several foreign governments tried to persuade him to accept leadership positions in their militaries, but he ended up turning down all of these offers. He worked as a railroad company executive until the mid-1870s, when he became involved in state government as supervisor of the Louisiana State Lottery and adjutant general (officer in charge) of the state's National Guard. In 1888, he was elected commissioner of public works for New Orleans. Beauregard died in New Orleans on February 20, 1893, after a brief illness.

Where to Learn More

Davis, William C. *The Commanders of the Civil War*. San Diego: Thunder Bay Press, 1999.

Williams, T. Harry. *P. G. T. Beauregard: Napoleon in Gray*. Baton Rouge: Louisiana State University Press, 1954, 1995.

Woodworth, Steven E. *The Failure of Confederate Command in the West*. Lawrence: University Press of Kansas, 1990.

Ambrose Bierce

Born June 24, 1842
Meigs City, Ohio
Died 1913 or 1914
Place of death unknown

Civil War veteran who authored
several short stories about the Civil War

A mbrose Bierce was one of America's best-known writers of the nineteenth century. As a Union soldier during the Civil War, Bierce witnessed the violence and horror of war firsthand. After the war ended, he drew upon those wartime experiences to write a number of popular short stories and essays. In addition, he ranked as one of the country's most famous newspaper columnists during the 1880s and 1890s.

Growing up in poverty

Ambrose Bierce was born in southeastern Ohio in 1842, but he spent most of his childhood in Indiana. He was the tenth of thirteen children born to Marcus Aurelius and Laura Bierce, poor farmers who struggled to provide food and clothing for their children. Ambrose spent a good deal of his childhood tackling farm chores under the watchful supervision of his disciplinarian mother. As a result, he received very little formal schooling. But his father loved to read books, and young Ambrose borrowed volumes from his father's modest library whenever he could. Literature thus became his

"To this day I cannot look over a landscape without noting the advantages of the ground for attack or defense."

Ambrose Bierce. *(Reproduced by permission of Corbis-Bettmann.)*

only source of relief from a childhood that he later recalled with great bitterness.

When Bierce was fifteen years old, he left the family farm to take a job as a printer's assistant on an abolitionist (antislavery) newspaper called the *Northern Indianan*. Two years later, his parents scraped together enough money to enroll him in the Kentucky Military Institute. A year later he moved to Elkhart, Indiana, where he worked as a saloon bartender.

Bierce's wartime experiences

In early 1861, America was torn in two by the Civil War. The nation's Northern and Southern states had long been angry with one another over a wide range of issues. The issue that most divided the two sides was slavery. Many Northerners felt slavery was wrong and wanted to abolish it. But the culture and economy of the South were closely linked to slavery, and Southerners resented Northern efforts to end the practice. The two sides finally went to war when the Southern states tried to secede from (leave) the Union and form their own country.

When the Civil War started, Bierce immediately volunteered to join the Union Army. His enlistment was due in part to the antislavery beliefs that his family had instilled in him. But Bierce also joined the army because he wanted to escape from the rural environment in which he had always lived. He became a private in Company C of the Ninth Indiana Volunteers in April 1861 and remained in the Union Army until January 1865, when he resigned as a lieutenant. He spent much of this period under the command of General W. B. Hazen (1830–1887), a tough officer for whom Bierce developed a great admiration.

During his service in the Civil War, Bierce experienced combat many times. In fact, he took part in a number of the war's worst battles, including Shiloh in Tennessee (April 1862) and Chickamauga in northwestern Georgia (September 1863). He fought well in these and other clashes, but fellow soldiers later said that his bravery sometimes bordered on recklessness. In June 1864, Bierce received a serious bullet wound to the head during a fierce battle at Kennesaw Mountain, Georgia. He recovered from the injury and returned to active military duty, only to be captured by Confederate soldiers. Bierce managed to escape from his captors, though. He slipped into the woods and slogged back to the Union Army, keeping one step ahead of his pursuers.

Exploring and writing

In January 1865, Bierce's application for a discharge from the Union military was approved. A few months later, Northern forces secured total victory over the South, formally ending the war. In the months immediately after the war ended, Bierce worked for the U.S. Treasury Department in Alabama. He helped the U.S. government confiscate (take possession of) property that previously had been owned by Confederate leaders.

Bierce's duties in Alabama made him very unpopular with local communities, and he began looking for another job. In the summer of 1866, he accepted an offer from W. B. Hazen, his old army commander, to accompany him on a small army expedition into the western territories. The four-man expedition traveled through remote wilderness all the way to San Francisco, California. Upon reaching the city, however, Bierce resigned from the military when he learned that his request to be commissioned as a captain had been denied (several years later, he received the brevet [honorary] rank of major in recognition of his Civil War service).

Within months of arriving in San Francisco, Bierce began writing for area newspapers. He soon became the editor for the city's *News-Letter.* But he became even better known for his essays and editorials on the issues and individuals shaping California at that time. His sarcastic writing style and willingness to criticize powerful politicians and businessmen soon made him the state's most controversial writer. In fact, people often referred to him as "the best-hated and best-loved man in California."

Bierce's Civil War stories

Bierce spent almost thirty years as a columnist for various San Francisco newspapers, including the *Argonaut,* the

Wasp, and the *San Francisco Examiner.* In 1871, he married Mollie Day, with whom he had two sons. A year later he moved to London, England, where his savagely witty newspaper columns made him a celebrity. After four years in Europe, though, he returned to San Francisco, where he resumed his journalism career.

In the 1890s, Bierce expanded his literary output by publishing a number of novels and short stories. The best known of these works was *Tales of Soldiers and Civilians,* published in 1891. This collection of short stories about the Civil War made Bierce even more famous. It included several powerful tales about the horrors of war. The best known of these stories is probably "An Occurrence at Owl Creek Bridge," which tells about a soldier who is about to be executed by enemy troops. But other selections like "Chickamauga," "One of the Missing," and "A Son of the Gods" also received significant critical and popular praise. Today, "An Occurrence at Owl Creek Bridge" and other Bierce stories continue to be included in many American short story anthologies [collections of stories, poems, or other writings].

Bierce freely admitted that his Civil War experiences had a big impact on his views of the world around him. The war's bloody violence and shocking casualties made him naturally suspicious of political and military leaders, and the sights and sounds of combat haunted his thoughts for the rest of his life. Years after the war had concluded, Bierce stated that "To this day I cannot look over a landscape without noting the advantages of the ground for attack or defense. I never hear a rifle-shot without [experiencing] a thrill in my veins. I never catch the peculiar odor of gunpowder without having visions of the dead and dying."

Leaves California

In the late 1890s, Bierce's reputation as one of the West's leading journalists and writers began to fade. He watched with anger and envy as other writers became more famous, even though many of them had less talent. He became particularly envious of Stephen Crane, whose 1895 Civil War novel *The Red Badge of Courage* received a level of

Stephen Crane's *The Red Badge of Courage*

The most famous Civil War book of all time is *The Red Badge of Courage*, by Stephen Crane (1871–1900). Crane, however, never experienced the Civil War first-hand. In fact, he was born six years after the conflict ended. Nonetheless, his realistic novel about a young soldier who overcomes his fears to fight bravely continues to be regarded as the best work of American literature about the Civil War. It also influenced the style of American writing for years to follow.

A native of Newark, New Jersey, Crane knew that he wanted to be a writer from a young age. His first novel, *Maggie: A Girl of the Streets* (1893) was not popular. But *The Red Badge of Courage* made Crane famous all across America, as readers rushed to buy his amazingly realistic Civil War tale. Eager to make use of Crane's notoriety (fame) and writing ability, several newspaper publishers subsequently hired him as a war correspondent. Crane spent the next few years reporting on wars in

Stephen Crane. *(Courtesy of the Library of Congress.)*

Cuba and Greece, even as he continued to write short stories and other fiction. In 1900, however, his life was cut short by tuberculosis, a disease that attacks the lungs and bones of its victims. A complete collection of Crane's prose and verse writings was published in 1925.

---

popular and critical acclaim that overshadowed Bierce's own war stories.

In 1900, Bierce left his longtime home outside San Francisco and became a political reporter in Washington, D.C. In 1906, he published a collection of sarcastic and satirical (using bitter humor to comment on human failings) definitions called *The Devil's Dictionary*. A multivolume collection of his essays, poetry, and other writings appeared over the following few years, too. Despite his best efforts, however, he never managed to regain the fame and influence he enjoyed in the 1880s and early 1890s.

By 1912, Bierce had grown weary of newspaper writing and life in Washington, D.C. He decided to leave his columnist position behind and travel to Mexico, where government and rebel forces were engaged in a bitter struggle for control of the country. "This fighting in Mexico interests me," Bierce told one friend. "If you should hear of my being stood up against a Mexican stone wall and shot to rags please know that I think it is a pretty good way to depart this life. It beats old age, disease or falling down the cellar stairs."

Bierce left for Mexico in 1913. In late December of that year he sent a letter to his secretary indicating that he was traveling with an army led by Pancho Villa (1878–1923), a Mexican rebel leader fighting to topple the country's authoritarian government (a government that demands absolute obedience from its citizens). He was never heard from again. Most historians believe that he died within months of writing that last letter, but no one really knows where or when Bierce died.

Where to Learn More

Ambrose Bierce (1814–1914?). [Online] http://www.creative.net~alang/lit/horror/abierce.sht (accessed on October 8, 1999).

The Ambrose Bierce Appreciation Society. [Online] http://idt.net/~damone/gbierce.html (accessed on October 8, 1999).

Bierce, Ambrose. *Ambrose Bierce's Civil War.* Edited by William McCann. Chicago: Regnery, 1956. Reprint, New York: Wings Books, 1996.

Morris, Roy. *Ambrose Bierce: Alone in Bad Company.* New York: Oxford University Press, 1998.

Wiggins, Robert A. *Ambrose Bierce.* Minneapolis: University of Minnesota Press, 1964.

John Wilkes Booth

Born May 10, 1838
Bel Air, Maryland
Died April 26, 1865
Port Royal, Virginia

Stage actor and Southern sympathizer who assassinated President Abraham Lincoln

John Wilkes Booth was a fanatical supporter of the Confederate cause during the Civil War. On April 14, 1865—as people throughout the North celebrated the end of the conflict—Booth made a deranged (insane) attempt to strike one final blow for the South. He shot **Abraham Lincoln** (1809–1865; see entry) as the president sat watching a play at Ford's Theatre in Washington, D.C. Lincoln died the following day. Although Booth and his accomplices (partners in crime) were soon captured, the assassination sent shock waves through the country. Lincoln's violent death made it much more difficult for the North and South to resolve their differences after the war.

Supports the South in the Civil War

John Wilkes Booth was born in Maryland in 1838. His father, Junius Brutus Booth (1796–1852), was the leading Shakespearean actor in the country at that time. His brother, Edwin Booth (1833–1893), became a well-known actor as

"Sic semper tyrannis! [Thus always to tyrants!]"

John Wilkes Booth. *(Courtesy of the National Archives and Records Administration.)*

well. John made a good living as an actor, but he never received the attention he felt he deserved.

By the time Booth reached his twenties, growing political tension in the United States had erupted into war. The Northern and Southern halves of the country had been arguing about a number of issues for many years. The most important of these issues was slavery. Many Northerners believed that slavery was wrong. They wanted the Federal government to take steps to outlaw slavery or at least keep it from spreading beyond the Southern states where it was already allowed. But slavery played an important role in the Southern economy and culture. Many Southerners resented Northern attempts to contain slavery. They felt that each state should decide for itself whether to allow the practice. They did not want the Federal government to pass laws that would interfere with their traditional way of life.

When the Civil War broke out in 1861, Booth's home state of Maryland remained part of the United States. It was one of four "border states" that allowed slavery, yet decided not to secede from (leave) the Union with the slaveholding states of the South. As a result, the people of Maryland had divided loyalties during the war. Booth's family tended to support the Union cause. But Booth himself believed in slavery because he thought that black people were inferior to white people. For this reason, he became a supporter of the Confederate cause.

Devises schemes to help the Confederacy

Despite his devotion to the South, Booth never volunteered to fight in the Confederate Army. It appeared that he was afraid to become a soldier, and that this fear embarrassed him. "I have begun to deem [believe] myself a coward, and to despise my own existence," he wrote in his diary. As a result, Booth started to dream of new ways to help the Confederacy. He wanted to do something important so that his name would live in history. At the same time, he developed an intense hatred of President Abraham Lincoln. In his unbalanced mind, Booth viewed Lincoln as a tyrant who was responsible for all of the country's troubles. He came up with a variety of schemes to harm the president. As Bruce Catton explained in *The American Heritage New History of the Civil War*,

Booth was "driven by an insane compulsion [impulse] of hatred and perverted loyalty to a cause which he had never felt obliged [required] to fight for as a soldier."

In 1861, shortly before Lincoln was inaugurated (sworn in) as president, Booth devised a plan to kidnap him. The plan failed when the president's travel plans changed unexpectedly. As the Civil War raged over the next few years, Booth formed a small band of anti-Union conspirators. They came up with several schemes to kidnap Lincoln, take him to the Confederate capital in Richmond, Virginia, and use him to negotiate an end to the war that favored the South. But all of these plans eventually fell apart.

When Confederate general **Robert E. Lee** (1807–1870; see entry) surrendered in April 1865 to end the Civil War, Booth realized that kidnaping the president would serve no purpose. Instead, he decided to kill Lincoln and several other important members of the government, including Vice President **Andrew Johnson** (1808–1875; see entry), Secretary of State **William Henry Seward** (1801–1872; see entry), and General **Ulysses S. Grant** (1822–1885; see entry). Booth thought that the Confederacy might survive if he killed the Union leaders. He also thought that he would be hailed as a hero throughout the South.

Booth assassinates President Lincoln

Booth and his helpers decided to put their plan into effect on April 14. That night, the president and his wife attended a play at Ford's Theatre in Washington called *Our American Cousin*. The Lincolns were joined in their fine balcony seats by Major Henry R. Rathbone and his fiancée, Clara Harris. Midway through the play, Booth slipped into the rear of the president's box in the theater. He then withdrew a one-shot pistol called a derringer from his jacket and shot Lincoln in the back of the head.

Major Rathbone leaped to his feet to stop the assassin, but Booth slashed the officer with a knife. He then jumped out of the balcony and landed on the stage below. Although he broke his leg in the fall, he still managed to get to his feet. Booth shouted "Sic semper tyrannis" (a Latin phrase meaning "Thus

A poster offers a reward for the capture of John Wilkes Booth. *(Courtesy of the Library of Congress.)*

A wood engraving shows the capture and death of John Wilkes Booth in a burning Virginia barn. *(Courtesy of Corbis Corporation.)*

always to tyrants") to the stunned audience, limped off the stage to the rear of the theater, and escaped on a waiting horse.

In the meantime, doctors in the audience rushed to Lincoln's aid. They carried him to a boarding house across the street from the theater, but found that they could do nothing to help him. The president died early the next morning. Most of the rest of Booth's plan collapsed, and the attacks on Johnson and Grant never took place. But one of his accomplices attacked Secretary Seward in his bedroom at the same time that Booth was attacking Lincoln. Seward suffered numerous knife wounds, but managed to hold off his attacker until the man fled into the night. He eventually recovered from his injuries.

The assassin is captured and killed

Booth rode through the night until he reached the farmhouse of Dr. Samuel Mudd. Mudd set Booth's broken leg for him, but later claimed that he had not known the identity of the assassin. With the help of fellow conspirator David E. Herold, Booth escaped south to Virginia. But Federal soldiers eventually tracked the two men to a tobacco barn near Port Royal. On April 26, the soldiers surrounded the barn and demanded that the men surrender. Herold gave himself up, but Booth refused. The soldiers then set fire to the barn in order to force the assassin out. Booth died of a gunshot wound while still inside the barn, but it remains uncertain whether he shot himself or whether one of the soldiers shot him.

The United States entered into a period of mourning after Lincoln's death. People in the North who had been celebrating the end of the Civil War suddenly plunged into a mood of deep anger and sadness. Some people questioned whether the assassination had been a conspiracy waged by Southern leaders, including Confederate president **Jefferson Davis** (1808–1889; see entry). A government commission investigated the matter, but the evidence suggested that Booth and his gang had acted on their own, without the knowledge of Confederate leaders.

Within a few weeks of Booth's death, eight other alleged (accused) participants in the assassination plot were captured and put on trial. All eight were convicted of being involved in the plan to kill Lincoln, and four of them were hanged—Mary E. Surratt, Lewis Paine, David E. Herold, and George A. Atzerodt. Three others were sentenced to life in prison, but they were pardoned (granted official forgiveness and released from further punishment) in 1869. (One of those was Samuel A. Mudd [1833–1883], the physician who treated Booth's injured leg but claimed to have no knowledge of either Lincoln's death or of Booth's involvement in the president's assassination.) The eighth person was sentenced to six years for helping Booth escape from Ford's Theatre.

Assassination ends up harming the South

Booth died thinking that he had helped the South by killing Lincoln. But historians point out that this was not really the case. "Confused motives had thronged [crowded into] Booth's cloudy mind, but one stood out with something resembling clarity. He thought that by removing Lincoln he was in some way helping his defeated South. He had not, of course, helped the South at all; he had in fact hurt it," T. Harry Williams wrote in *The Union Restored.* "By his act Booth had damaged the hopes of the entire nation for an easy 're-construction' [the period immediately after the Civil War, when the United States struggled to resolve its differences and readmit the Southern states to the Union]. . . . Booth had shot the one man who might have provided the leadership needed so urgently at this unique moment in history."

Lincoln believed that the country could never be whole again unless the South was welcomed back with open arms. He wanted to give the Southern states significant control over their own affairs and help them rebuild their ruined cities and farmlands. At his second inauguration a few weeks before his death, the president had expressed his desire to act with "malice toward none; with charity for all . . . to bind up the nation's wounds" and "to achieve and cherish a just and lasting peace among ourselves."

After Lincoln's death, power in the U.S. government shifted to lawmakers who were determined to punish the South for the war and for the loss of their leader. Vice President Johnson assumed the presidency following Lincoln's assassination, and both he and leaders in Congress indicated that their Reconstruction policies toward the South would be very stern. The nation struggled to resolve its differences for many years.

Where to Learn More

Abraham Lincoln's Assassination. [Online] http://members.aol.com/RVS Norton/Lincoln.html (accessed on October 8, 1999).

Assassination of President Lincoln and the Trial of the Assassins. [Online] http://www.tiac.net/users/ime/famtree/burnett/lincoln.htm (accessed on October 8, 1999).

Clarke, Asia Booth. *John Wilkes Booth: A Sister's Memoir.* Jackson: University Press of Mississippi, 1996.

Dr. Samuel A. Mudd Society, Inc. *Dr. Samuel A. Mudd House Museum Home Page.* [Online] http://www.somd.lib.md.us/MUSEUMS/Mudd.htm (accessed on October 8, 1999).

Furtwangler, Albert. *Assassin on Stage.* Urbana: University of Illinois Press, 1991.

Jakoubek, Robert. *The Assassination of Abraham Lincoln*. Brookfield, CT: Millbrook Press, 1993.

January, Brendan. *The Assassination of Abraham Lincoln*. New York: Children's Press, 1998.

National Park Service. *Ford's Theatre National Historic Site*. [Online] http://www.nps.gov/foth/index2.htm (accessed on October 8, 1999).

Nottingham, Theodore J. *The Curse of Cain: The Untold Story of John Wilkes Booth*. Nicholasville, KY: Appaloosa Press, 1997.

Surratt Society. *Surratt House Museum*. [Online] http://www.surratt.org/ (accessed on October 8, 1999).

Belle Boyd

Born 1843 or 1844
Martinsburg, Virginia (now West Virginia)
Died 1900
Kilborn, Wisconsin

Confederate spy known as
"Cleopatra of the Secession"

elle Boyd was one of the most famous Confederate spies of the Civil War, but not necessarily one of the most successful. She carried information to Confederate general **Thomas "Stonewall" Jackson** (1824–1863; see entry) that helped him win battles in Virginia's Shenandoah Valley in 1862. But Boyd loved the thrills of spying and basked in the attention she received as a spy. As a result, she became less effective over time and eventually lost much of her value to the Confederate cause.

Home state changes loyalties

Belle Boyd was born in Martinsburg, Virginia, in 1843. This was a time of great political tension in the United States. For years, the North and the South had been arguing over several issues, including slavery. By 1861, this ongoing dispute had convinced several Southern states to secede from (leave) the United States and attempt to form a new country that allowed slavery, called the Confederate States of America. Boyd's home state of Virginia was one of the Southern

> Belle Boyd was a daring and flamboyant young woman who enjoyed the thrill of spying for the Confederacy.

Belle Boyd. *(Reproduced by permission of Corbis-Bettmann.)*

states that decided to join the Confederacy. But Northern political leaders were determined to keep the Southern states in the Union. The two sides soon went to war.

Some of the earliest fighting of the Civil War took place in the western part of Virginia. Many people in this mountainous region remained loyal to the Union despite Virginia's decision to secede. They felt they had more in common with the neighboring free states of Pennsylvania and Ohio than with the slave economy of the eastern part of Virginia. By June 1861, Union loyalists in western Virginia were trying to form a new state that would separate from Virginia and rejoin the Union. Boyd's hometown of Martinsburg eventually became part of this new state of West Virginia.

Of course, not all residents of western Virginia were loyal to the Union. Boyd and her family continued to support the Confederacy, even after Union forces moved into the area where they lived. Boyd expressed her pro-Confederate feelings in a dramatic and violent way. On July 4, 1861, a Union soldier came to her family's house to replace their Confederate flag with a U.S. flag. Boyd shot the soldier, and he later died of his wounds. She was put on trial for the crime, but received only minor punishment.

Boyd becomes a spy for the Confederacy

Before long, Boyd decided to help the Confederate cause by acting as a spy. As an attractive young woman, she figured she could get close to Union soldiers in the area, obtain information about their troop strength and military strategies, and take that information to the Confederate forces. She ran her spying operations out of her parents' hotel in Martinsburg, in the Shenandoah Valley.

In March 1862, General Thomas "Stonewall" Jackson entered the Shenandoah Valley with eight thousand Confederate troops. Over the next three months, he roamed across the region in a dazzling display that thoroughly baffled his Union Army counterparts. On several occasions, Jackson's army defeated much larger Union forces in battle. At other times, he and his troops seemed to melt into the valleys and woodlands of the Shenandoah region, frustrating pursuing Union armies.

Part of what allowed Jackson to avoid capture was information he received from local Confederate supporters. Boyd was one of the most valuable sources of information. At one point, she found out that the Union forces planned to surround Jackson's army and take the general prisoner. She rode fifteen miles to Jackson's camp and delivered this information to his staff personally. Another time, Boyd learned that three Union generals were combining forces against Jackson. During the heat of battle, she ran across from the Union lines to the Confederate lines to carry this information to the Southern leader. According to legend, she had bullet holes in the hoops of her skirt but was not hurt. After Confederate forces won the battle, Jackson thanked Boyd personally and made her an honorary member of his staff.

According to legend, Belle Boyd had bullet holes in the hoops of her skirt. *(Courtesy of Corbis Corporation.)*

Arrest and exile

On July 29, 1862, at the age of nineteen, Boyd was arrested for spying against the United States. She was taken to the Old Capitol Prison in Washington, D.C. Even after she was caught, Boyd continued to express her strong support for the Confederate cause. She waved a Confederate flag out the window of the train that carried her to prison, and while there she was often heard singing the Southern song "Dixie" at the top of her lungs. Within a few months, Boyd was released and allowed to return to the South as part of a prisoner exchange. (In the early war years, the North and the South regularly exchanged the people they had captured for their own people who were held by the other side.)

Boyd spent some time in hiding with relatives in the South. When she returned to Martinsburg in June 1863, she was again arrested as a spy. She spent six more months in prison, then was released because she was suffering from the disease typhoid. Knowing that she would return to spying when she regained her health, Union officials deported her (forced her to leave the country). She spent a few months in exile in England, then attempted to return to the United States on a Confederate supply ship. But the ship was captured, and Boyd was taken prisoner on a Union ship.

Boyd fell in love with the Union soldier in charge of prisoners on the ship, Lieutenant Samuel Wylde Hardinge. As a result of their relationship, Hardinge was charged with aiding a Confederate spy, forced to leave the Union Navy, and put in prison. Meanwhile, Boyd was sent back to England, where she became a celebrity. She appeared on stage, telling dramatic stories about her life as a spy, and even wrote a book about her experiences, *Belle Boyd in Camp and Prison*. Hardinge joined Boyd in England after his release from prison. Their wedding in August 1864 was a huge social event. But Boyd soon convinced her husband to return to the United States as a Confederate spy. He was captured and died in prison, leaving her a widow at the age of twenty-one.

Turns spy life into a stage career

After the Civil War ended in 1865, Boyd returned to the United States. She continued her stage career for many years. She seemed to enjoy the attention she attracted as a former spy. In fact, she often used the titles "Cleopatra of the Secession" and "Siren of the Shenandoah" in her stage shows. Boyd married two more times over the years. She died in 1900 while making a public appearance in Kilborn, Wisconsin. The Women's Auxiliary of the Grand Army of the Confederacy paid for her burial there.

Although Boyd became famous as a Confederate spy, her fame actually made her much less effective in her work. Most other spies worked behind the scenes and tried not to show their true loyalties or attract unnecessary attention to themselves. But Boyd was a daring and flamboyant (flashy) young woman who enjoyed the thrill of spying. She carried valuable tactical (military) intelligence to Stonewall Jackson during his campaign in the Shenandoah Valley, but lost her value to the Confederacy as her fame grew.

Where to Learn More

Belle Boyd House. [Online] www.travelwv.com/bellepic.htm (accessed on October 8, 1999).

Boyd, Belle. *Belle Boyd in Camp and Prison.* New York: Blelock, 1865. Reprint, Baton Rouge: Louisiana State University Press, 1998.

Markle, Donald E. *Spies and Spymasters of the Civil War.* New York: Hippocrene Books, 1994.

Scarborough, Ruth. *Belle Boyd: Siren of the South.* Macon, GA: Mercer University Press, 1983.

Mathew Brady

Born 1822 or 1823
Warren County, New York
Died January 15, 1896
New York City, New York

Civil War photographer
His studio produced many of the war's most famous photographs

M athew Brady is the most famous of the many American photographers who documented the Civil War in pictures. He did not personally take many of the photographs that made him famous. Instead, failing eyesight forced him to hire teams of photographers to take care of the actual camera work. But it was Brady who led the effort to use photography as a way of recording the events of the Civil War for future generations. "[Mathew Brady] would serve history and country," wrote Carl Sandburg in *The Photographs of Abraham Lincoln.* "He would prove what photography could do by telling what neither the tongues nor the letters of soldiers could tell of troops in camp, on the march, or mute and bullet-riddled on the ground."

"[Mathew Brady proved] what photography could do by telling what neither the tongues nor the letters of soldiers could tell of troops in camp, on the march, or mute and bullet-riddled on the ground."

Carl Sandburg

Child of immigrants

Mathew Brady was born around 1823 to Irish immigrants who settled in New York state in the early 1820s. The youngest of five children, Brady spent his early years working on the family farm. It was during his midteens that Brady

Mathew Brady. *(Courtesy of the Library of Congress.)*

first began to suffer from problems with his eyesight. This condition became steadily worse as he grew older.

In 1839, Brady moved to New York City, where he worked as a department store clerk. He spent much of his free time, however, learning about the fascinating new world of photography. Over the previous few years, the discoveries of inventors Louis-Jacques-Mandé Daguerre (1789–1851) and Samuel F. B. Morse (1791–1872) had made it possible to take the first photographs. The process of creating these early photographs—called daguerreotypes in honor of Louis Daguerre—was very primitive. For example, cameras were far too heavy to be held by hand, photographic subjects had to remain still for fifteen seconds or more to avoid looking blurry, and processing of pictures required cumbersome (difficult to handle) chemicals and equipment.

Master of photography

Despite these factors, however, people viewed photography as an exciting new invention. Determined to build a career out of this new technology, Brady studied how to be a photographer and opened his own studio in New York in 1844. The high quality of his work quickly attracted attention around the city. In 1845, he won two first prizes in a daguerreotype competition held by the American Institute of the City of New York. A year later the magazine *Spirit of the Times* hailed his photography as "brilliantly clear and beautiful."

By the late 1840s, Brady's reputation for excellence had made him the preferred portrait photographer of the rich and famous. His subjects ranged from politicians like President Martin Van Buren (1782–1862) and Senator John Calhoun (1782–1850) to such celebrities as writer Edgar Allan Poe (1809–1849) and circus showman Phineas T. Barnum (1810–1891). In 1851, Brady published a book of photographs called *Gallery of Illustrious Americans* that further cemented his reputation as one of the nation's master photographers. He also married Julia Handy, the daughter of a prominent Maryland lawyer, around this time.

In 1853, Brady opened a new studio in New York, even though his eyesight had become so bad that he rarely took photographs himself. Instead, he relied on talented assistants to take portraits and other pictures. In 1856, Brady hired Alexander Gardner (1821–1882) to work for him. Gardner proved to be a valuable employee. A talented and well-educated photographic artist, he assisted Brady as he made the transition from daguerreotype to the wet-plate process, a new photographic technology that used negatives to produce multiple copies of pictures. This process became the basis for all modern photography.

In the late 1850s, Brady decided to open another studio in Washington. But instead of managing the new studio—called the National Photographic Art Gallery—himself, he remained in New York and sent Gardner to manage it. Gardner managed the new studio with great skill. He and other photographers in the Washington studio took all the pictures that were produced there, but Brady still insisted that all of the photos be credited to him. This rule also was applied in Brady's New York studio. This policy gave people the false impression that Brady was the one who was taking all the great photographs produced in his studios, and it eventually caused bitter splits between the studio owner and some of his most talented camera operators.

Brady and Lincoln

In 1860, Brady's studio took several portraits of **Abraham Lincoln** (1809–1865; see entry) that were used in his presidential campaign. The two men established a friendly relationship. After Lincoln won the 1860 election, Brady and his assistants received special status as semiofficial photographers to the White House. In addition to taking pictures of Lincoln's family, friends, and cabinet members, they also took many portraits of the president himself. Alexander Gardner alone took more than thirty photographs of Lincoln during his presidency.

When the Civil War between the North and South began in April 1861, Brady's studios were flooded with Northern soldiers who wanted to leave pictures with their loved ones before heading off to war. Brady was inspired by the sight of these young men in uniform. He believed that photographs could provide a powerful historical record of the conflict. As a result, Brady decided that he wanted to accompany the Union Army as it marched against the soldiers of the Confederacy. "A spirit in my feet said, 'Go!' and I went," Brady later said.

First, Brady obtained permission from Lincoln to accompany Union troops into the field. He then worked with his assistants to address the many challenges of taking photographs outside of a studio setting. The photographers eventually modified a wagon so that it could serve as a sort of portable darkroom, complete with shelves and drawers for photographic chemicals, lenses, cameras, and other equipment.

Brady at the First Battle of Bull Run

In July 1861, Brady and a team of assistants accompanied a Union army led by General Irvin McDowell (1818–1885) as it marched out of Washington. Their destination was a small village in Virginia called Manassas, located about thirty miles southwest of the capital, where a Confederate army had gathered.

Many Northerners assumed that the Civil War would be over in a matter of a few months. They believed that Union forces were vastly superior to the Confederate Army. As a result, they viewed the upcoming battle at Manassas as a certain victory that would begin the process of restoring the rebellious Confederate states to the Union. Northern confidence in victory was so high that hundreds of Washingtonians packed up picnic baskets and followed the Union troops to Manassas as if they were going to a show.

But when the Union and Confederate armies met at Manassas in the first major battle of the Civil War, the Southern army registered a decisive victory. The battle—known in the North as the First Battle of Bull Run in recognition of nearby Bull Run Creek—ended in a disastrous retreat for the North, as soldiers and civilians alike fled back to Washington in a frightened herd. Brady's cameramen took some pictures of the chaotic scene, but all of their pictures were ruined when the panicked crowd knocked his wagon over.

Antietam photographs shock the North

Brady's first journey onto the battlefield had not gone as he had hoped. But his determination to produce a photographic record of the war remained strong. As Northerners adjusted to the reality that the war might last for quite awhile, Brady organized his photographers into two-man teams that accompanied Union armies all around the country.

One of these teams, comprised of Alexander Gardner and James Gibson, accompanied the Union army commanded by General **George B. McClellan** (1826–1885; see entry) when it clashed in September 1862 with a large rebel force led by Confederate general **Robert E. Lee** (1807–1870; see entry). This one-day struggle along Antietam Creek outside of Sharpsburg, Maryland, produced more than twenty-six thousand casualties, making it the single bloodiest day in American military history.

A Mathew Brady photograph shows two dead soldiers lying in a ravine. *(Courtesy of the Library of Congress.)*

The Battle of Antietam (known in the South as the Battle of Sharpsburg) forced Lee to discard his plans to invade the North. Instead, he retreated back into Virginia to regroup. In the meantime, Gardner and Gibson wandered over the Antietam battlefield. Their photographs of the dead soldiers who lay scattered across the countryside provided vivid evidence of the toll that the war was taking on both sides.

When Brady saw the photographs that Gardner and Gibson had taken, he immediately made plans to exhibit them at his studio in New York. The photographs created excitement throughout the city. Citizens rushed to the gallery to see the horrible but powerful pictures for themselves. "Mr. Mathew Brady has done something to bring us the terrible reality and earnestness of the war," commented the *New York Times*. "If he has not brought bodies and laid them in our dooryards and along our streets, he has done something very like it."

Brady struggles with mounting debts

Shortly after taking the photographs at Antietam, Gardner left Brady and started his own studio. Gardner had argued with Brady over business issues for some time. In addition, he was tired of giving credit to Brady for photographs that he himself had taken. Gardner's departure proved to be a major blow to Brady. His studios suffered financially in Gardner's absence, and his former assistant quickly emerged as a major competitor. In fact, Gardner was commonly viewed as Washington's leading photographer by the end of the Civil War.

By 1864, Brady's studios were in serious financial trouble. His photographers continued to follow Union armies as they marched across the South, but the cost of outfitting his teams of photographers was huge. In addition, Brady overestimated the money he could make on his Civil War photographs. Demand for his photographs increased somewhat after the Confederacy surrendered in the spring of 1865, but the increased income was not enough to cover his many debts. In 1868, Brady was forced to declare bankruptcy.

Despite his financial problems, Brady managed to reopen a modest studio in Washington. In 1875, Brady received a financial boost when the U.S. government agreed to purchase many of the photographs that his studios had accumulated during the war. His reputation as a portrait photographer also brought him a steady income for several years. Famous figures like women's rights advocate Susan B. Anthony (1820–1906), inventor Thomas Edison (1847–1931), and Supreme Court Chief Justice Salmon P. Chase (1808–1873) all traveled to Brady's studio for portraits during the 1870s. But growing health problems and financial difficulties finally forced Brady to close his studio in 1881.

During the last fifteen years of his life, Brady scraped together a living from occasional photography work. His wife died in 1887, but he remained in Washington rather than return to his native New York. One woman who knew Brady during this period described him as a "sad little man." Brady entertained the woman with "tales of his glory days as the prince of New York photographer and his exploits during the Civil War," wrote George Sullivan in *Mathew Brady: His Life and Photographs.* "[But] he also complained to her of his financial woes, his poor health, and loneliness, which had deepened since the death of his wife."

In the mid-1890s, Brady returned to New York, where he moved into a small apartment. In 1895, a Civil War veterans' group asked Brady to prepare a retrospective (review of past work) of his wartime photographs for display at New York's Carnegie Hall. The honor excited Brady, who had become a largely forgotten figure. But in late 1895, he was hospitalized with kidney problems. Brady died on January 15, 1896, two weeks before his scheduled exhibition at Carnegie Hall.

By the time Brady died, most Americans had forgotten how important his activities were in creating a photographic record of the Civil War. Today, however, many of the photographs produced by Brady and his assistants rank among the most famous in American history. Many of them are used in history books about the war, and they form one of the most highly prized collections in the Library of Congress.

Where to Learn More

Hoobler, Dorothy, and Thomas Hoobler. *Photographing History: The Career of Mathew Brady.* New York: Putnam, 1977.

Kunhardt, Dorothy Meserve, and Philip B. Kunhardt, Jr. *Mathew Brady and His World.* Alexandria, VA: Time-Life Books, 1977.

National Portrait Gallery, Smithsonian Institution. *Mathew Brady's Portraits.* [Online] http://www.npg.si.edu/exh/brady/index2.html (accessed on October 8, 1999).

Panzer, Mary. *Mathew Brady and the Image of History.* Washington, D.C.: Smithsonian Institution Press, 1997.

Sullivan, George. *Mathew Brady: His Life and Photographs.* New York: Cobblehill Books, 1994.

Van Steenwyk, Elizabeth. *Mathew Brady: Civil War Photographer.* Danbury, CT: Franklin Watts, 1997.

Braxton Bragg

Born March 22, 1817
Warrenton, North Carolina
Died September 27, 1876
Galveston, Texas

Confederate general
Was victorious at Battle of Chickamauga but
failed in two other campaigns in 1862 and 1863

General Braxton Bragg was one of the most controversial generals in the Confederate Army. In September 1863, Bragg guided the South's Army of Tennessee to victory in the Battle of Chickamauga. This was the Confederacy's only major triumph in the western theater (the region of the country between the Mississippi River and the Appalachian Mountains) during the entire Civil War. Despite this victory, however, the general is better known for his failures as commander of the Army of Tennessee. During the eighteen months that he led that army, Bragg's stormy relationship with subordinate (lower-ranking) officers greatly reduced its effectiveness. In fact, his unpopularity with his own troops is often cited as a factor in the failure of two major offensive campaigns he undertook in 1862 and 1863.

A life in the military

Braxton Bragg was born in 1817 in North Carolina to a wealthy planter. When Bragg was a teenager, his father managed to arrange his enrollment in the U.S. Military Acad-

"[Bragg] loved to crush the spirit of his men. The more of a hang-dog look they had about them, the better was General Bragg pleased. Not a single soldier in the whole army ever loved or respected him."

Soldier Sam Watkins

Braxton Bragg. *(Courtesy of Corbis Corporation.)*

emy at West Point, the nation's premier military school. He entered West Point at the age of sixteen and established himself as a top cadet. He graduated in 1837, ranking fifth in a class of fifty students.

After graduating from West Point, Bragg entered the U.S. Army. He became known as an intelligent and efficient officer, but also gained a reputation for being argumentative and stubborn. One of his first military assignments took him to Florida, where he fought in the Seminole Wars (1835–42). This clash between the U.S. government and the Seminole Indians eventually pushed the tribe out of Florida and onto reservations in Oklahoma. In the late 1840s, Bragg served with great distinction in the Mexican War (1846–48), a struggle between Mexico and the United States over possession of the vast territories in the American West. In 1848, U.S. military victories forced Mexico to give up its claims on California, New Mexico, and other lands in the West in exchange for $15 million.

In 1849, Bragg returned to the eastern United States and married Eliza Brooks Ellis, the daughter of a wealthy Louisiana plantation owner. He remained in the military until 1856, when he resigned at the rank of lieutenant colonel. He then settled in his wife's home state of Louisiana and became a wealthy planter himself.

Devoted to the Confederate cause

Bragg's comfortable life in Louisiana came to an end in early 1861, when America's Northern and Southern sections went to war. These regions had been angry with one another for years over the continued existence of slavery in America. The Northern states felt that slavery was immoral and wanted to abolish (completely get rid of) it. The South, however, wanted to keep slavery because many of its economic and social institutions had been built on the practice. In addition, Southerners argued that individual states had the constitutional right to disregard Federal laws that they did not like. This belief in "states' rights" further increased the divisions between the two sides. As Northern calls to make slavery illegal grew louder, Southerners became increasingly resentful and defensive. The two sides finally went to war in early 1861 when the Southern states tried to secede from (leave) the Union and form their own country that allowed slavery, called the Confederate States of America.

When the Civil War began, Bragg immediately volunteered his services to the Confederacy. He strongly believed in the theory of states' rights. He also felt a great loyalty to his adopted home state of Louisiana, which voted to join the Confederacy in January 1861. When Confederate leaders learned of Bragg's decision to fight on the side of the South, they wasted no time in appointing the veteran soldier to a position of responsibility. He was made a brigadier general and ordered to Pensacola, Florida, where he trained volunteer soldiers for the upcoming war.

Bragg's skill at turning inexperienced recruits into disciplined soldiers attracted a good deal of attention. In September 1861, he was promoted to major general by Confederate president **Jefferson Davis** (1808–1889; see entry), even though the two men had clashed in the 1850s over various military issues. A month later, Bragg was assigned command of Confederate troops in western Florida and all of Alabama.

Takes command of Army of Tennessee

In February 1862, Bragg joined the Army of Mississippi, led by General Albert S. Johnston (1803–1862), as chief of staff and corps commander. Two months later, he commanded a major part of the Confederate force at the Battle of Shiloh in Tennessee. Union general **Ulysses S. Grant** (1822–1885; see entry) barely avoided a catastrophic defeat in this clash, which claimed the life of Johnston.

In recognition of his performance at Shiloh, Bragg was promoted to full general on April 12, 1862. Several weeks later, the Army of Mississippi's new commander, **Pierre G. T. Beauregard** (1818–1893; see entry), took an unauthorized medical leave. President Davis promptly removed Beauregard from command and appointed Bragg—whom he had come to trust—to lead the army.

Upon taking command, Bragg devised a plan to invade Kentucky. Kentucky was one of four "border states" that allowed slavery but remained part of the Union. The invasion was successful in its early stages, as Bragg skillfully moved his troops through Tennessee and into Kentucky. In the fall of 1862, though, Bragg's campaign faltered. On October 8, Union forces under the direction of General Don Carlos Buell (1818–1898) stopped Bragg's army at Perryville, Kentucky. The Confederate general retreated back to Tennessee, where he was hit with heavy criticism.

Political enemies of President Davis offered particularly harsh words of disapproval about Bragg's failed invasion. Some even suggested that Bragg had been given command of the army (which was now known as the Army of Tennessee) only because he was friendly with Davis. These critics hoped that attacks on Bragg might also hurt Davis, whom they wanted to replace. "You have the misfortune of being regarded as my personal friend," Davis wrote to Bragg. "And are pursued therefore with malignant censure [evil insults] by men regardless of truth and whose want [lack] of principle to guide their conduct renders them incapable of conceiving that you are trusted because of your known fitness for command, and not because of friendly regard."

Chickamauga

At the end of 1862, Bragg's army was tested again when the Union's Army of the Cumberland moved into central Tennessee in hopes of seizing control of the area. Bragg reacted by setting up a strong defensive position at Stones River, near the town of Murfreesboro. The Union force, commanded by General William Rosecrans (1819–1898), attacked Bragg's position on New Year's Eve, 1862. The battle raged for three days, as both armies desperately fought for possession of the battlefield. The clash finally ended on January 2, 1863, after Bragg learned that Union reinforcements were on the way to help Rosecrans. He reluctantly retreated from the region, giving up on his hopes of establishing Confederate control over the area.

The Battle of Stones River (also known as the Battle of Murfreesboro) badly damaged both armies. Rosecrans lost more than thirteen thousand of his forty-seven thousand troops, while Bragg's thirty-eight thousand–man force suffered more than ten thousand casualties. These heavy losses forced both commanders to remain inactive for the next several months. By June 1863, however, Rosecrans's army had recovered. Armed with reinforcements that swelled the size of his Army of the Cumberland to about sixty thousand troops, Rosecrans launched a skillful military campaign that pushed Bragg's army all the way across Tennessee. By early September, Bragg had abandoned the city of Chattanooga, even though it was a major Confederate railroad center and supply depot.

Encouraged by Bragg's evacuation of Chattanooga, Rosecrans tried to acquire even more rebel territory. But when Bragg received reinforcements in northern Georgia, he turned to confront his pursuer. In mid-September he counterattacked near a small stream known as Chickamauga Creek. Over the course of two days (September 19 and 20) the brutal Battle of Chickamauga raged, until Bragg's Army of Tennessee finally gained the advantage and chased Rosecrans' troops from the field. Rosecrans retreated all the way back to Chattanooga. Bragg gave chase, but his progress was slowed by continued bickering with his junior (lower-ranked) officers over military strategy and other issues.

Chattanooga

By this time, many of Bragg's officers had developed a great dislike for their stern, quick-tempered commander. They disagreed with many of his strategic decisions and did not feel any loyalty to him. As time passed, this dissatisfaction with Bragg could be detected throughout his army. "None of General Bragg's soldiers ever loved him," wrote Sam Watkins, a soldier in the Army of Tennessee. "They had no faith in his ability as a general. He was looked upon as a merciless tyrant. . . . He loved to crush the spirit of his men. The more of a hang-dog look they had about them, the better was General Bragg pleased. Not a single soldier in the whole army ever loved or respected him." By mid-1863, hostility toward Bragg had become so great that some of his officers had begun urging Davis to relieve the general of his command.

Davis ignored these calls, though. Instead, he watched with great interest as Bragg marched on Chattanooga in an effort to finish off Rosecrans's battered Army of the Cumberland. In October, Bragg surrounded the city and began a siege (a blockade designed to prevent the city from receiving food and

Union major general William S. Rosecrans (above) fought against Confederate general Braxton Bragg in several battles. *(Courtesy of the Library of Congress.)*

other supplies) in hopes of starving the Union troops into surrendering.

As the weeks passed, however, the situation at Chattanooga began to turn against Bragg. Union general Ulysses S. Grant replaced Rosecrans with General George H. Thomas (1816–1870), who managed to open a supply route into the city. At the same time, Bragg's relationships with his officers and troops continued to worsen with each passing day. On November 24, Grant ordered an attack on Bragg's army in hopes of breaking the siege. This offensive easily broke through the Confederate Army, which fought in half-hearted fashion. The following day, Grant's forces pushed the entire Army of Tennessee out of the area and back into Georgia. The poor performance of Bragg's army at the Battle of Chattanooga shocked Davis and convinced him that Bragg could no longer manage his men effectively. Davis quickly replaced him with General **Joseph E. Johnston** (1807–1891; see entry).

Bragg spent most of the rest of the war serving as a military advisor to Davis in Richmond. In March 1865, he returned to the Army of Tennessee to take command of one of its divisions. But by this time Union control of the South was nearly complete, and all of the Confederate armies surrendered over the next few weeks. After the war was over, Bragg moved to Texas and settled in Galveston. He died on September 27, 1876.

Where to Learn More

Connelly, Thomas L. *Autumn of Glory: The Army of Tennessee, 1862–1865.* Baton Rouge: Louisiana State University Press, 1971.

Hallock, Judith Lee. *Braxton Bragg and Confederate Defeat.* Tuscaloosa: University of Alabama Press, 1991.

Woodworth, Steven E. *Jefferson Davis and His Generals: The Failure of Confederate Command in the West.* Lawrence: University Press of Kansas, 1990.

John Brown

**Born 1800
Torrington, Connecticut
Died December 2, 1859
Charlestown, Virginia**

**Radical abolitionist
Led an unsuccessful attempt to ignite
a slave uprising in the South in 1859**

John Brown was a highly controversial member of the movement to abolish (put an end to) slavery in the years leading up to the Civil War. He believed that slavery was morally wrong and committed himself to doing anything in his power to destroy it. "Slavery throughout its entire existence in the United States is none other than a mad, barbarous [cruel], unprovoked, and unjustifiable war of one portion of its citizens upon another portion, in utter disregard and violation of those eternal and self-evident truths set forth in our Declaration of Independence," he stated.

As Brown grew more and more furious about slavery, he came to believe that violence was both necessary and justified in the fight to abolish it. In 1856, he participated in the cold-blooded murder of five slavery supporters in Kansas. Three years later, he led a raid on a federal armory (a storage facility for weapons and ammunition) in Harpers Ferry, Virginia. Known as "John Brown's Raid," this was the first step in a plan to arm slaves and lead them in a violent uprising throughout the South. Brown's plan failed, and he was captured and executed. But his actions added to the bit-

"Slavery . . . is none other than a mad, barbarous, unprovoked, and unjustifiable war of one portion of its citizens upon another portion. . . ."

John Brown. *(Courtesy of the National Archives and Records Administration.)*

ter feelings between the North and the South that led to the Civil War.

Taught to hate slavery

John Brown was born in Torrington, Connecticut, in 1800. His father, Owen Brown, was a tanner (a person who turns animal hides into leather) and shoemaker. A deeply religious man, Owen Brown raised his children to live by the teachings of the Bible. He also taught them to hate slavery because he believed that it violated God's commandments.

Black people were taken from Africa and brought to North America to serve as slaves for white people beginning in the 1600s. The basic belief behind slavery was that black people were inferior to whites. Under slavery, white slaveholders treated black people as property, forced them to perform hard labor, and controlled every aspect of their lives. States in the Northern half of the United States began outlawing slavery in the late 1700s. But slavery continued to exist in the Southern half of the country. Over time, it became an essential part of the South's economy and culture.

In 1812, the Brown family moved to Ohio. Around this time, John Brown saw a Southern slaveowner whip a slave about his own age. "This brought me to reflect on the wretched [miserable or unfortunate], hopeless condition of fatherless and motherless slave children," he recalled. "I sometimes would raise the question, 'Is God their father?'"

Brown did not have much interest in school, so instead he learned his father's business as a teenager and helped raise livestock. In 1820, he married Deanntha Lusk. They had seven children together over the next fifteen years. Sadly, his wife died during the birth of the last baby. Realizing that he could not raise this large family on his own, Brown married Mary Ann Day in 1836. They added thirteen more children over the years. Brown worked at a number of different jobs to support his family, including farming, tanning, and herding sheep.

Becomes active in the abolition movement

In 1837, slavery supporters murdered the editor of an abolitionist newspaper in Illinois. This event sparked protest meetings across the North. Brown attended one of the meetings and dedicated himself to the abolition of slavery. "Here, before God, in the presence of these witnesses, I consecrate [declare sacred] my life to the destruction of slavery," he stated. By the mid-1840s, Brown lived in Springfield, Massachusetts, and worked in the wool business. During this time he met **Frederick Douglass** (1818?–1895; see entry), an escaped slave who became a well-known abolitionist speaker and writer. He also organized a group of men called the League of Gileadites to protect fugitive slaves from being returned to their masters in the South.

In 1849, Brown moved his family to North Elba, New York, to join an experimental mixed-race farming community. A wealthy abolitionist had set up the community in order to prove that blacks and whites could live together peacefully. The following year, the U.S. Congress passed the Fugitive Slave Act. This measure granted slaveowners sweeping new powers to capture and reclaim escaped slaves. It also required people in the North to assist the slaveowners in retrieving their property.

Many Northerners resented the Fugitive Slave Act. They were able to ignore slavery when it was confined to the South, but not when they saw black people being tracked down like animals and carried off in chains within their own cities. The Fugitive Slave Act ended up increasing the anti-slavery and anti-Southern feelings of many people in the North. Brown felt that the Fugitive Slave Act justified the use of violence in the fight against slavery. He began criticizing abolitionist groups for being too passive. He grew determined to take action.

Contributes to "Bleeding Kansas"

The 1850s were a time of great political tension in the United States. Thanks to the efforts of Brown and other abolitionists, growing numbers of Northerners believed that slavery was wrong. Some people wanted to outlaw it, while others just wanted to prevent it from spreading beyond the Southern states where it was already allowed. But many Southerners felt threatened by Northern efforts to contain slavery. They believed that each state should decide for itself whether to allow the practice. They did not want the national government to pass laws that would interfere with their traditional way of life. This dispute grew more heated as the United States expanded westward. Both sides wanted to spread their political ideas into the new territories and states.

For many years, the representatives of the Northern and Southern states in the U.S. government had reached a series of political compromises on the issue of slavery. To resolve the question of westward expansion, for example, they established a pattern of allowing one slave state and one free state to enter the Union at the same time. In this way, the number of slave and free states remained in balance. In 1854, however, the Kansas-Nebraska Act disrupted this pattern. It allowed the people living in a territory to decide whether to join the Union as a slave state or a free state. The act was named after the next two territories scheduled to enter the Union. It soon became clear that Nebraska voters would elect to enter the United States as a slave state. But the decision of Kansas voters was uncertain.

People on both sides of the slavery issue tried to affect the outcome of the vote in Kansas. Slavery supporters from neighboring Missouri came to Kansas in large numbers. These "border ruffians," as they were called, voted illegally and used violence to intimidate their opponents. In the meantime, antislavery people flocked into Kansas as well. In 1856, Brown traveled to Kansas with his family and a wagon load of weapons. They settled along Pottawatomie Creek, near the abolitionist settlement of Lawrence. Brown had chosen Kansas as the place where he would make a stand against slavery.

In May 1856, a proslavery mob attacked Lawrence. They fired artillery shells into a hotel and burned down several homes. Brown vowed to take revenge for the attack on Lawrence. On May 24, he and a small band of followers attacked several proslavery settlements along Pottawatomie Creek. They captured five men who supported slavery and brutally hacked them to death in front of their wives and children. Afterward, each side followed with more violent acts of retaliation. Over the summer of 1856, more than two hundred people died in what became known as "Bleeding Kansas." Brown became the focus of a great deal of fear and hatred among Southerners.

"John Brown's Raid"

Brown disappeared for awhile following the killings in Kansas. He grew a long, white beard in order to disguise his appearance. He quietly traveled throughout the North, raising money and collecting weapons to support a new, ambitious plan to overthrow slavery by force. Brown planned to invade the South with a band of guerilla fighters. He convinced himself that once the fighting started, slaves across the South would join the rebellion. He wanted to help the slaves gain their freedom by igniting a large-scale slave uprising. Once the slaves were free, he planned to create a revolutionary state for black Americans in the mountains of Virginia and Maryland.

As the first step in his plan, Brown chose to raid the small town of Harpers Ferry, Virginia. He planned to capture the federal armory there, take all the weapons, and supply them to the large numbers of slaves he expected to join the

A Civil War–era view of Harpers Ferry, Virginia (now part of West Virginia).
(Photograph by James Gardner. Courtesy of the National Archives and Records Administration.)

uprising. On October 16, 1859, Brown and twenty-one followers—including several members of his family—set out to capture the armory in Harpers Ferry.

The first part of his scheme unfolded according to plan. The radical abolitionists seized the armory and took several prominent Virginia plantation owners prisoner. But it soon became clear that Brown's plan had serious flaws. For one thing, local slaves were unsure what was happening and did not join Brown's raiders. For another thing, he had not expected any resistance from the white citizens of Harpers Ferry. But they reacted angrily and managed to surround Brown's position.

Brown and his followers remained trapped inside a nearby building the whole next day, yet they refused to surrender. On October 18, federal troops under Lieutenant Colonel **Robert E. Lee** (1807–1870; see entry) arrived to resolve the situation. They captured Brown and seven of his raiders after a brief but bloody battle. The rest of Brown's gang, including two of his sons, were killed.

Executed for his crimes

Just one week later, Brown was put on trial before a Virginia court. Brown laid on a cot during the proceedings because he was too badly wounded to sit up. But he still found the strength to defend his actions. "I believe that to interfere, as I have done, in the behalf of God's despised poor is not wrong but right," he stated. "Now, if it is deemed [considered] necessary that I should mingle my blood further with the blood of my children and the blood of millions in this slave country whose rights are disregarded by wicked, cruel, and unjust enactments [laws], I say let it be done." Brown also presented his feelings about slavery and encouraged others who felt the same way to continue his mission.

The Virginia jury found Brown and his men guilty of murder, treason (betraying the country), and inciting a slave rebellion after just forty-five minutes of deliberation. The judge then sentenced Brown to death by hanging. As he sat in prison awaiting execution, Brown remained calm and never wavered in his commitment to the abolitionist cause.

He died on December 2, 1859. His last words predicted that the fight over slavery would eventually result in an all-out war: "The crimes of this guilty land will never be purged [washed] away but with blood. I had, as I now think vainly, flattered myself that without very much bloodshed it might be done."

Actions increase tension between North and South

Brown's actions at Harpers Ferry—and his death a few weeks later—had a major impact on communities all across America. In the North, reaction was mixed. Some people criticized his violent methods and agreed that he deserved to be executed. But other Northerners saw Brown as a hero who was willing to die for his beliefs. They recognized that he had used bad judgment and made some mistakes, but claimed that the reasons behind his actions were noble. This view gained support as Brown maintained his dignity and composure in the period before his death. Many prominent people praised him for his bravery and dedication to abolishing slavery. At the time of Brown's execution, church bells tolled in salute throughout the North, and many people observed a moment of silence.

In the South, on the other hand, Brown's raid created a wave of hysteria in many white communities. Even though Brown had been unable to convince any slaves to join his rebellion, the idea of a slave uprising played into the South's greatest fears. Many Southerners worried that Northern abolitionists would do anything to end slavery—even sacrifice the lives of thousands of Southern whites. The reaction to Brown's execution in some parts of the North further increased Southern anger and fear. Southerners considered Brown a murderer and were outraged that some Northerners seemed to approve of his actions.

In this way, Brown's raid increased the bitter feelings between the two sections of the country. As a result, more and more Southerners began to support the idea of seceding from (leaving) the United States. Just as Brown had predicted, the Civil War began a little more than a year after his death. "[Brown's] raid and subsequent execution did not directly cause the Civil War," according to William C. Davis, Brian C. Pohanka, and Don Troiani in *Civil War Journal: The Leaders*, "but his ideals and beliefs became the standard under which thousands upon thousands of men and boys marched off to do battle in their own land."

Where to Learn More

Cox, Clinton. *Fiery Vision: The Life and Death of John Brown*. New York: Scholastic, 1997.

Davis, William C., Brian C. Pohanka, and Don Troiani. *Civil War Journal: The Leaders*. Nashville, TN: Rutledge Hill Press, 1997.

Dubois, W. E. B. *John Brown: A Biography*. Armonk, NY: M. E. Sharpe, 1997.

Finkelman, Paul, ed. *His Soul Goes Marching On: Responses to John Brown and the Harpers Ferry Raid*. Charlottesville: University Press of Virginia, 1995.

Harpers Ferry National Historical Park. [Online] http://www.nps.gov/hafe/home.htm (accessed on October 9, 1999).

John Brown and the Valley of the Shadow. [Online] http://jefferson.village.virginia.edu/jbrown/master.html (accessed on October 9, 1999).

John Brown Farm State Historic Site. [Online] http://lakeplacid.com/lphs/jbf1.htm (accessed on October 9, 1999).

John Brown Historical Association of Illinois. [Online] http://www.cyberword.com/johnbrown/ (accessed on October 9, 1999).

Kansas State Historical Society. *Adair Cabin / John Brown Museum*. [Online] http://www.kshs.org/places.adair.htm (accessed on October 9, 1999).

Oates, Stephen B. *To Purge This Land with Blood: A Biography of John Brown*. Amherst: University of Massachusetts Press, 1984.

Renehan, Edward J. *The Secret Six: The True Tale of the Men Who Conspired with John Brown*. New York: Crown Publishers, 1995.

Stein, R. Conrad. *John Brown's Raid on Harpers Ferry in American History*. Berkeley Heights, NJ: Enslow, 1999.

Tackach, James. *The Trial of John Brown: Radical Abolitionist*. San Diego: Lucent Books, 1998.

Villard, Oswald G. *John Brown, 1800–1859: A Biography Fifty Years After*. Boston: Houghton Mifflin, 1910. Reprint, Gloucester, MA: P. Smith, 1965.

Warren, Robert Penn. *John Brown: The Making of a Martyr*. New York: Payson & Clarke, 1929. Reprint, Nashville: J. S. Sanders and Co., 1993.

Ambrose Burnside

Born May 23, 1824
Liberty, Indiana
Died September 13, 1881
Bristol, Rhode Island

Union general

Best known for his decisive defeat at the Battle of Fredericksburg and his unsuccessful "Crater" attack during the siege of Petersburg

Ambrose Burnside is best known for his disastrous command of the Union's Army of the Potomac from November 1862 to January 1863. During the course of this three-month period, Burnside's army suffered a major defeat at Fredericksburg, Virginia, at the hands of Confederate general **Robert E. Lee** (1807–1870; see entry). Burnside then tried to rally his army by launching an offensive across Virginia's Rappahannock River, but the Union march fell apart when bad weather reduced the army's route to a muddy quagmire. After his removal from command of the Army of the Potomac, Burnside served the North well by helping to hold Knoxville, Tennessee, against Southern forces. But in late 1864, his scheme to break Confederate defenses at Petersburg failed miserably. This attack, known as the Battle of the Crater, ended Burnside's military career.

Soldier and inventor

Ambrose Everett Burnside was born on May 23, 1824, to a former South Carolina slaveowner who settled in Indiana

"It can hardly be in human nature for men to show more valor or generals to manifest less judgement."

Newspaper account of Burnside's involvement in the Battle of Fredericksburg

Ambrose Burnside. *(Courtesy of the Library of Congress.)*

after freeing his slaves. He received a good education as a youngster, and in 1843 he enrolled in the prestigious U.S. Military Academy at West Point, New York. He served in the Mexican War (1846–48) after his 1847 graduation from West Point, helping guard forts and military supply centers.

In 1848, the Mexican War came to an end, as the United States acquired vast new territories in the West from the weaker Mexican government. Continuing his service with the army, Burnside served at various federal forts in these newly acquired territories. In 1849, he was wounded in a clash with Apache Indians, but he made a quick recovery.

By the early 1850s, Burnside had built a reputation among his fellow soldiers as a likable, intelligent officer who seemed to be on track for a successful career in the military. In 1853, though, he surprised his colleagues by resigning from the army in order to open a rifle-making factory. Burnside had developed a new breech-loading rifle (a rifle that could be loaded from the side) that he felt was greatly superior to the rifles currently being used by U.S. soldiers. He thought that his new design would make him very wealthy. Unfortunately, he was forced to declare bankruptcy after a few years because he could not convince the federal government to buy his rifles. He had to turn his factory and his rifle design over to creditors (other businessmen to whom Burnside owed money). A few years later, these businessmen became rich using Burnside's rifle design. They sold more than fifty-five thousand of his rifles—called "Burnside Carbines"—and millions of rounds of matching ammunition to the Union Army during the Civil War. But since Burnside had been forced to give up possession of the rifle design in order to pay off his debts, he never received any money from these sales.

Early Civil War successes

In the late 1850s, Burnside worked as an engineer on the Illinois Central Railroad and served as major general of the Rhode Island militia (a group of citizens who volunteer to provide military services). He returned to the regular army in the spring of 1861, when longstanding tensions between America's Northern and Southern states finally exploded into war.

America's Northern and Southern regions had been angry with one another for years over a variety of issues. The major issue dividing the two sections, however, was slavery. The Northern states felt that slavery was immoral and wanted the federal government to pass laws that would end the practice. The South, however, wanted to keep slavery because many of its economic and social institutions relied on it. They also argued that each state should be able to decide for itself whether to allow slavery. As Northern calls to end slavery grew stronger over the years, Southerners became increasingly resentful and defensive. The two sides finally went to war when the Southern states tried to secede from (leave) the Union and form their own country that accepted slavery in early 1861.

Burnside enjoyed many military successes during the first eighteen months of the war. Serving as a colonel in the First Rhode Island Volunteers, Burnside helped organize the establishment of new defenses around Washington, D.C. Weeks later, his performance at the First Battle of Bull Run at Manassas, Virginia, convinced the Lincoln administration to promote him to brigadier general.

In early 1862, Burnside's reputation continued to grow. He organized an expedition down the North Carolina coast that destroyed a small Confederate fleet and captured Roanoke Island. After seizing the island (and capturing twenty-six hundred Confederate soldiers stationed there), Burnside continued to move down the coast. Over the course of several weeks he captured Southern positions in North Carolina at New Berne, Beaufort, and Fort Macon. In recognition of his successful expedition, Burnside was promoted to major general on March 18, 1862. In July, he was named commander of the Army of the Potomac's Ninth Corps.

Burnside and the Army of the Potomac

During the summer of 1862, President **Abraham Lincoln** (1809–1865; see entry) twice offered Burnside command of the Army of the Potomac. Lincoln had lost faith in the army's current commander, General **George B. McClellan** (1826–1885; see entry), and he wanted to make a change. Burnside, though, turned down the offers because of deep

self-doubts about his ability to direct such a large military force. Disappointed by Burnside's decision, Lincoln reluctantly kept McClellan in command.

In September 1862, Burnside fought by McClellan's side in Maryland in the Battle of Antietam, a vicious day-long battle against General Lee's Confederate Army of Northern Virginia. This clash between the war's two largest armies killed or wounded more than twenty-three thousand Union and Confederate soldiers, making it the single bloodiest day in Civil War history. The Union viewed Antietam as a victory for their side, since the battle put an end to a brief Confederate invasion of the North. But many historians believe that if McClellan and Burnside had acted more decisively, they might have been able to crush Lee's army altogether. Instead, Lee's army retreated into Virginia, where it operated for the next three years.

Ambrose Burnside (reading a newspaper) sits with three others, including famed photographer Mathew Brady (in front of tree) at the Army of Potomac headquarters. *(Courtesy of the Library of Congress.)*

Burnside reluctantly takes command

In the weeks following Antietam, Lincoln ordered McClellan to pursue Lee's army and resume the battle. But McClellan moved his army so slowly that the president finally decided to change commanders. He removed McClellan from command of the Army of the Potomac and once again asked Burnside to lead the army. Burnside was not sure that he could handle such a big responsibility, but he reluctantly accepted the assignment on November 7, 1862.

Burnside's first command decisions pleased Lincoln. The general moved his army forward at an increased speed, and he showed a much greater willingness to engage the enemy than had McClellan. Burnside's plan was to march on the Confederate capital of Richmond, Virginia, in hopes of drawing Lee's army out for another battle. Once Lee committed to defending the capital, Burnside hoped to use his superior firepower and troop size to demolish the Confederate Army.

At first, Burnside's strategy succeeded. Lee's hungry and tired Army of Northern Virginia was forced to set up defenses at Fredericksburg, Virginia, in an effort to stop the Union march on Richmond. But when the two armies resumed their bloody fight on December 13, Burnside's plan fell apart.

Battle of Fredericksburg

Once Burnside reached Lee's position at Fredericksburg, a small town located along the Rappahannock River, he ordered a full frontal assault on the Confederate defenses. Lee and his lieutenants had established strong positions, however, and they easily pushed back every Union offensive. Union casualties mounted with shocking speed throughout the day, but Burnside refused to admit that his plan was flawed. As a result, thousands of courageous Northern troops sacrificed their lives in doomed attempts to break through the rebel (Confederate) lines. "It can hardly be in human nature for men to show more valor [courage] or generals to manifest [show] less judgement," wrote one newspaper reporter who witnessed the battle.

By the end of the day, the Army of the Potomac had suffered nearly thirteen thousand casualties. Lee's army, on the other hand, suffered fewer than five thousand casualties. When Burnside realized how badly he had been defeated, he at first vowed to lead an attack personally the next day. During the night, though, his lieutenants convinced him to break off the offensive and withdraw to Washington.

Burnside's "Mud March"

Lee's decisive victory at Fredericksburg stunned Lincoln. As the president listened to reports about the battle, he wondered if Burnside was the right man to lead the Army of the Potomac. Despite growing doubts, however, he decided to give Burnside one last chance to prove himself.

In January 1863, Burnside launched another campaign against Lee's Army of Northern Virginia, which had set up camp around Fredericksburg for the winter. But within hours of setting out from Washington, the Union advance was slowed by a heavy rainstorm. Burnside ordered his troops on, but the storm continued for days. The roadways upon which they were traveling disintegrated into muddy pits. The conditions made it impossible for the army to make any progress. Supply wagons became hopelessly stuck and soldiers became cold and exhausted as they slogged through the muddy mess. Finally, after days of struggling through the mud, Burnside admitted defeat. Angry and humiliated, he ordered the Army of the Potomac to return to camp.

Burnside's "Mud March," as it came to be known, further damaged the general's reputation. It also convinced Lincoln that he needed to change generals once again. On January 25, 1863, Major General Joseph Hooker (1814–1879) replaced Burnside as commander of the Army of the Potomac.

In March 1863, Burnside was reassigned to lead the Department of the Ohio. Over the next few months he made significant contributions to the Union cause. He captured Confederate cavalry leader John Hunt Morgan (1825–1864) and supervised the arrest and conviction of Congressman **Clement L. Vallandigham** (1820–1871; see entry) on charges of treason. Burnside also served the Union well in the fall of 1863, when he helped fend off a Confederate attempt to seize the city of Knoxville, Tennessee, from Federal control.

Battle of the Crater

Burnside returned to the war's eastern theater in the spring of 1864, when he received orders to take his old spot as commander of the Army of the Potomac's Ninth Corps. In May he took part in the Wilderness Campaign of Union general **Ulysses S. Grant** (1822–1885; see entry). This bloody campaign against Lee's Army of Northern Virginia eventually drove the Confederate Army back to Petersburg, Virginia. Once Lee reached Petersburg, however, he established defenses that repulsed Grant's aggressive assaults. Grant responded by initiating a siege (a blockade intended to prevent the city's inhabitants from receiving food and other supplies) of Petersburg in June 1864.

Shortly after the siege began, Colonel Henry Pleasants (who had been a mining engineer before the war) approached Burnside with an idea to tunnel under a key section of the rebel defenses and blow it up. Waiting Union forces could then rush through the gap and destroy Lee's army once and for all. Pleasants's scheme intrigued Burnside, who received reluctant approval from Grant to undertake the plan.

Burnside's regiment began work on the tunnel on June 25. By the end of July, the Union troops had tunneled to a point directly under the Confederate line and placed four tons of gunpowder at the end of the tunnel. Early in the morning of July 30, Burnside's troops lit the fuse. A few moments later, the Confederate fortifications erupted in a terrific explosion of fire, dirt, and timber. The blast buried an entire Confederate regiment and opened a huge hole in Lee's defenses. But Burnside proved unable to take advantage of the situation. Rather than appoint a competent commander to lead the assault, he had arranged to have his division commanders draw straws. Division commander James H. Ledlie received the assignment, but he turned out to be unreliable: he drank too much and did not adequately prepare his men for the offensive. In fact, Ledlie did not even join in the attack. Instead, he hid in the Union trenches drinking rum.

Ledlie's men, meanwhile, charged down *into* the crater that had been created by the explosion rather than around it. This move gave the rebel soldiers time to recover from the explosion and close the hole. Leaderless and disorganized, the Union troops became trapped inside the thirty-foot-deep pit as Confederate troops rushed to the edge and opened fire. James M. McPherson noted in *Battle Cry of Freedom* that more than four thousand Northern soldiers were killed or wounded in the subsequent slaughter, as "rebel artillery and mortars found the range and began shooting at the packed bluecoats [Union soldiers] in the crater as at fish in a barrel."

Calling the so-called Battle of the Crater "the saddest affair I have witnessed in the war," Grant placed the blame for the disaster squarely on Burnside's shoulders (though he also stripped Ledlie of his command). Grant relieved Burnside of his command and sent him on military leave. Burnside resigned from the army a few months later.

Burnside's Beard

For much of his career, General Ambrose Burnside maintained a very unusual-looking beard. Unlike other soldiers who kept mustaches or full beards, Burnside shaved his chin area but let his mustache and cheek whiskers grow out until they joined together across his face. People originally called this peculiar style "burnsides," but over time the two syllables became reversed, and the name came to be associated primarily with the part of a man's face directly in front of his ears. Today, people refer to the area of beard down the side of a man's face as "sideburns."

Governor of Rhode Island

After the Civil War ended in 1865, Burnside became involved in politics in Rhode Island. Despite his controversial military record, he was elected governor of the state for three consecutive one-year terms from 1866–68. In 1874, he was elected to the U.S. Senate. He served there until he died in 1881.

Where to Learn More

Davis, William C. *The Commanders of the Civil War.* San Diego: Thunder Bay Press, 1999.

Marvel, William. *Burnside.* Chapel Hill: University of North Carolina Press, 1991.

Warner, Ezra J. *Generals in Blue.* Baton Rouge: Louisiana State University Press, 1964.

Williams, T. Harry. *Lincoln and His Generals.* New York: Knopf, 1952. Reprint, Westport, CT: Greenwood Press, 1981.

Joshua L. Chamberlain

Born September 8, 1828
Brewer, Maine
Died February 24, 1914
Brunswick, Maine

Union general
Hero at the Battle of Gettysburg

oshua L. Chamberlain was one of the Union Army's great heroes at the Battle of Gettysburg in Pennsylvania in July 1863. His brave defense of the Union's vulnerable left flank saved the North from certain defeat in the clash. Chamberlain received the Congressional Medal of Honor for his valor at Gettysburg, and he went on to serve the Union with distinction for the remainder of the war.

Attends Bowdoin College

Joshua Lawrence Chamberlain was born in 1828 in Brewer, Maine. He was the oldest of three boys. His parents originally named him Lawrence Joshua, but their son decided to reverse the order of the names when he became an adult. Chamberlain's father, Joshua Chamberlain Jr., was a successful farmer who also held several political offices in the community. He wanted Joshua to be a soldier, but his eldest son thought that he might want to be a missionary instead (a missionary is a person who does religious or charitable work in a distant or foreign territory).

"Out of [the] silence [of night] rose new sounds [of wounded soldiers] . . . a smothered moan . . . some begging for a drop of water, some calling on God for pity; and some on friendly hands to finish what the enemy had so horribly begun; some with delirious, dreamy voices murmuring loved names, as if the dearest were bending over them. . . ."

Joshua L. Chamberlain.
(Courtesy of the Library of Congress.)

Chamberlain enrolled at Bowdoin College in Brunswick, Maine, where he initially struggled to keep up with his schoolwork. "The first two years in college were on the whole a pretty severe experience," he admitted. "Well remembered are those weary nights when some problem would be given out for the next morning's demonstration over which [I] sat staring at the words until the stars were lost in the flush of dawn." As time passed, however, Chamberlain became a good student.

As Chamberlain continued his studies in theology (the study of religion) and foreign languages, he met two women who had a significant impact on his life. In 1851, he met Fannie Adams, the daughter of a minister, when Chamberlain became the choir director for a local church. They were married on December 7, 1855, and eventually had three children (although their only son died a few hours after he was born).

The second notable woman that Chamberlain met during his studies at Bowdoin College was **Harriet Beecher Stowe** (1811–1896; see entry), a devout abolitionist (person who worked to end slavery in America). In 1851, Chamberlain attended several gatherings at which Stowe read excerpts from a novel that she was in the process of writing. This work, called *Uncle Tom's Cabin,* was fiercely antislavery in its outlook. Chamberlain was profoundly moved by the passages that Stowe read at the gatherings. The author's words helped him decide that slavery was an awful practice that should not be permitted to continue in the United States. "Slavery and freedom cannot live together," he later said. *Uncle Tom's Cabin,* meanwhile, became the most famous antislavery book of all time when it was published a year later.

Chooses a life of teaching

After concluding his studies at Bowdoin, Chamberlain accepted the school's offer of a professorship. He became one of the college's brightest young professors, teaching courses in foreign languages and rhetoric (writing and speaking effectively). He also bought a house in Brunswick, where his family thrived.

In 1861, however, long-simmering disputes between America's Northern and Southern states boiled over into war. For years, the two regions had been arguing over slavery. Many Northerners believed that slavery was wrong and wanted to abolish it. But the economy of the South had been built on slavery, and Southerners resented Northern efforts to halt or contain the practice. In early 1861, these differences over slavery and other issues convinced several Southern states to secede from (leave) the United States. They announced their intention to form a new country, the Confederate States of America, that would continue to protect slavery. But Northern political leaders were determined to keep the Southern states in the Union. In April 1861, the two sides finally went to war over their differences.

Takes a sabbatical to go to war

When the Civil War began, Chamberlain decided that he wanted to do his part to help keep the Union together. He wrote to Maine governor Israel Washburn (1813–1883), who was in charge of organizing troops from Maine to serve in the Union Army. "I have always been interested in military matters and what I do not know in that line I know how to learn," Chamberlain stated in his letter.

The administrators at Bowdoin College, however, did not want to see one of their most talented young instructors leave to go fight in a war. They refused Chamberlain's request for a leave of absence. Instead, they offered him a big promotion and a two-year sabbatical (an extended leave of absence given to university professors to travel, rest, or study) in Europe. But Chamberlain was determined to serve in the Union Army. He accepted the college's offer of a European study sabbatical, but instead of departing for Europe, he reported for military service.

When Chamberlain joined the army, Washburn offered him command of a new volunteer regiment called the Twentieth Maine, part of the Union's Army of the Potomac. This offer was not completely unexpected. The Union Army often filled officers' positions with educated men, even if they did not have any military experience. But Chamberlain sensed that he might not be able to handle all the responsibilities of command immediately. Noting that he would prefer to "start a little lower and learn the business first," Chamberlain instead asked to be named lieutenant colonel, the second-highest ranking position in the regiment.

A quick learner

On August 8, 1862, he reported to Colonel Adelbert Ames (1835–1933), commander of the Twentieth Maine. Over the next several weeks, Chamberlain quickly distinguished himself as a sharp young officer. Ames learned to trust his second-in-command, impressed by the former professor's intelligence and desire to learn. In fact, Chamberlain seemed to spend nearly all of his waking moments talking with veteran officers in order to improve his knowledge of military strategy and other subjects. "I study . . . every military work I can find and it is no small labor to master the evolutions of a battalion and brigade," he said in a letter to his wife. "I am bound [determined] to understand everything." Joshua was joined in the regiment around this time by his younger brothers Tom and John, who would fight by his side for the remainder of the war.

In September 1862, Chamberlain and the other soldiers of the Twentieth Maine were stationed near Sharpsburg, Maryland, site of the bloody Battle of Antietam. The Twentieth Maine was never ordered into the battle, but the troops saw plenty of evidence of war's terrible toll. Chamberlain recalled that the sight of one dead Confederate soldier holding a Bible in his lifeless hands haunted him for the rest of his life. "I saw him sitting there gently reclined against the tree . . . this boy of scarcely sixteen summers," he stated. "His cap had fallen to the ground on one side, his hand resting on his knee. It clasped a little testament opened at some familiar place. He wore the gray. He was my enemy, this boy. He was dead—the boy, my enemy—but I shall see him forever."

Chamberlain takes command

In the last months of 1862, the Twentieth Maine regiment took part in some of the Civil War's fiercest engagements, including two conflicts in Virginia—the Battle of Fred-

Chamberlain Recalls Fredericksburg

Joshua Chamberlain witnessed many terrible scenes of warfare during his period of service in the Union Army. One of the worst of these battles took place at Fredericksburg, Virginia, where a large federal army under the command of General **Ambrose Burnside** (1824–1881; see entry) failed in its attempt to dislodge troops led by General Robert E. Lee from their defensive positions. After the war, Chamberlain recalled what it was like to listen to wounded soldiers after night fell on the Fredericksburg battlefield: "Out of that silence . . . rose new sounds more appalling still . . . a strange ventriloquism, of which you could not locate the source, a smothered moan . . . as if a thousand discords were flowing together into a key-note weird, unearthly, terrible to hear and bear, yet startling with its nearness; the writhing concord [similar-sounding moans] broken by cries for help . . . some begging for a drop of water, some calling on God for pity; and some on friendly hands to finish what the enemy had so horribly begun; some with delirious, dreamy voices murmuring loved names, as if the dearest were bending over them; and underneath, all the time, the deep bass note from closed lips too hopeless, or too heroic to articulate [speak about] their agony."

When the sun rose the following day, Chamberlain and his regiment were forced to spend the entire day hiding behind the stacked bodies of fallen comrades as Confederate troops tried to pick them off. "The living and the dead were alike to me," Chamberlain remembered. "I slept [but] my ears were filled with the cries and groans of the wounded and the ghastly faces of the dead almost made a wall around me. We lay there hearing the dismal [gloomy] thud of bullets into the dead flesh of our lifesaving bulwarks [defensive barriers]." On the night of December 14, Chamberlain and his regiment finally received orders to withdraw from their gruesome positions. They and the rest of Burnside's army then left the area, leaving Fredericksburg to the rebel victors.

ericksburg in December 1862 and the Battle of Chancellorsville in May 1863. These clashes featured long stretches of terrible violence that claimed the lives of thousands of Union and Confederate soldiers. But the Twentieth Maine performed well, and Chamberlain became known both for bravery and concern for his troops.

In the spring of 1863, Union Army leaders transferred Ames to command of another brigade and promoted Chamberlain to colonel of the Twentieth Maine. Chamberlain's leadership qualities continued to blossom in his new position, and the soldiers under his command developed a solid respect for him. His horror of war continued to stay strong during this time. But Chamberlain felt that his military service had given him a rare opportunity to improve himself, and he sometimes confessed that he loved the excitement and challenges of his new existence. "No danger and no hardship ever makes me wish to get back to that college life again," he wrote. "I would spend my whole life campaigning rather than endure that again."

Battle of Gettysburg

In the summer of 1863, the Twentieth Maine and the rest of the Army of the Potomac marched into Pennsylvania to stop an invading Confederate force led by General **Robert E. Lee** (1807–1870; see entry). Lee hoped that by bringing the war into the Northern states, he could capture Union supplies and create a surge of antiwar sentiment in the North. The Confederate commander knew that President **Abraham Lincoln** (1809–1865; see entry) would not be able to continue the war against the South if he did not have the support of the Northern people. But Lee's progress was stopped outside of Gettysburg, Pennsylvania, by the Army of the Potomac, a ninety thousand–man force led by General **George Meade** (1815–1872; see entry).

The first major clash between Meade's forces and Lee's seventy-five thousand–man Army of Northern Virginia erupted on July 1, 1863. The Union Army barely held its ground during the first day of fighting. As the morning of July 2 approached, both armies knew that the next several hours might determine the winner of the whole battle. Meade and his Union officers prepared their defenses for the upcoming Confederate attack, but mix-ups created a big hole in the Union defenses. A wooded hill on the far left flank of the Union defenses was accidentally left unprotected. If the Confederates gained possession of this hill, known as Little Round Top, they would be able to sweep in behind the Union defenses and crush Meade's army.

Defending Little Round Top

The Battle of Gettysburg resumed on July 2, as Lee continued with his efforts to push Meade out of the area. But the Confederates were slow to reach the Union's left flanks. A Federal (Union) officer eventually realized that Little Round Top had been left unprotected, and the North scrambled to send troops to defend it before the rebel (Confederate) soldiers reached the area. The last of four regiments sent to defend the hill from the Confederates was the Twentieth Maine. Chamberlain and his men set up defensive positions on the top of Little Round Top, at the very end of the Union line of defenses. "It was a critical moment," remembered one soldier in Chamberlain's regiment. He noted that if the advancing Confederate line "was permitted to turn the Federal flank, Little Round Top was untenable [not capable of being de-

The center of the Federal position viewed from Little Round Top in Gettysburg, Pennsylvania. *(Courtesy of the Library of Congress.)*

fended], and with this little mountain in the Confederates' possession, the whole [Union] position would be untenable. It was a most fortunate fact for the Union cause that in command of the Twentieth Maine was Colonel Joshua Lawrence Chamberlain."

Once the Twentieth Maine arrived at Little Round Top, Chamberlain rushed to arrange the 350 men under his command behind trees and boulders. Ten minutes later, Confederate troops came charging up the hill in a furious attack. Chamberlain's troops pushed back the first assault, only to be hit with another one a few minutes later. The fight for possession of the hill became vicious and desperate, as Chamberlain's men pushed back wave after wave of attack, despite being badly outnumbered. "The edge of the conflict swayed to and fro, with wild whirlpools and eddies," Chamberlain recalled. "At times I saw around me more of the enemy than of my own men; gaps opening, swallowing, closing again. . . . All around, a strange, mingled roar."

By mid-afternoon, Chamberlain's regiment had lost nearly half of its men and was nearly out of ammunition. Chamberlain himself had been wounded. But the former professor refused to give up control of the hill. Instead, he ordered his troops to prepare for a bayonet charge into the midst of their Confederate attackers (bayonets were long blades that could be attached to the ends of rifles). Chamberlain's daring strategy worked. As his battered soldiers charged down the hill, hundreds of stunned rebel soldiers surrendered. The rest of the Confederate troops fled, but many of them fell under a final deadly burst of gunfire from one of Chamberlain's companies. "We ran like a herd of wild cattle," admitted the Confederate commander at Little Round Top. "The blood stood in puddles in some places on the rocks; the ground was soaked with blood."

Chamberlain's brave and daring stand at Little Round Top enabled the Union Army to withstand the Confederate offensive. A day later, Lee mounted one final attempt to break the Union Army. When it failed, however, he was forced to retreat to Virginia. The South never invaded the North again. Chamberlain, meanwhile, received the Congressional Medal of Honor for his exploits. He and the other members of the Twentieth Maine were praised throughout the North for their bravery and fighting spirit.

Wounded at Petersburg

In November 1863, Chamberlain was forced to give up his command when he came down with malaria, an infectious disease. Transferred to Washington, he performed light duties during his recovery. In May 1864, his doctors said he was ready to resume his command of the Twentieth Maine. He promptly rejoined the Army of the Potomac, which was engaged at the time in a bloody stalemate with Lee's Army of Northern Virginia.

But Chamberlain's return to active duty lasted only a few weeks. In June 1864, he took part in a Union assault on Petersburg, Virginia, where Lee's army had erected strong defenses. The Union offensive failed, and Chamberlain was seriously wounded in the attack. A single Confederate bullet smashed through both of his hips and his pelvis. As the bullet continued through his body, it also tore into important arteries and nicked his bladder. Yet Chamberlain stayed on his feet despite his wound. He leaned on his sword with one hand and waved his men forward with the other until they had passed him by. He then collapsed in a bloody heap.

When Chamberlain was dragged from the field of battle, nobody thought that he would live. His doctors believed that his wounds were mortal, and Chamberlain himself dictated a farewell letter to his wife. Union commander **Ulysses S. Grant** (1822–1885; see entry) immediately promoted him to brigadier general as a way of honoring him before he died. Obituaries mourning Chamberlain's death even appeared in several Northern newspapers. But the former language professor stubbornly refused to die. As the days passed by, he delighted his doctors and superior officers by beginning a slow but remarkable recovery.

Confederate surrender at Appomattox

In November 1864, Chamberlain returned to active duty at Petersburg, where Lee's troops had been trapped by Grant's Army of the Potomac. Over the next few months, Chamberlain participated in several important Union victories, even though his earlier wounds caused him great suffering. Walking was extremely painful for Chamberlain, and he sometimes had to be helped onto his horse. But still he pressed on, performing so well in battles at Quaker Road and Five Forks that he was promoted to the rank of major general.

On April 9, 1865, Lee surrendered to Grant, and the Civil War finally came to an end. The two generals made arrangements to hold a formal surrender ceremony on April 12. Of all the soldiers in the Union Army, Grant selected Chamberlain to preside over the ceremony.

Governor and college president

When the war ended, Chamberlain returned to his native Maine. His war injuries continued to bother him—he had been wounded six different times during the course of the war—but he became a leading figure in state politics. He served as governor of the state for four years, and in 1871 he began a twelve-year tenure as president of Bowdoin College in Brunswick. On February 24, 1914, Chamberlain finally died from health problems associated with the war wounds he had suffered fifty years earlier.

Where to Learn More

Bowdoin College Library. *Joshua Lawrence Chamberlain Collection.* [Online] http://www.bowdoin.edu/dept/library/arch/manscrpt/jlcg.htm (accessed on October 9, 1999).

Chamberlain, Joshua L. *The Passing of the Armies.* New York: G. P. Putnam, 1915. Reprint, Lincoln: University of Nebraska Press, 1998.

Chamberlain, Joshua Lawrence. *Bayonet! Forward!: My Civil War Reminiscences.* Gettysburg, PA: S. Clark Military Books, 1994.

The Joshua Chamberlain Home Page. [Online] http://maineiac.freeservers.com/jlc/ (accessed on October 9, 1999).

Longacre, Edward. *Joshua Chamberlain: The Soldier and the Man.* Conshohocken, PA: Combined Publishing, 1999.

Official Home Page of Joshua L. Chamberlain. [Online] http://www.joshuachamberlain.com/ (accessed on October 9, 1999).

Pejepscot Historical Society. *Joshua L. Chamberlain Area.* [Online] http://www.curtislibrary.com/chamberlain/htm (accessed on October 9, 1999).

Perry, Mark. *Conceived in Liberty: Joshua Chamberlain, William Oates, and the American Civil War.* New York: Viking Press, 1997.

Pullen, John J. *Joshua Chamberlain: A Hero's Life and Legacy.* Mechanicsburg, PA: Stackpole Books, 1999.

Soul of the Lion: Joshua Lawrence Chamberlain. [Online] http://world.std.com/~khebert/ (accessed on October 9, 1999).

Trulock, Alice Rains. *In the Hands of Providence: Joshua Lawrence Chamberlain and the American Civil War.* Chapel Hill: University of North Carolina Press, 1992.

Wallace, Willard M. *Soul of the Lion: A Biography of General Joshua L. Chamberlain.* New York: T. Nelson, 1960.

Mary Boykin Chesnut

Born March 31, 1823
Statesburg, South Carolina
Died November 22, 1886
Camden, South Carolina

Civil War diarist

Thousands of Americans recorded their thoughts and experiences during the Civil War period in diaries and journals. Since that time, many of these diaries have been studied by historians, and some of them have been published in book form. The most famous diary of the Civil War was written by Mary Boykin Chesnut. Chesnut was a well-educated woman from a wealthy and influential Southern family. She married James Chesnut Jr., who became a U.S. senator from South Carolina shortly before the start of the Civil War. Thanks to her political connections and her skills as an observer and writer, Chesnut was able to provide an inside view of the Confederacy for future generations to read and study.

Raised in a prominent Southern family

Mary Boykin Miller Chesnut was born on March 31, 1823, in Statesburg, South Carolina. She was the first of four children born to Stephen Decatur Miller, a prominent politician, and his wife Mary Boykin Miller. Chesnut's father served as a state senator, a U.S. congressman, and governor of South Carolina during her childhood.

"I have nothing to chronicle but disasters. . . . The reality is hideous."

Mary Boykin Chesnut.
(Reproduced by permission of The Granger Collection, New York.)

Chesnut was educated in some of the best private girls' schools in the southeastern United States, including a boarding school in Charleston where the students were taught in French. In 1840, she married James Chesnut Jr., the son of one of the largest landowners in South Carolina. She then went to live at Mulberry Plantation, where her husband's family owned numerous slaves. The Chesnuts never had any children, so Mary had a great deal of time to read books and entertain.

Swept up in the secession movement

In 1858, James Chesnut Jr. was elected to represent South Carolina in the U.S. Senate. The Chesnuts moved to Washington, D.C., where Mary became friends with many prominent politicians and their wives. But this was a time of great political tension in the United States. The Northern and Southern sections of the country had been arguing over several issues—including slavery and the power of the national government to regulate it—for many years.

Growing numbers of Northerners believed that slavery was wrong. Some people wanted to outlaw it, while others wanted to prevent it from spreading beyond the Southern states where it was already allowed. But slavery played a big role in the Southern economy and culture. As a result, many Southerners felt threatened by Northern efforts to contain slavery. They believed that each state should decide for itself whether to allow slavery. They did not want the national government to pass laws that would interfere with their traditional way of life.

This ongoing dispute came to a crisis in November 1860, when **Abraham Lincoln** (1809–1865; see entry) was elected president of the United States. Lincoln was a Northerner who opposed slavery, although he wanted to eliminate it gradually rather than outlaw it immediately. Following Lincoln's election, many people in the South felt that the national government could no longer represent their interests. Several Southern states decided to secede (withdraw) from the United States and form a new country that allowed slavery, called the Confederate States of America. But it soon became clear that Northern leaders were willing to fight to keep the

Southern states in the Union. The two sides went to war a few months later.

Inspired to record historic events in her diary

Chesnut's husband was the first Southern senator to resign from his position in the U.S. Congress following Lincoln's election. Before long, he became a delegate (representative) in the provisional (temporary) Confederate Congress. The Chesnuts moved to Montgomery, Alabama, where a number of influential Southerners were meeting to establish a government for their new nation. Chesnut's home was one of the most popular gathering places for Confederate officials. On many occasions, her living room was full of important people socializing, exchanging information, and holding political debates.

In February 1861, Chesnut began recording what she saw and heard during these meetings in a diary. "From the beginning of secession, she recognized the depth of the political and social upheaval in which her region was engaged, and she felt herself qualified by education, social position, and native intelligence to report what she observed," Elisabeth Muhlenfeld explained in *Mary Boykin Chesnut: A Biography*.

South Carolina senator James Chesnut Jr., husband of diarist Mary Boykin Chesnut. *(Reproduced by permission of The Granger Collection, New York.)*

One of Chesnut's best friends during this time was Varina Davis, wife of Confederate president **Jefferson Davis** (1808–1889; see entry). This friendship gave her access to the top officials in the new government, which put her in a unique position to record what was going on in the Confederacy. In fact, the observations she made in her journal cov-

Excerpts from Mary Boykin Chesnut's Diary

One of the reasons that Chesnut's diary became the most famous remembrance of the Civil War was that she covered such a wide range of topics. During the four years that she kept a journal, she recorded her thoughts on all of the most important people and events of the war. The following excerpts provide a sample of some of the issues she covered.

In April 1861, Confederate forces fired upon Fort Sumter to begin the Civil War. This fort, located in the harbor of Charleston, South Carolina, was held by Federal troops. Southern leaders viewed these troops as a symbol of Northern authority and were determined to remove them. The Confederacy gained control of the fort after two days of intense bombing. Chesnut watched the battle from the roof of a house in Charleston:

> There was a sound of stir all over the house, pattering of feet in the corri-

dors. All seemed hurrying one way, I put on my double gown and went too. It was to the housetop. The shells were bursting. . . . The regular roar of the cannon— there it was. . . . The women were wild there on the housetop. Prayers came from the women and imprecations [curses] from the men. And then a shell would light up the scene. . . . We watched up there, and everybody wondered that Fort Sumter did not fire a shot.

In April 1862, Union admiral **David Farragut** (1801–1870; see entry) led a daring navy mission up the Mississippi River that ended with the capture of the Southern port city of New Orleans, Louisiana. The fall of New Orleans was one in a series of significant Confederate defeats in the Civil War's western theater. Like many other Southerners, Chesnut grew depressed upon hearing the news:

> Battle after battle—disaster after disaster. . . . How could I sleep? The power they [Union forces] are bringing

ered everything from parties and romances, to rumors and disagreements, to battles and funerals.

Chesnut witnessed some of the major events of the Civil War. Her husband participated in the April 1861 bombing of Fort Sumter in Charleston Harbor, which marked the official start of the war, as she watched from a rooftop in town. Following the Confederate victory in the first major battle of the war, the First Battle of Manassas (also known as the First Battle of Bull Run) in July 1861, she visited wounded Confederate soldiers in Richmond, Virginia. Chesnut moved to Richmond in 1862, when her husband became the person-to bear against our country is tremendous. . . . Every morning's paper enough to kill a well woman [or] age a strong and hearty one. . . . New Orleans gone—and with it the Confederacy. Are we not cut in two? The Mississippi ruins us if it is lost. . . . I have nothing to chronicle but disasters. . . . The reality is hideous.

Chesnut received more bad news in 1864. She learned that a close friend's son had been killed in battle. This event prompted her to write the following passage about the horrors of war:

When I remember all—the true hearted—the light hearted—the gay and gallant [courageous] boys—who have come laughing singing—dancing in my way—in the three years past—I have looked into their brave young eyes—And helped them—as I could every way—And then seen them no more forever—they lie stark—and cold—dead upon the battle field or mouldering away in hospitals or prisons—which is worse—I think if I consider the long array of those bright youths and loyal men—who have gone to their death almost before my very eyes—my heart might break too. Is any thing worth it? This fearful sacrifice—this awful penalty we pay for war?

After the war ended in 1865, Chesnut returned to her South Carolina plantation to find that it had been badly damaged by Union troops. Many of her former slaves were still there, but she realized that the South had changed forever:

My negroes—now free citizens of the U.S.A.—are more humble & affectionate & anxious to be allowed to remain as they are than the outside world—the readers of Mrs. [Harriet Beecher] Stowe [author of the antislavery novel *Uncle Tom's Cabin*]—could ever conceive—not one expressed the slightest pleasure at the *sudden* freedom—but they will all *go* after a while—if they can better their condition.

al aide to President Davis. They lived near the Confederate White House and entertained generals and other important people. She moved to Columbia, South Carolina, in 1864, where she helped out in an army hospital. She recorded all of these experiences in her diary.

During the early years of the war, Chesnut kept her journal in an elegant red leather-bound book with a little brass lock. As the war went on, and the South suffered from severe supply shortages, however, she ended up writing on scraps of paper and in the back of old cookbooks. Calling herself "a close observer . . . of men and manners," she tried to record things as they happened without coloring the facts with her own opinions.

Diary is finally published forty years after the war ends

Chesnut stopped writing in her diary in June 1865, shortly after the Civil War ended in a Union victory. She and her husband returned to Mulberry Plantation to find it badly damaged, and all of her family's possessions and crops destroyed. Their fortune gone, she began running a small dairy business to help make ends meet. In the 1870s, she translated several French novels and tried her hand at writing fiction.

In 1881, Chesnut began revising her Civil War diary for publication. During the war, she was too busy to provide a complete record of events as they occurred. Instead, she made detailed notes that she could look back on later to help her remember. She always intended to flesh out her description of the war. Chesnut worked on the project for several years, but never finished the revision to her satisfaction. She struggled through legal and financial troubles, and had to deal with the death of her husband and her mother during this time. She also suffered from heart problems herself. Chesnut died on November 22, 1886, in Camden, South Carolina.

Shortly before her death, Chesnut asked a trusted younger friend, Isabella Martin, to take care of her diaries and finish preparing them for publication. But after looking at the journals, Martin felt that they were too personal to be published. She recognized the historical value of the documents, but she worried about embarrassing the people who were mentioned. So she set the diaries aside for many years.

In 1904, Martin met a writer from New York named Myrta Lockett Avary. Avary read Chesnut's journals and insisted on publishing them. Excerpts first appeared in the popular magazine *Saturday Evening Post* under the title "A Diary from Dixie." In 1905, the excerpts were compiled into a book of the same name. But the book was much different from the original journal entries Chesnut had written during the Civil War. Martin, who served as editor of the book, cut nearly half of the material in order to avoid offending people. It still received good reviews, however, and was frequently quoted by Civil War historians over the years.

A novelist named Ben Ames Williams published another edition of Chesnut's diaries in 1949. This edition was more complete than the first, but Williams still cut or changed Chesnut's original words. The complete, unchanged journal did not appear until 1981. *Mary Chesnut's Civil War,* edited by historian C. Vann Woodward, won the Pulitzer Prize upon its publication. It has since become the most famous diary of the Civil War period. Muhlenfeld called it "a stunning eyewitness account of the society that was the Confederacy."

Where to Learn More

Chesnut, Mary Boykin Miller. *A Diary from Dixie.* Boston: Houghton Mifflin, 1949. Reprint, New York: Random House, 1997.

Chesnut, Mary Boykin Miller. *The Private Mary Chesnut: The Unpublished Civil War Diaries.* New York: Oxford University Press, 1984.

DeCredico, Mary A. *Mary Boykin Chesnut: A Confederate Woman's Life.* Madison, WI: Madison House, 1996.

Muhlenfeld, Elisabeth. *Mary Boykin Chesnut: A Biography.* Baton Rouge: Louisiana State University Press, 1981.

Woodward, C. Vann, ed. *Mary Chesnut's Civil War.* New Haven, CT: Yale University Press, 1981.

Pauline Cushman

Born June 10, 1833
New Orleans, Louisiana
Died December 2, 1893
San Francisco, California

Stage actress who served as a Union spy

P auline Cushman used her skills as an actress to pretend that she supported the Confederate cause during the Civil War. In reality, she collected information about Confederate spies and strategies and passed it along to Union authorities. In 1863, Cushman was captured and sentenced to death by Confederate general **Braxton Bragg** (1817–1876; see entry). If the sentence had been carried out, she would have been the only female spy executed by either side during the war. But Union troops arrived in Shelbyville, Tennessee, in time to save her.

Cushman was one of the more glamorous yet effective Union spies of the Civil War. She was brave and daring, yet always conducted her activities in a quiet, professional manner.

Decides to serve her country

Pauline Cushman was born in New Orleans, Louisiana, in 1833. Her name was originally Harriet Wood, but she changed it when she decided to become an actress. Cushman lived in Michigan for awhile, then moved to New York to look for jobs in the theater. When she had trouble launching her acting career in New York, she returned to New Orleans, got married, and started a family. Sadly, her children died as babies, and her husband died shortly after the start of the Civil War.

Pauline Cushman.
(Reproduced by permission of AP/Wide World Photos.)

The war grew out of a steady increase in tension between the Northern and Southern regions of the United States. The two sides had disagreed on a number of issues for many years, including whether to allow slavery. By 1861, this ongoing dispute had convinced several Southern states to secede from (leave) the United States and attempt to form a new country that allowed slavery, called the Confederate States of America. But Northern political leaders were determined to fight to keep the Southern states in the Union.

Even though Cushman had been born in the South, she remained loyal to the Union. Figuring that she had no family ties anymore, she decided to serve her country as a spy. Her first assignment was in St. Louis, Missouri. While she appeared on stage as an actress, she also used her charm and good looks to uncover Confederate spies and their means of communication with Confederate leaders.

Acts like a Confederate sympathizer

Cushman's next assignment was in Nashville, Tennessee. Union forces controlled this area, but it was still full of people who supported the Confederate cause. At one point, a Confederate sympathizer offered the actress $300 to propose a toast to Confederate president **Jefferson Davis** (1808–1889; see entry) on stage. Cushman consulted with Union officials about it, then accepted the offer. After she made the toast, she was fired from her job with the theater company and thrown out of the Union as a Confederate sympathizer. But since she had publicly proclaimed her support for the Confederacy, many people were willing to believe that she was a loyal Southerner.

Cushman created a cover story—that she was looking for her brother, a Confederate officer—and used it to go behind Confederate lines. She attracted the interest of several Confederate officers, who invited her to accompany them to their army camps. In this way, Cushman gathered a great deal of valuable information for the Union Army.

In May 1863, Cushman passed information about the strength and location of Confederate troops in Tennessee to Union general William Rosecrans (1819–1898). But Confederate general Braxton Bragg became suspicious of her activities and held her for questioning. Cushman panicked and tried unsuccessfully to escape. When Bragg's forces recaptured Cushman, they discovered her secret notes that proved she was a Union spy. Tired of dealing with spies, Bragg sentenced her to death by hanging.

Escapes a death sentence

For some reason, Bragg's order to execute Cushman was not carried out immediately. Some sources say that she was ill, and the hanging was delayed until she recovered her health. Other sources say that a Union raid caused chaos in the Confederate camp and caused the soldiers to forget about the order. At any rate, Confederate forces evacuated the area a short time later and left Cushman behind. Union troops rescued her near Shelbyville, Tennessee.

Pauline Cushman in uniform. *(Reproduced by permission of Corbis-Bettmann.)*

News of Cushman's death sentence and dramatic rescue soon spread across the country. After all, she almost became the first female spy to be executed by either side in the Civil War. But all the attention meant that Cushman could not serve as a Union spy anymore. She was too well known. The Union Army made her an honorary major in recognition of her service. For the remainder of the war, she helped the Union cause by advising the army on the geographic terrain of Tennessee, which she had come to know well (good maps were difficult to find at that time).

Meets a tragic end

After the Civil War ended in 1865, Cushman returned to her acting career. She was proud of her successful wartime service—she liked to be introduced in the theater as "Major

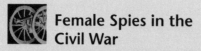

Female Spies in the Civil War

Women acted as spies for both the North and the South during the Civil War. Like the men who fought as soldiers, they risked their lives in order to serve their country. Female spies from both sides had a strong belief in the Union or Confederate cause. This belief made them want to contribute to the war effort. But roles for women were extremely limited in those days. Women were not allowed to serve as soldiers, so nursing and spying were their main choices for wartime activities.

Traditional attitudes had limited women to roles as mothers and home-makers before the Civil War. Many American men tended to think of women as delicate, refined ladies. Such attitudes actually helped some female spies. They were sometimes able to avoid detection because men could not believe women were smart enough or devious enough to serve as spies. Some men thought women were not capable of understanding anything of a technical or strategic nature. As a result, these men spoke freely about military matters in the presence of women. Female spies used this situation to their advantage and relayed the information to their side.

Cushman"—but did not talk about her spy activities on the stage. Her days as an actress gradually came to an end, and she was largely forgotten by the American people. The U.S. government even refused to give her a military pension for her service to the country.

Toward the end of her life, Cushman worked as a dressmaker's assistant and a cleaning woman in order to make ends meet. She also became addicted to drugs. Cushman committed suicide in San Francisco, California, in 1893 (some sources say 1894). Reversing its earlier policy, the government gave her a full military funeral and buried her in a veterans' cemetery. Cushman is remembered as one of the more glamorous yet effective Union spies of the Civil War. She was brave and daring, yet always conducted her activities in a quiet, professional manner.

Where to Learn More

Axelrod, Alan. *The War Between the Spies: A History of Espionage During the American Civil War.* New York: Atlantic Monthly Press, 1992.

Markle, Donald E. *Spies and Spymasters of the Civil War.* New York: Hippocrene Books, 1994.

Sarmiento, F. L. *Life of Pauline Cushman.* Philadelphia: J. E. Potter, 1865.

Jefferson Davis

Born June 3, 1808
Southwestern Kentucky
Died December 6, 1889
New Orleans, Louisiana

President of the Confederate States of America

Jefferson Davis served as the president of the Confederate States of America during its four years of existence. He was the South's political leader during the Civil War and the counterpart of U.S. president **Abraham Lincoln** (1809–1865; see entry). "On each side there was one man who stood at storm center, trying to lead a people who would follow no leader for long unless they felt in him some final embodiment [expression] of the deep passions and misty insights that moved them," Bruce Catton wrote in *The Civil War*. "This man was the President, given power and responsibility beyond all other men . . . Abraham Lincoln, in Washington, and Jefferson Davis, in Richmond."

Davis faced an extremely difficult job as president of the Confederacy, but he was well qualified to do it. He had proven himself as a military leader during the Mexican War (1846–48), and he was a respected U.S. senator who had also served as secretary of war. Davis also had some shortcomings that made his job more difficult. For example, he was stubborn, he found it difficult to admit when he was wrong, and he had trouble dealing with other strong personalities. Although he could not lead

"The Union is a creature of the states. It has no inherent power. All it possesses was delegated by the states."

Jefferson Davis. *(Photography by Mathew Brady. Courtesy of the National Archives and Records Administration.)*

the South to victory in the Civil War, Davis remained deeply committed to the Confederate cause until the end.

Supports slavery as a youth

Jefferson Davis was born on June 3, 1808, in southwestern Kentucky. He was the youngest child in a large family. His father, Samuel Davis, was a tobacco farmer and horse breeder who moved the family to Louisiana when Jefferson was two years old. A short time later, the Davises bought a plantation (a large farming estate) near Woodville, Mississippi. They also purchased a number of slaves to work in their cotton fields.

Black people were taken from Africa and brought to North America to serve as slaves for white people beginning in the 1600s. The basic belief behind slavery was that black people were inferior to whites. Under slavery, white slaveholders treated black people as property, forced them to perform hard labor, and controlled every aspect of their lives. States in the Northern half of the United States began outlawing slavery in the late 1700s. But slavery continued to exist in the Southern half of the country because it played an important role in the South's economy and culture.

Growing up in Mississippi, Davis came to believe that slavery offered the best possible life for black people. He felt that blacks were incapable of living on their own, so they needed white people to give them food, clothing, shelter, and religion. He thought that black people in Africa lived as savages, while black slaves in the South were relatively civilized. Compared to many other slaveowners, the Davis family treated their slaves well. For example, they taught their slaves to read and write and allowed them to handle discipline among themselves, rather than resorting to whipping and other harsh punishments. Since his only experience was with his family's slaves, however, young Davis did not realize that many other people were cruel to their slaves.

Receives military training

After Davis's father died in 1824, his older brother, Joseph, took over care of the family and the plantation.

Joseph was a successful and respected man, and he managed to obtain an appointment to the prestigious U.S. Military Academy at West Point for his youngest brother. But Davis proved to be a troublemaker at the school. He often skipped class, kept his room messy, and hung out at a local tavern that was strictly off-limits to students. Davis managed to graduate from West Point in 1828, but he finished near the bottom of his class.

Like most West Point graduates, Davis took a position with the U.S. Army. His first assignment was as a frontier soldier in the Pacific Northwest, where his job was to keep the peace between white settlers and Indians. He served in the infantry (the military division in which soldiers fight on foot) until 1833, then transferred to the cavalry (the military division in which soldiers fight on horseback). During this time, he developed a reputation for arguing with his superior officers.

In 1835, Davis resigned from the army in order to marry Sarah Knox Taylor. She was the daughter of his commanding officer, future U.S. president Zachary Taylor (1784–1850). Zachary Taylor was not impressed with Davis and discouraged the union, so the young couple eloped (ran away secretly to get married). Davis convinced his new bride to move to his family's plantation in Mississippi. Shortly after they arrived, however, they both contracted malaria (a serious disease carried by infected mosquitoes). Davis recovered, but his wife died just a few months after their wedding. Since he had asked her to move to the South, he felt responsible for her death. He spent the next several years in seclusion on his family's plantation. In 1845, he married Varina Howell, the nineteen-year-old daughter of a Mississippi landowner. They eventually had six children together—four boys and two girls.

Argues for states' rights in the U.S. Congress

Also in 1845, Davis was elected to represent Mississippi in the U.S. Congress. At this time, he became known as a defender of slavery and of states' rights. The role of the national, or federal, government was still being defined in the mid-1800s. People who supported states' rights wanted to limit the power of the federal government. They wanted individual states to have the right to decide important issues for themselves without interference from the national government. "The Union is a creature of the states," Davis once said. "It has no inherent power. All it possesses was delegated [granted] by the states."

In the eyes of Davis and other Southern politicians, one of the most important issues that should be decided by the states was slavery. Growing numbers of Northerners believed that slavery was wrong, and they urged the federal government to take steps to limit it. Some people wanted to outlaw slavery altogether, while others just wanted to prevent it from spreading beyond the Southern states where it was already allowed. But slavery played a big role in the Southern economy and culture. As a result, Davis and many other Southerners felt threatened by Northern efforts to contain slavery. They believed that each state should decide for itself whether to allow slavery. They did not want the national government to pass laws that would interfere with their traditional way of life.

After serving two years in the U.S. House of Representatives, Davis resigned to join the army fighting the Mexican War. The United States fought Mexico to gain territory that eventually formed parts of Arizona, New Mexico, Utah, and California. As colonel of the First Mississippi Rifles, Davis proved himself to be a good military leader who maintained his cool under fire. His performance earned the respect of his former father-in-law, Zachary Taylor, and several other important military men. By the time a foot wound forced him to leave his command, he had become a well-known war hero.

Backs the decision of Southern states to secede from the Union

Upon leaving the army in 1848, Davis was elected to the U.S. Senate. In 1853, President Franklin Pierce (1804–1869) asked Davis to join his cabinet (a group of trusted advisors who head various departments of the government) as secretary of war. Davis performed well in this position. He increased the size of the U.S. Army in a short period of time, and also introduced new, state-of-the-art weapons. When Pierce's term ended in 1857, Davis reclaimed his seat in the U.S. Senate.

Davis continued to argue in favor of slavery and states' rights in the U.S. Congress. Along with other Southern lawmakers, he warned that the Southern states would secede from (leave) the United States if an antislavery candidate was elected president in 1860. "We would declare the government at an end, even though blood should flow in torrents throughout the land," Davis stated.

Davis knew that the North would not allow the South to leave without a fight. For this reason, he hoped that the federal government would agree not to interfere with slavery in the South or in new states and territories. But his hopes for compromise were dashed when Abraham Lincoln, who opposed slavery, was elected president. The Southern states reacted by seceding from the United States and forming a new country that allowed slavery, called the Confederate States of America. With their enemies in control of the U.S. government, they felt that the only way they could protect their rights as independent states was to leave the Union.

Jefferson Davis served as secretary of war during the administration of President Franklin Pierce (above). *(Courtesy of the Library of Congress.)*

Becomes president of the Confederate States of America

Davis and the other Southern lawmakers resigned their seats in the U.S. Congress in January 1861. Then Davis went home to his plantation in Mississippi. He told his family and friends that he did not want to play a role in the political leadership of the Confederacy, but that he would accept a military command if the North and South went to war. In February 1861, however, a messenger arrived at Davis's home and informed him that he had been selected as president of the new nation. He was stunned by the news, but felt it was his duty to accept the position. Davis became provisional (temporary) president of the Confederacy on February 9,

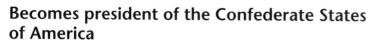

The Two Civil War Presidents: Davis and Lincoln

Jefferson Davis and Abraham Lincoln never met. But the two men are forever linked in history as the presidents of the opposing sides in the American Civil War. They share a number of striking similarities, but also some notable differences.

Both men were born in Kentucky, separated by only one hundred miles in distance and eight months in age. But Davis moved south to Mississippi as a boy, while Lincoln moved north to Illinois. Davis's family grew prosperous by using slaves to work on their cotton plantation. As a result, Davis became a strong supporter of slavery. In the meantime, Lincoln raised himself from poverty through education and hard work. He strongly opposed slavery.

When the Civil War began in 1861, Davis seemed to be more qualified to lead his country's war effort. After all, he had graduated from West Point, proven himself as a military leader during the Mexican War, and served the U.S. government as secretary of war. In contrast, Lincoln had very limited military experience. Although he had joined the Illinois militia during the Black Hawk War (a war between the Sauk

tribe and the U.S. government in 1832), he later joked that he had "fought mosquitoes and led a charge on an onion patch."

Although Davis had more military training, Lincoln possessed many other traits that made him a great commander in chief. For example, he was able to analyze situations quickly and make good decisions. He was also better at dealing with difficult people than Davis and more able to handle the extreme pressure of the job. Both men faced well-organized and vocal opposition to their policies during their time in office. In fact, both are more highly regarded and popular now than they were during the Civil War.

Since the two men played opposite roles during a crucial period in American history, historians have often drawn comparisons between them. In most cases, these comparisons reflect negatively on Davis. But as William C. Davis, Brian C. Pohanka, and Don Troiani noted in *Civil War Journal: The Leaders,* "It is unfair in many ways to criticize Davis because he was not Abraham Lincoln; nobody else has been Abraham Lincoln either."

1861, and then was elected to a six-year term as president on November 6, 1861.

Despite Davis's protests, many people in the South believed that he was the most qualified man for the job. "Few men in the United States in 1861 seemed better prepared by training and experience to undertake the leadership of a nation at war than Jefferson Davis," Steven E. Woodworth wrote in *Jefferson Davis and His Generals*. "Davis had graduated from West Point, managed a large plantation, commanded an entire regiment in battle . . ., and been an unusually active secretary of war and an effective senator. He was honest, courageous, determined, and completely devoted to his duty as he understood it."

For six weeks, Davis tried to negotiate a peaceful settlement with the North. He still wanted to avoid a war if possible. One of the issues he hoped to resolve was the presence of federal troops at Fort Sumter, located in the middle of the harbor at Charleston, South Carolina. He viewed these troops as a symbol of Northern authority and asked Lincoln to remove them. When negotiations failed, Davis ordered Confederate forces to open fire on Fort Sumter on April 12, 1861. The Confederacy gained control of the fort, but the Civil War had begun.

Faces difficult task as president during the Civil War

Davis faced a number of challenges once the war started. He had to appoint military leaders and raise an army to defend the Confederacy. Since the United States Army was controlled by the North, he had to convince individual Southern states to send men, weapons, ammunition, and supplies for the war effort. One of Davis's first mistakes involved choosing his close friends to be generals in charge of the Confederate Army, regardless of their qualifications. For example, he appointed his West Point classmate Leonidas Polk (1806–1864) as commander of all Confederate troops in the West (the area west of the Appalachian Mountains). But Polk had never served in the military. After leaving West Point, he had immersed himself in the study of religion and become an Episcopal bishop. After a few early victories in minor skirmishes, Polk turned out to be a disaster as a general.

On the other hand, Davis failed to take advantage of the talents of other military men. For example, the flamboyant **Pierre G. T. Beauregard** (1818–1893; see entry) had led the capture of Fort Sumter and had been a hero at the First

Battle of Bull Run (also known as the First Battle of Manassas) in Virginia. But Davis and Beauregard did not get along. As a result, Davis went out of his way to avoid giving Beauregard any significant responsibility after mid-1862. Of course, Davis also had some notable successes in his choice of generals. For example, he placed another fellow West Pointer, **Robert E. Lee** (1807–1870; see entry), in charge of the Confederacy's most vital army. Lee won a number of important battles over much larger Union forces and became the South's greatest general.

Part of the problem Davis experienced in selecting Confederate military leaders was due to his own personality. He trusted his own abilities far beyond those of others, and he found it difficult to admit that he was wrong. "Davis was all iron will and determination, a rigid man who might conceivably be broken but who could never be bent, proud almost to arrogance and yet humbly devoted to a cause greater than himself," Catton explained. The president was highly involved in military matters throughout the war. He made frequent visits to troops in the field and often consulted with his generals about strategy. As a result, the Southern people and media tended to place the blame on him when things went badly.

Another problem Davis encountered in leading the Confederacy during the war years involved the culture of the South. The Southern states had seceded from the Union in order to assert their right to make important decisions for themselves, without interference from the national government. Yet Davis needed to create a strong national government for the Confederacy in order to manage the war effectively. The South would have no chance of winning against larger, better organized Union forces if each state insisted on fighting on its own. "The kind of government Southerners wanted was not the kind that could fight and win an extended war," Catton noted. "The administration had to have broad wartime powers, but when Davis tried to get and use them he was bitterly criticized; fighting against strong centralized government, he had to create such a government in order to win." This issue created problems between Davis and the Confederate Congress.

Davis also suffered personal tragedies during the Civil War. In 1863, Union forces conquered Mississippi and destroyed his plantation, forcing members of his family to become refugees. In 1864, his six-year-old son, Joseph, fell from the balcony of the Confederate White House in Richmond, Virginia, and was killed. But the pressures of his job as president did not allow Davis to grieve for his son. At that time, Union general **Ulysses S. Grant** (1822–1885; see entry) had pushed the Confederate Army back almost to Richmond. The responsibility of sending thousands of young men to their deaths in battle also wore on the president. He developed physical problems, such as severe headaches and stomach ulcers, that were related to the stress of his job.

Refuses to admit defeat

In April 1865, it became clear that Union forces were about to capture the Confederate capital of Richmond. Davis and other leaders of the Confederate government fled south to Greensboro, North Carolina. Once they arrived, they learned that the South's main army had given up the fight—Lee had surrendered to Grant at Appomattox, Virginia. But Davis refused to admit defeat and vowed to continue fighting. Some of his advisors worried that the president had lost touch with reality, because everyone else seemed to recognize that the Southern cause was lost.

As Union forces approached Greensboro, Davis took his family even further south. He was finally captured near Irwinville, Georgia, on May 10, 1865. As Union troops surrounded their camp, Davis's wife, Varina, threw her shawl over him to hide his face. The Northern press changed the story in order to humiliate Davis and make him seem like a coward. They claimed that he had tried to avoid capture by wearing women's clothing.

Davis was charged with treason (betraying his country) and put in prison. At first, his captors treated him very harshly. They chained his legs, limited his food and exercise, and prevented him from seeing his family. But this treatment only made Davis a hero in the eyes of the Southern people. The U.S. government eventually offered to pardon (officially forgive) him for his crimes, but Davis refused to accept the offer. He insisted that he had committed no crime because the South's secession was legal. He wanted to make his case before a Virginia jury. But Northern leaders did not want

Davis's case to go to trial, because they were afraid a jury would decide he was right. Instead, the government dropped the charges and released Davis in 1867, after he had spent two years in captivity.

Shows no regret for his actions

Davis recovered in Canada for a while after his release from prison, then returned to Mississippi. Since his home had been destroyed and he had very little money, he relied on the help of Southern supporters to care for his family. In 1881, Davis published a book about the Civil War from his point of view, called *The Rise and Fall of the Confederate Government*. He justified his own actions and refused to apologize, which made some people angry. "Were the thing to be done over again, I would do as I then did," he stated. "Disappointments have not changed my conviction." Davis lived out his remaining years near Biloxi, Mississippi, and never tried to have his American citizenship reinstated (it was eventually restored by President Jimmy Carter [1924–] over one hundred years later). He died on December 6, 1889, at the age of eighty-two. His was the largest funeral ever held in the South, with an estimated two hundred thousand mourners attending.

Immediately after the Civil War, many people blamed Davis for the South's defeat. But historians now believe that there was nothing Davis could have done to bring victory to the South. "Davis certainly made mistakes, but no one can point to one thing or another that he could have done that would have changed the outcome of the war," William C. Davis, Brian C. Pohanka, and Don Troiani wrote in *Civil War Journal: The Leaders*. Davis's popularity grew over time, as Southerners came to regard him as a representative of everything that was good about the Old South. He did the best he could in a difficult situation, and he remained devoted to the Confederate cause until the end of his life.

Where to Learn More

Beauvoir, Jefferson Davis Home and Presidential Library. [Online] http://www.beauvoir.org (accessed on October 9, 1999).

Burch, Joann Johansen. *Jefferson Davis: President of the Confederacy.* Springfield, NJ: Enslow, 1998.

Davis, Jefferson. *The Rise and Fall of the Confederate Government.* New York: D. Appleton, 1881. Reprint, New York: Da Capo Press, 1990.

Davis, William C., Brian C. Pohanka, and Don Troiani. *Civil War Journal: The Leaders.* Nashville, TN: Rutledge Hill Press, 1997.

Eaton, Clement. *Jefferson Davis.* New York: Free Press, 1977.

Jefferson Davis Memorial Home Page. [Online] http://www.pointsouth. com/csanet/greatmen/davis/davis.htm (accessed on October 9, 1999).

King, Perry Scott. *Jefferson Davis.* Philadelphia: Chelsea House, 1990.

The Papers of Jefferson Davis Home Page. [Online] http://www.ruf.rice. edu/~pjdavis/jdp.htm (accessed on October 9, 1999).

Strode, Hudson. *Jefferson Davis, American Patriot.* New York: Harcourt Brace, 1955.

Woodworth, Steven E. *Jefferson Davis and His Generals: The Failure of Confederate Command in the West.* Lawrence: University Press of Kansas, 1990.

Martin R. Delany

Born May 6, 1812
Charleston, Virginia (now West Virginia)
Died January 24, 1885
Wilberforce, Ohio

Black abolitionist and political activist
First black field officer in the Union Army

M artin R. Delany was one of America's leading black political activists of the nineteenth century. In the 1840s, he became a leading abolitionist (person who works to end slavery). From the 1850s through the 1870s, his political beliefs changed, and he became one of the country's best-known supporters of black emigration (leaving one country to settle in another country) to Africa and pan-Africanism (a belief that all black peoples should unite to improve their lives). Delany is also well known for his Civil War activities. He was a leading recruiter of black soldiers for the Union Army, and in 1865 he became the first black soldier ever to be named a field officer in the U.S. military.

Exposed to prejudice at early age

Martin Robinson Delany was born in 1812 in Charleston, Virginia (now West Virginia). His father was a slave. But since his mother was free, Martin and his four brothers and sisters were also considered to be free blacks. Their mother's legal status thus saved them from child-

"[Black] elevation must be the result of self-efforts, and the work of [their] own hands. No other human power can accomplish it."

Martin R. Delany.
(Reproduced by permission of Archive Photos, Inc.)

105

hoods of enslavement. But even though he did not experience slavery firsthand, Delany grew up around slavery. In addition, he was exposed to terrible racial prejudice against blacks from a very early age. When he was a youngster, for instance, his father was sent to prison for a significant period of time because he resisted a white man's attempts to beat him. Such incidents showed young Delany that blacks occupied an inferior position in Virginia society. Nonetheless, he grew up with a healthy sense of his own worth, in part because his grandmother made him aware of his proud African heritage.

In 1819, the state of Virginia passed a law that made it illegal for any black children—whether free or enslaved—to attend school or receive any kind of educational instruction. A white salesman traveling through Virginia, though, gave the Delany family some educational materials so that the children could learn to read and write. Three years later, local authorities arrested Delany's mother and charged her with violating the 1819 law. Concerned that the courts might punish her by separating her from her children, she promptly gathered her family together and fled to Chambersburg, Pennsylvania. Delany's father joined them in Chambersburg one year later, after buying his freedom from his master.

Joins abolitionist movement

In 1831, Delany left his family to study religion and medicine in Pittsburgh, Pennsylvania. During his stay in Pittsburgh, he became increasingly involved in efforts to help fugitive slaves from the American South gain their freedom in the Northern states or Canada. He also made a visit to the South in 1839 in order to study slavery practices. As he journeyed through Texas, Louisiana, and Arkansas, he was shocked at the poor living conditions and vicious treatment that many slaves endured. When he returned to the North, he felt an even greater dedication to end slavery in the United States.

During the 1840s, Delany became an increasingly visible figure in the Northern antislavery movement. In 1843, he started a magazine called *Mystery,* which he used to speak out against slavery and to call for equal rights for blacks in America's Northern states. That same year he married Cathrine A. Richards, with whom he had a total of thirteen children over the years. In 1847, he stopped publication of *Mystery* and became a coeditor of the famous antislavery newspaper *The North Star* with abolitionist leader **Frederick Douglass** (c. 1818–1895; see entry) for the next two years.

Calls for emigration from United States

The 1850s were busy for Delany. In 1850, he enrolled in Harvard Medical School, where he hoped to continue his medical education. But the faculty forced Delany and two other black men to leave the school's medical program after one term because of protests by some white students. Cyril E. Griffith wrote in *The African Dream* that the Harvard incident provided Delany with yet "another concrete example to his expanding catalogue of injustices northern whites committed against black men. [Delany saw it as] further evidence that black self-determination [the right of a people to decide their own political status] would be difficult to achieve in America."

As the 1850s progressed, Delany's views increasingly placed him in disagreement with Douglass and other black abolitionist leaders. He charged that many white abolitionists did not really believe in racial equality, and complained that free blacks continued to rely too much on whites for direction. "We find ourselves occupying . . . a secondary, underling [inferior] position, in all our relations to" white abolitionists, he stated. "[Black] elevation must be the result of self-efforts, and the work of [their] own hands. No other human power can accomplish it."

Delany also came to believe that the best way for black Americans to improve their lives was to leave the United States and relocate in areas with a large nonwhite population, like Central America, South America, the West Indies, and Africa. Once they emigrated, they could unite with other blacks and work together for the benefit of all black peoples without relying on anyone else. In an 1852 book titled *The Condition, Elevation, Emigration and Destiny of the Colored Peo-*

ple of the United States, Politically Considered, Delany wrote that black people hunger for "the day when they may return to their former national position of self-government and independence, let that be in whatever part of the habitable world it may. . . . Our race is to be redeemed [restored]; it is a great and glorious work, and we are the instrumentalities [tools or agents] by which it is to be done. But we must go from among our oppressors; it never can be done by staying among them."

Delany spent the rest of the decade advancing his dream of mass black emigration from the United States to a new homeland. He helped organize a National Emigration Convention that met throughout the 1850s, and in 1859 he led a delegation (group of representatives) called the Niger Valley Exploring Party to Africa. This group explored sections of Liberia and Nigeria, scouting for places that black Americans might join with Africans to build a healthy new society.

Delany and the American Civil War

When Delany returned to North America in 1860, he was confident that he could convince large numbers of blacks to resettle in Africa with him. He was joined by other organizations that urged free black Americans and Canadians to build new lives for themselves in Africa, the West Indies, and other areas of the world with large black populations. But as Cyril Griffith noted in *The African Dream,* "this pressure . . . to leave the continent came at the very moment when the Civil War presented them with the opportunity to participate in the struggle to free millions of their brethren [brothers] enslaved in the South."

The American Civil War began in April 1861, when differences between the nation's Southern and Northern states finally erupted into armed conflict. The two sides had been arguing over several issues—including slavery and the power of the national government to regulate it—for many years. Many Northerners believed that slavery was immoral. Some people wanted to outlaw it, while others wanted to prevent it from spreading beyond the Southern states where it was already allowed. But slavery played a big role in the

Southern economy and culture. As a result, many Southern-ers felt threatened by Northern efforts to contain slavery. They believed that each state should decide for itself whether to allow slavery. They did not want the national government to pass laws that would interfere with their traditional way of life. The two sides finally went to war when the Southern states tried to secede from (leave) the United States and form their own country that allowed slavery, called the Confeder-ate States of America.

In 1861 and 1862, Delany continued trying to arrange a mass exodus (departure) of free blacks to a region of western Nigeria called Yorubaland. But interest in his emigration plans faded, especially after President **Abraham Lincoln** (1809–1865; see entry) issued his Emancipation Proclamation on January 1, 1863. This proclamation declared that all slaves within the Confederacy were free and called for the inclusion of blacks into the United States armed services. When black Americans learned of Lincoln's announcement, they reacted with joy and expressed optimism for their future. As prospects for a brighter future in America increased, they be-came less interested in Delany's calls for relocating thousands of miles away.

Delany, meanwhile, contributed his efforts to the Union cause. In 1863, he began recruiting free blacks for sev-eral all-black Union army units. One of these units was the Fifty-fourth Massachusetts regiment, which eventually be-came one of the most famous fighting units of the entire war. Delany soon became known as one of the North's best re-cruiters. He tirelessly urged black volunteers to come forward, proclaiming that "millions of your brethren still in bondage implore [urgently request] you to strike for their freedom." Despite his recruiting work, however, Delany recognized that black soldiers often encountered discrimination even within the Union Army. He worked hard to change unfair rules and treatment wherever he found them.

In addition to his recruiting activities, Delany worked on behalf of blacks in other ways. He lobbied (attempted to influence) the Federal government to form an entirely inde-pendent army composed exclusively of black troops. He also urged the Union to promote deserving blacks to positions of authority (black men were not allowed to become officers at this time). In February 1865, he was granted a meeting with President Lincoln in which he explained his proposals. Lincoln was very impressed with Delany, and he agreed that blacks should not be disqualified for officer positions just because of the color of their skin. Lincoln quickly arranged to make Delany an officer in the U.S. Army. On February 27, 1865, Delany was commissioned (given official rank) as a major, becoming the first black man to hold a field command in American history.

Postwar career

Delany spent the last few months of the Civil War continuing his recruiting activities. After the North defeated the South to end the Civil War in the spring of 1865, he became a military aide to the Freedmen's Bureau. This organization was charged with helping former slaves secure education, employment, and other assistance. Leaving his family in Wilberforce, Ohio, he traveled to South Carolina to begin his new duties.

Delany devoted a great deal of time and effort to his new job. But his calls for black self-reliance sometimes clashed with government policies, so he became a controversial figure within the Bureau. He and many other officers assigned to the Freedmen's Bureau were discharged from the army in the summer of 1868. Around this same time, Congress adopted the Fourteenth Amendment, which gave blacks the legal status of citizens for the first time in the nation's history.

Delany remained in South Carolina during the 1870s, where controversy continued to follow him. He continued to urge black Americans to take pride in their ancestry, and remained a leading defender of Africa's proud history and future potential. But he also allied himself with the Southern Democrats, who had been fiercely proslavery before and during the Civil War.

Delany joined with the Democrats because he thought that Republicans were no longer making much of an effort to secure civil rights for blacks. He believed that Southern blacks had a better chance of improving their lives if they

Secretary of War Stanton Issues a Historic Order

In February 1865, Martin Delany was commissioned (given official rank) as the first black field officer in U.S. history. The following letter, written by U.S. secretary of war Edwin M. Stanton (1814–1869), formally announced this historic appointment:

Secretary of War Edwin M. Stanton.

> The Secretary of War of the United States of America
>
> To all who shall see these presents, Greetings;
>
> Know ye, that, reposing [having] special trust and confidence in the patriotism, valor [courage or bravery], fidelity [faithfulness to duty], and abilities of MARTIN R. DELANY, the President does hereby appoint him Major, in the One Hundred and Fourth Regiment of the United States Colored Troops, in the service of the United States, to rank as such from the day of his muster [enlistment or entrance] into service, by the duly appointed commissary [officer] of musters, for the command to which said regiment belongs.
>
> He is therefore carefully and diligently [with dedication] to discharge the duty of Major by doing and performing all manner of things thereunto belonging. And I do strictly charge, and require, all officers and soldiers under his command to be obedient to his orders as Major. And he is to observe and follow such orders and directions, from time to time, as he shall receive from me or the future Secretary of War, or other superior officers set over him, according to the rules and discipline of war. This appointment to continue in force during the pleasure of the President for the time being.
>
> Given under my hand at the War Department, in the City of Washington, D.C., this twenty-sixth day of February, in the year of our Lord one thousand eight hundred and sixty five.

cooperated with the Democratic Party, which was dominant throughout the South. His alliance with the Democrats, however, drew heavy criticism from other members of South Carolina's black community. Delany ran for political office on several occasions during this decade, but each effort ended in defeat. In the early 1880s, he resumed his medical practice, rejoining his family in Wilberforce, Ohio, in 1884. He died one year later.

Where to Learn More

Griffith, Cyril E. *The African Dream: Martin R. Delany and the Emergence of Pan-African Thought.* University Park: Pennsylvania State University Press, 1975.

Levine, Robert S. *Martin Delany, Frederick Douglass, and the Politics of Representative Identity.* Chapel Hill: University of North Carolina Press, 1997.

Martin Delany Home Page. [Online] http://www.libraries.wvu.edu/delany/home/htm (accessed on October 9, 1999).

Sterling, Dorothy. *The Making of an Afro-American: Martin R. Delany, 1812–1885.* Garden City, NY: Doubleday, 1971. Reprint, New York: Da Capo Press, 1996.

Frederick Douglass

Born February 1818?
Tolbert County, Maryland
Died February 20, 1895
Washington, D.C.

Abolitionist, writer, and speaker
Escaped from slavery to become one of the most prominent activists in the antislavery movement

Frederick Douglass began his life as a slave. After escaping to the North in 1838, Douglass became a leading figure in the fight to abolish (put an end to) slavery in the United States and gain equal rights for black Americans. He was an accomplished writer and speaker who used the power of words to convince people that slavery was wrong. He was one of the country's first great black leaders.

Born a slave

Frederick Douglass was born in Tolbert County, in eastern Maryland, around 1818. He never knew the exact date of his birth because he was born a slave. Black people were taken from Africa and brought to North America to serve as slaves for white people beginning in the 1600s. The basic belief behind slavery was that black people were inferior to whites. Under slavery, white slaveholders treated black people as property, forced them to perform hard labor, and controlled every aspect of their lives. States in the Northern half of the United States began outlawing slavery in the late

"This war with the slaveholders can never be brought to a desirable termination until slavery, the guilty cause of all our national troubles, has been totally and forever abolished."

Frederick Douglass. *(Courtesy of the Library of Congress.)*

1700s. But slavery continued to exist in the Southern half of the country because it played an important role in the South's economy and culture.

Most slave owners tried to prevent their slaves from learning much about themselves or the world around them. They believed that educated slaves would be more likely to become dissatisfied with their lives. For this reason, Douglass received no information about his birth. "By far the larger part of slaves know as little of their ages as horses know of theirs," he explained, "and it is the wish of most masters within my knowledge to keep their slaves thus ignorant." Douglass knew who his mother was, but she lived on a different plantation (a large farming estate). He did not know the identity of his father, but he suspected that it was Aaron Anthony, the white master of the plantation where he lived. His last name was originally Bailey, but he changed it to Douglass after he escaped from slavery.

Douglass spent his early years under the care of his grandmother. He had a relatively pleasant childhood—often playing with other children along the banks of nearby Tuckahoe Creek—until he was six years old. At that time, he was assigned to be the personal slave of the plantation owner's child. He was required to perform certain duties each day. Whenever he misbehaved or failed to perform his duties, he was punished severely. He also saw other slaves treated cruelly, including his Aunt Hester, who was tied up and beaten for disobedience. "Her arms were stretched up at their full length so that she stood upon the ends of her toes," he recalled. "[The master] then said to her, 'Now you damned bitch, I'll learn you how to disobey my orders.' And soon the warm, red blood came dripping to the floor."

Learns to read

A few years later, Douglass was sold to a new owner, Hugh Auld, and went to live on a different plantation. Auld's wife taught him to read the Bible, even though educating slaves was frowned upon in the South. Douglass soon realized that education would provide him with a means to escape slavery. He continued learning by tricking the white children of the plantation into sharing their books and homework assignments with him. At the age of fifteen, Douglass was sent to the city of Baltimore to become a laborer. He learned a trade in the shipbuilding industry—how to use a gooey substance called caulk to seal the parts of a boat together and make them watertight. His owner rented him out to shipbuilding companies and received payment for the work he did. During his time working on the docks in Baltimore, Douglass saw boatloads of slaves being transported around the country. "I've seen men and women chained and put on a ship to go to New Orleans and I still hear their cries," he noted.

Escapes to freedom

Douglass managed to save some money over the next few years and bought his first book, a collection of famous speeches. He memorized all of the speeches in the book and practiced reciting them. He also came into contact with a network of free black people during this time. Not all black people in the United States were slaves in the early 1800s. Some former slaves were set free when their white owners died or no longer needed their services. Other former slaves saved money and purchased their freedom from their owners. When free blacks had children, the children were also free. In contrast, slaves who escaped from their owners were not legally free. Although some fugitive slaves lived on their own in places where slavery was not allowed, they risked being captured and returned to slavery at any time.

One of the free blacks Douglass met in Baltimore was Anna Murray. They fell in love, and she encouraged him to try to escape from slavery. In 1838, Murray sold a poster bed and gave Douglass the money so that he could travel to a Northern state where slavery was not allowed. The journey would be dangerous, since Southern states placed restrictions on black people's travel in order to prevent slaves from escaping. Douglass obtained papers that enabled him to pass as a sailor. Many slaves were hired out as sailors in those days, and they frequently traveled from port to port. Posing as a sailor, Douglass took a train north to Delaware, then caught a ship to Pennsylvania (a free state). Once he had reached the North, he continued on to New York, where he met and married Murray. The couple then moved to New Bedford, Massachusetts, where Douglass worked several jobs as a laborer.

Joins the abolitionist movement

Shortly after he escaped to the North, Douglass learned about the abolitionist movement. Abolitionists were people who dedicated themselves to fighting against slavery. One of the most vocal abolitionists was William Lloyd Garrison (1805–1879), who published a newspaper called *The Liberator*. "*The Liberator* became my meat and my drink," Douglass recalled. "My soul was set all on fire. Its sympathy for my brethren [brothers] in bonds, its faithful exposures of slavery, and its powerful attacks on the institution sent a thrill of joy through my soul such as I had never felt before."

In 1841, Douglass attended a meeting of Garrison's abolitionist group, the American Anti-Slavery Society, in Nantucket, Massachusetts. Upon hearing that there was an escaped slave in the audience, Garrison asked him to say a few words. Douglass kept the audience on the edge of their seats for two hours with stories about what it was like to be a slave. "I stand before you this night as a thief and a robber," he told them. "I stole this head, these limbs, this body from my master and ran off with them." Before long, Douglass began touring the country speaking at abolitionist meetings.

In 1845, Douglass wrote a book about his experiences as a slave, *Narrative of the Life of Frederick Douglass*. It was popular among people who opposed slavery and sold thirty thousand copies over the next five years. Since the book was so well written, some people doubted that a former slave could have written it. But these people became convinced as soon as they heard Douglass speak. Douglass's success as an antislavery writer and speaker helped him bring his message to large numbers of people. But as he grew more famous, his life also became more dangerous. After all, Douglass was still a fugitive slave. His master knew where he was and could send a slave catcher to capture him and return him to the South at any time.

To protect himself from returning to slavery, Douglass went to England (where slavery was not allowed) in 1845. While he was there, his abolitionist friends collected money to buy his freedom from his owner. Douglass returned to the United States in 1847 as a free man. He then settled in Rochester, New York, and began publishing a newspaper called *The North Star*. He chose the title because fugitive slaves often used *The North Star* to guide them as they escaped to the North.

Black spokesman during the Civil War

Douglass and his family—which grew to include five children—lived a comfortable life during the 1850s. But this was a time of great political tension in the United States. For years, the North and the South had been arguing over several issues, including slavery. Thanks to the efforts of Douglass and other abolitionists, growing numbers of Northerners believed that slavery was wrong. Some people wanted to outlaw it, while others wanted to prevent it from spreading beyond the Southern states where it was already allowed. But slavery played a big role in the Southern economy and culture. As a result, many Southerners felt threatened by Northern efforts to contain slavery. They believed that each state should decide for itself whether to allow slavery. They did not want the national government to pass laws that would interfere with their traditional way of life.

The front page of Frederick Douglass's newspaper, *The North Star*. (*Courtesy of the Library of Congress.*)

By 1861, this ongoing dispute had convinced several Southern states to secede from (leave) the United States and attempt to form a new country that allowed slavery, called the Confederate States of America. But Northern political leaders were determined to keep the Southern states in the Union. The two sides soon went to war. Douglass was glad to see the Civil War begin because he believed it would result in the abolition of slavery. From the start of the war, he pressured President **Abraham Lincoln** (1809–1865; see entry) to make emancipation (granting freedom from slavery or oppression) the North's main priority. "This war with the slaveholders can never be brought to a desirable termination [end] until slavery, the guilty cause of all our national troubles, has been totally and forever abolished," he stated.

Douglass also argued that black men should be allowed to serve as soldiers in the Union Army. When the government finally accepted this idea in late 1862, Douglass became an active and effective recruiter of black soldiers. He spoke to crowds of free black men across the North to convince them to join the fight for freedom of their race. "I urge you to fly to arms and smite [strike] with death the power that would bury the government and your liberty in the same hopeless grave," he said. "He who would be free, themselves must strike the blow." Two of his first recruits were his own sons, Charles and Lewis, who joined the Fifty-Fourth Massachusetts regiment. By the end of the Civil War, two hundred thousand black men had served the Union. They made up about 10 percent of the Union forces, fought in every major battle in the last two years of the conflict, and helped ensure victory for the North.

Holds government posts after the war

Douglass was recognized as one of the most important black leaders in the United States by the time the Civil War ended in 1865. His speaking and publishing ventures had made him quite wealthy. He bought a nice home outside of Washington, D.C., overlooking the Anacostia River. He accepted several high-profile government jobs during the postwar years, including marshal of the District of Columbia and U.S. minister to the Caribbean nation of Haiti.

In 1882, Douglass published the third and final volume of his life story, *The Life and Times of Frederick Douglass*. In 1883, his wife of forty-four years passed away. Douglass took his wife's death very hard and seemed to have a nervous breakdown. But he managed to overcome his grief and dedicated himself once again to gaining equal rights for Americans. He wrote and spoke about the importance of helping freed slaves and the value of granting women the right to vote.

In 1884, Douglass created a stir by remarrying. His new wife, Helen Pitts, was a white woman, twenty years younger than him, who had worked as a secretary in his office. The controversy surrounding his marriage troubled Douglass. He felt that by marrying a white woman, he helped prove that whites and blacks could live together as equals. But some people, including his children, resented it. The episode showed that America still held racial prejudices, and that Douglass still refused to be bound by them.

Douglass suffered a stroke on February 20, 1895, and died at the age of seventy-eight. He rose from slavery to become one of the greatest speakers and activists of his time. He committed his life to attaining freedom and equality for all people. He never stopped trying to make the United States live up to the values of liberty and justice outlined in the Constitution. "He had an enormous ability to capture in words the meaning of what America is about—freedom," William C. Davis, Brian C. Pohanka, and Don Troiani concluded in *Civil War Journal: The Leaders.*

Where to Learn More

Blight, David W. *Frederick Douglass' Civil War: Keeping Faith in Jubilee.* Baton Rouge: Louisiana State University Press, 1989.

Davis, William C., Brian C. Pohanka, and Don Troiani. *Civil War Journal: The Leaders.* Nashville, TN: Rutledge Hill Press, 1997.

Douglass, Frederick. *The Life and Times of Frederick Douglass.* Hartford, CT, Park Publishing, 1881. Reprint, Grand Rapids, MI: Candace Press, 1996.

Douglass, Frederick. *My Bondage and My Freedom.* New York: Miller, Orton and Mulligan, 1855. Reprint, Urbana: University of Illinois Press, 1987.

Douglass, Frederick. *Narrative of the Life of Frederick Douglass.* Boston: Anti-slavery Office, 1845. Reprint, New Brunswick, NJ: Transaction Publishers, 1997.

Frederick Douglass Museum & Cultural Center. [Online] http://www.ggw. org/freenet/f/fdm/index.html (accessed on October 9, 1999).

Frederick Douglass National Historic Site. [Online] http://www.nps.gov/ frdo/freddoug.html (accessed on October 9, 1999).

Frederick Douglass Papers. [Online] http://www.iupui.edu/~douglass/ (accessed on October 9, 1999).

Huggins, Nathan. *Slave and Citizen: The Life of Frederick Douglass.* Boston: Little, Brown, 1980.

McFeeley, William S. *Frederick Douglass*. New York: Norton, 1991.

Russell, Sharman. *Frederick Douglass*. New York: Chelsea House, 1992.

Emma Edmonds

Born December 1841
New Brunswick, Canada
Died September 5, 1889
La Porte, Texas

Union soldier, nurse, and spy
Disguised herself as a man to serve in the Union Army

Historians estimate that more than four hundred women disguised themselves as men in order to serve as either Union or Confederate soldiers during the Civil War. Of all these women, Emma Edmonds was the most remarkable. Adopting the name "Franklin Thompson," she joined the Union Army early in the war and served for two years without revealing her true identity. She started out as a battlefield nurse, then made eleven successful missions behind Confederate lines as a spy. Edmonds used a variety of disguises during her spy missions. For example, she posed as a black man, a middle-aged Irish woman, a black woman, and a white Southern businessman. Many years after the war ended, the U.S. government recognized her contributions and awarded her a veteran's pension.

An adventurous tomboy

Emma Edmonds was born on a farm in New Brunswick, Canada, in December 1841. Her full name was Sarah Emma Edmonds, but she used her middle name for

"I am naturally fond of adventure, a little ambitious, and a good deal romantic—but patriotism was the true secret of my success."

Emma Edmonds. *(Courtesy of Corbis Corporation.)*

most of her life. Edmonds had a difficult life as a young girl. Her father had always wanted a son and took out his disappointment on his daughter. To please him, she dressed as a boy from the age of six and worked hard in the fields. She also learned to enjoy rough-and-tumble, outdoor activities like swimming, horseback riding, and climbing trees. After her mother died, though, her father became more and more abusive towards her. When she was sixteen, Edmonds ran away from home. She left Canada and went to the United States in search of freedom.

After spending some time on the East Coast, Edmonds settled in Flint, Michigan. She had trouble finding a good job as a young woman, so she pretended to be a man named Franklin Thompson. She then found a job selling Bibles for a publishing company. But this was a time of great political tension in the United States. For years, the North and the South had been arguing over several issues, including slavery. By 1861, this ongoing dispute had convinced several Southern states to secede from (leave) the United States and attempt to form a new country that allowed slavery, called the Confederate States of America. But Northern political leaders were determined to keep the Southern states in the Union. Before long, the two sides went to war.

Civil War soldier and nurse

By the time the Civil War started, Edmonds had developed strong feelings about the United States and considered it her home country. She wanted to help defend the Union against the Southern rebellion. But roles for women were limited in those days. They were not allowed to be soldiers, and they were discouraged from taking on other jobs that were not considered ladylike. But Edmonds did not want to sew clothing and blankets for the soldiers, or work in an office or factory, or be a nurse in a city hospital far from the lines of battle. She wanted to be in the middle of the action. So she decided to enlist in the Union Army as Franklin Thompson.

Disguised as a man, Edmonds went to an army recruiting office to volunteer. Luckily, the officials there did not require a complete physical examination. Instead, they just asked her some questions. On May 14, 1861, Franklin

Thompson was accepted as a private in the Second Michigan Volunteer Infantry unit of the Union Army. Edmonds (Thompson) received special training to serve as a field nurse. She would work in a tent hospital near the front lines of battle, providing medical treatment to wounded soldiers. She served in this capacity in the first major battle of the Civil War—the First Battle of Bull Run in Virginia in July 1861.

Edmonds continued working as a soldier and nurse until March 1862, and no one discovered her true identity. But then two things happened that made her want to contribute even more to the Union war effort. First, she learned that a fellow soldier who had been a close friend since she had moved to the United States had been killed by the Confederates. His death made her want to do anything in her power to make the war end sooner. Next, she heard that an important Union spy had been caught and executed in the Confederate capital of Richmond, Virginia. Without information from this spy, the Union generals in charge of her unit could not move ahead with their plans. After thinking about these two things, Edmonds volunteered to become a spy.

Secret agent for the Union

By this time, Edmonds was a master of disguise. After all, she had fooled everyone for almost a year by pretending to be a man. To increase her value as a spy, she also studied weapons, military strategies, local geography, and biographies of the South's military leaders. For her first mission, she used a chemical called silver nitrate to darken her skin and posed as a black man named Cuff. She knew that the Confederate Army used black slaves as laborers in their camps, so she hoped Cuff would not attract much attention. The disguise worked. She crossed into Confederate territory and began working in the kitchen of an army camp. She overheard valuable information there, then slipped back to the Union side to report her findings.

For her next assignment, Edmonds tied pillows around her waist, put on a dress, and posed as a heavy Irish peddlar woman named Bridget O'Shea. Once again, she crossed into Confederate territory without attracting attention. She wandered into the Confederate Army camp and

Emma Edmonds disguised as a black man in the Confederate lines.
(Reproduced by permission of Corbis Corporation [Bellevue].)

sold thread, paper, matches, soap, and tea to the soldiers. She also took note of the Confederate defenses and collected other valuable information. When she was finished, she stole a horse to ride back to the Union line. She was shot at and wounded in the arm by Confederate forces, but she escaped. Another time, Edmonds went behind enemy lines disguised as a middle-aged black woman. While doing laundry for the Confederate soldiers, she found official papers in an officer's coat. She slipped out of the camp in the middle of the night and took the papers to Union leaders.

In late 1862, Edmonds's unit was transferred from Virginia to Kentucky. Kentucky was one of four "border" states that allowed slavery but remained loyal to the Union. Many people in Kentucky and the other border states, however, secretly supported the Confederate cause. As a result, a great deal of information about Union forces and strategy in the state was passed to the Confederates. Edmonds was assigned to go to the city of Louisville to learn the identity of Confederate sympathizers and spies there. This time she posed as a young Southern gentleman named Charles Mayberry. She got a job, attended society parties, and generally blended into the population of Louisville. Over time, she successfully uncovered the Confederate spy network that had been operating in the city.

Forced to leave the army

In 1863, Edmonds contracted malaria, a serious disease carried by mosquitoes. She could not check into the military hospital, because everyone there knew her as Private Franklin Thompson. She decided that the only way to prevent her unit from discovering that she was a woman was to leave the army. Without telling anyone, she went to a private hospital in Cairo, Illinois, on April 22. She checked into the hospital under her real name and spent several weeks recovering. Afterward, she hoped to rejoin her old unit. But then she saw an official notice listing Private Franklin Thompson as a deserter, meaning that he had left the army without permission before his term of service ended. Edmonds knew that she would be punished if she went back as Thompson.

Instead of creating a new male identity, Edmonds joined a relief organization as herself. She worked as a female nurse in Washington, D.C., until the end of the war in 1865. The following year, she published a book about her wartime adventures called *Nurse and Spy in the Union Army.* In it, she finally revealed the secret she had kept for so many years. The book sold many copies, and she donated all the profits to the U.S. war relief fund.

Wife and mother honored for wartime service

In 1867, Edmonds met and married Linus Seeyle. They had three sons together. The family lived in Cleveland, Ohio, for awhile, and then moved to Kansas and Texas. Over the years, Edmonds kept in touch with some members of her old Union Army regiment. She was very proud of her wartime service, but she was always disappointed that the government still considered Franklin Thompson a deserter.

In 1884, some of her fellow Civil War veterans urged her to file for a veteran's pension (a monthly payment the government provides to retired service people). She asked the government to review her case, mostly because she hoped to have the desertion charge removed from her record. Government investigators found numerous witnesses willing to state that Emma Edmonds Seeyle and Franklin Thompson were the same person, and that Thompson had provided valuable service to the Union cause as a soldier, nurse, and spy. On March 28, 1884, the U.S. Congress granted Thompson an honorable discharge from the army and awarded Edmonds a veteran's pension of $12 per month.

Edmonds died in La Porte, Texas, on September 5, 1889. She was buried in the military section of the Washington Cemetery in Houston, Texas. At the time of her death, she was the only female ever admitted to the Grand Army of the Republic—an organization of Union Civil War veterans that had over four hundred thousand members. Her incredible story has continued to capture people's imagination for generations. As Edmonds once wrote about her exciting Civil War experiences, "I am naturally fond of adventure, a little ambitious, and a good deal romantic—but patriotism was the true secret of my success."

Where to Learn More

Edmonds, Sarah Emma. *Nurse and Spy in the Union Army: Comprising the Adventures and Experiences of a Woman in Hospitals, Camps, and Battlefields.* Hartford, CT: W. S. Williams, 1865.

Markle, Donald E. *Spies and Spymasters of the Civil War.* New York: Hippocrene Books, 1994.

Reit, Seymour. *Behind Rebel Lines: The Incredible Story of Emma Edmonds, Civil War Spy.* San Diego: Harcourt Brace Jovanovich, 1988.

Seguin, Marilyn. *Where Duty Calls: The Story of Sarah Emma Edmonds, Soldier and Spy in the Union Army.* Boston: Branden, 1999.

David G. Farragut

Born July 5, 1801
Campbell's Station, Tennessee
Died August 14, 1870
Portsmouth, New Hampshire

Navy admiral who commanded successful Union offensives at New Orleans and Mobile Bay

David G. Farragut is the most famous figure to emerge from the fierce Civil War struggle for control of the seas. A life-long sailor, he was nearing his sixtieth birthday when the war began. But despite his age and his Southern background, Farragut became the best commander in the Union Navy. In fact, his successful naval assaults on the Southern ports of New Orleans and Mobile Bay are recognized as major Civil War victories for the North.

A childhood at sea

Born in Tennessee, David Glasgow Farragut was introduced to sailing at an early age by his father, George Farragut. Young Farragut learned the basics of sailing in all kinds of weather, for his father took him out on the sea in both peaceful and stormy conditions. When Farragut was eight years old, his father died, leaving him an orphan. But he was adopted by Commodore David Porter (1780–1843), a family friend who was also an officer in the U.S. Navy.

"Damn the torpedoes! Full speed ahead!"

David G. Farragut. *(Courtesy of the Library of Congress.)*

On December 17, 1810, Farragut received an appointment as a midshipman. A midshipman is a student enrolled in training to be a commissioned naval officer. The following summer he served on the *Essex,* a ship commanded by Commodore Porter that sailed as far as the West Indies. One year later, the twelve-year-old Farragut found himself in the thick of the War of 1812.

The War of 1812 was a conflict between the United States and Great Britain that lasted until 1815. This war came about for two reasons. First, the United States became angry with England after it captured some American ships and sailors who were attempting to trade with France (France and England were already at war). Second, the two nations grew upset with one another over American claims on British-held territory in North America's western regions.

As the War of 1812 unfolded and the *Essex* sailed against British warships, young Farragut proved himself to be a remarkably steady and courageous boy. In addition to serving as an aide to Porter, he also helped the older sailors operate the ship's heavy cannons and massive sails. By the time that America and England reached a truce in early 1815, Farragut knew that he wanted to spend the rest of his life in the navy.

Farragut spent the next forty-five years roaming across the oceans of the world. His naval assignments took him as far as the Caribbean and Mediterranean seas, though he also spent considerable amounts of time captaining ships along the coastlines of the United States. Farragut's duties during this time ranged from commanding warships during the Mexican War (1846–48) to supervising the establishment of a naval shipyard in San Francisco Bay in the mid-1850s.

Farragut moves his family north

During the late 1850s, Farragut became concerned about the hostile atmosphere that was building between America's Northern and Southern regions. The two sides had become bitterly frustrated with each other over several emotional issues, including slavery and the concept of states' rights. Many Northerners believed that slavery was wrong and wanted to abolish it. They also defended the idea that the federal government had the authority to pass laws that applied to all citizens of the United States. But the economy of the South had been built on slavery, and Southerners resented Northern efforts to halt or contain the practice. In addition, they argued that the federal government did not have the constitutional power to institute national laws on slavery or anything else. Fearful that the national government might pass laws that would interfere with their traditional way of life, white Southerners argued that each state should decide for itself whether to allow slavery. Finally, America's westward expansion worsened these disputes because both sides wanted to spread their way of life—and their political ideas—into the new territories and states.

In late 1860 and early 1861, a number of Southern states became so angry that they finally followed through on their long-time threat to secede from (leave) the United States and form a new country that allowed slavery, called the Confederate States of America. The U.S. government, though, declared that those states had no right to secede and that it was willing to use force to make them return to the Union. In the spring of 1861, the two sides finally went to war over their differences.

The Southern-born Farragut watched all of these events unfold with great sadness and anger. He and his wife, Virginia Loyall Farragut, had by this time settled in Norfolk, Virginia, a Southern town that they liked very much. But Farragut fiercely opposed secession. Determined to do his part to restore the Union, he quickly packed up his family and moved them north to a cottage in New York. He then reported for duty as a member of the U.S. Navy.

An important mission

During the first few months of the war, Farragut served on naval committees and boards far from any military action. In late 1861, however, the leadership of the U.S. Navy interviewed him for an important mission. They wanted someone to lead a daring assault on the strategically vital Confederate port of New Orleans. According to Secretary of the Navy Gideon Welles (1802–1878), Farragut assured him that he would restore New Orleans to Federal control, or never return. "I might not come back . . . but the city will be ours." When Welles heard Farragut's determination, he decided that he was the right man for the job.

Located in southern Louisiana near where the Mississippi River flows into the Gulf of Mexico, New Orleans was used by many Confederate ships looking to obtain supplies from Europe. Farragut's superiors recognized that if he could capture the city, their larger plan to clamp a naval blockade (a line of ships designed to prevent other vessels from entering or exiting an area) over the entire Southern coastline would have a much greater chance of success.

Farragut knew that New Orleans had strong defenses, including a small fleet of ships and two big military outposts (Fort Jackson and Fort St. Philip) that guarded New Orleans against attacks from the south. But the veteran naval commander received plenty of support for the upcoming attack. When he set sail for the Gulf of Mexico in the spring of 1862, he led a fleet of 46 warships armed with a total of 286 cannons.

The Battle of New Orleans

Farragut's fleet reached the forts in mid-April. Standing on the deck of the flagship *Hartford,* Farragut promptly ordered an attack on Fort Jackson and Fort St. Philip. The two rebel (Confederate) fortresses immediately returned fire. For the next few days, the two sides tried to hammer each other into giving up. By April 22, Farragut realized that he could not get past the two forts and up the river to New Orleans by force. His ships were beginning to run low on ammunition, and the rebel outposts showed no signs of wilting despite suffering severe damage.

Farragut then came up with a bold plan to sail past the forts under cover of darkness and proceed on to New Orleans. Many of his officers tried to convince him not to attempt this strategy, but their commander held firm. He spent April 23 visiting each ship in his fleet in order to encourage his sailors and make sure that everyone understood their orders. By that evening, Farragut wrote, "everyone looked forward to the conflict with firmness, but with anxiety."

Farragut's fleet began their move up the river at 2 A.M. on the morning of April 24, when the night was darkest. As the Union ships sailed up the river, they were met with a hail of cannon fire from the forts and the Confederate warships that had been assigned to guard the city. Some of the rebel ships even pushed flaming rafts down the river to smash into Farragut's ships. But the Union fleet fought back furiously as they pushed their way upstream. As the nighttime battle lit up the sky, one reporter said that "the river and its banks were one sheet of flame, and the messengers of death were moving . . . in all directions."

The battle on the river was horribly violent. But as the Federal fleet pressed on, it became clear to everyone that Farragut's bold strategy was working. His fleet successfully glided past the guns of Fort Jackson and Fort St. Philip, then manhandled the smaller Confederate flotilla (small fleet of ships). By dawn, Farragut's path to New Orleans was clear. He captured the city on April 25, and the soldiers at Fort St. Philip and Fort Jackson surrendered three days later.

Secretary of the Navy Gideon Welles. *(Courtesy of the National Archives and Records Administration.)*

News of Farragut's great triumph delighted President **Abraham Lincoln** (1809–1865; see entry), Secretary Welles, and other Union leaders. Down in the Southern capital of Richmond, meanwhile, the loss of New Orleans stunned Confederate military leaders. "The capture of New Orleans ranks as one of the strategic milestones of the war," wrote Ivan Musicant in *Divided Waters: The Naval History of the Civil War.* "At a blow, the South's largest city, premier [main] port of entry, and the mouth of the Mississippi, fell to the Union."

Sailing on Vicksburg

Farragut's bravery and skill at New Orleans made him a celebrity in the North. But his next assignment did not end in victory. In the weeks following his capture of New Orleans, he tried to convince his superiors to approve an attack on Mobile Bay, Alabama. He wanted to move against Mobile Bay because it was one of the last Confederate harbors that remained open to rebel ships. But he was instead told to take his fleet further up the Mississippi River to the city of Vicksburg.

Vicksburg, Mississippi, was another strategically important Southern city that remained under the control of the Confederacy. But Farragut's voyage up the river proved to be a dangerous one. His lack of familiarity with the river's currents and layout made passage very difficult, and shortages of supplies hurt the fleet's effectiveness as well. Farragut later admitted that "the elements of destruction in this river are beyond anything I ever encountered."

In May 1862, Farragut reached Vicksburg. But a lack of adequate Union ground troops in the area made it impossible to take the city, and Farragut soon retreated back to New Orleans. A few weeks later, Farragut received orders directing him to make a second attempt on Vicksburg. But this midsummer effort also ended in failure for Farragut. He finally ordered his fleet to return to the Gulf of Mexico for the winter. Vicksburg remained under Confederate control until July 1863. The troops defending the city finally surrendered when an extended Union siege (surrounding a city in order to prevent supplies from entering) organized by **Ulysses S. Grant** (1822–1885; see entry) threatened them with starvation.

The Battle of Mobile Bay

In 1863, Farragut supervised the Union ships operating along the Gulf coast. He also moved against a number of targets along the Texas coastline, capturing Galveston and Corpus Christi. In addition, he helped the Union take Port Hudson, a rebel fortress that stood near Vicksburg. Farragut occasionally requested permission to attack Mobile Bay, which had become the only port on the coast still open to Confederate blockade-runners (ships that attempted to slip past the Union naval blockade to deliver supplies to the South). But other military plans always seemed to have a higher priority. Farragut did not receive orders to move on Mobile Bay until mid-1864.

On August 5 of that year, Farragut led a fleet of fourteen ships and four special warships known as monitors into Mobile Bay. He knew that the mission was a dangerous one. After all, Confederate defenses in the bay included Fort Morgan, three gunboats, an armored vessel called the *C.S.S. Tennessee,* and an underwater minefield. As Farragut's fleet cruised into the bay, the gunfire between the Union and Confederate forces became so heavy that smoke drifted across the water in thick clouds. Farragut finally lashed himself to a mast high above the deck of the *Hartford* so that he could see what was going on.

"Full speed ahead!"

As the Union fleet sailed into the bay, one of its four monitors—the *Tecumseh*—struck an underwater mine. The mine (then known as a torpedo) blew a huge hole in the ship, and it quickly sank to the bottom of the bay with its captain and ninety-two sailors still trapped on board. The other Union vessels hesitated when the *Tecumseh* went down, but Farragut ordered them forward, shouting "Damn the torpedoes! Full speed ahead!"

Farragut's flagship charged into the heart of the bay, even though it drew heavy fire. One of Farragut's lieutenants remembered that sailors on the *Hartford* "[were] being cut down by scores. . . . The sight was sickening beyond the power of words to portray. Shot after shot came through the side, mowing down the men, deluging [flooding] the decks with blood, and scattering mangled fragments of humanity." But Farragut pressed forward, and he successfully guided the *Hartford* and the rest of the Union ships through the minefield and out of the range of Fort Morgan's guns. Farragut quickly turned his cannons on the bay's small Confederate fleet, and the rebel vessels surrendered a short time later.

Farragut's mission to seize control of Mobile Bay had succeeded, though he later admitted that the battle was "one of the hardest-earned victories of my life." Over the next three weeks, Union forces took control of Fort Morgan and two other rebel strongholds on Mobile Bay. The city of Mobile remained in Confederate hands, but Farragut's capture of the bay effectively ended its usefulness as a blockade-running port.

America's first admiral

In November 1864, Farragut returned home to New York because of health problems and his desire to take a break. He was given a big public reception and presented with a gift of $50,000 so he and his wife could buy a home of their liking. Farragut also received recognition from the U.S. Navy for his wartime exploits. In 1866, one year after the Confederacy finally surrendered and the Union was restored, he became the first man in American history to hold the rank of admiral in the U.S. Navy. He died of a heart attack in 1870, midway through an inspection tour in Portsmouth, New Hampshire.

Where to Learn More

Duffy, James P. *Lincoln's Admiral: The Civil War Campaigns of David Farragut*. New York: John Wiley & Sons, 1997.

Hearn, Chester G. *Admiral David Glasgow Farragut: The Civil War Years*. Annapolis, MD: U.S. Naval Institute Press, 1998.

Latham, Jean Lee. *David Glasgow Farragut: Our First Admiral*. Champaign, IL: Garrard, 1967. Reprint, New York: Chelsea House, 1991.

Lewis, Charles Lee. *David Glasgow Farragut: Admiral in the Making*. Annapolis, MD: U.S. Naval Institute, 1941. Reprint, New York: Arno Press, 1980.

Musicant, Ivan. *Divided Waters: The Naval History of the Civil War*. New York: HarperCollins, 1995.

Reynolds, Clark G. *Famous American Admirals*. New York: Van Nostrand, 1978.

Nathan Bedford Forrest

Born July 13, 1821
Chapel Hill, Tennessee
Died October 29, 1877
Memphis, Tennessee

Highly feared Confederate cavalry commander

onfederate cavalryman Nathan Bedford Forrest ranks as one of the most controversial figures in Civil War history. Forrest was a ferocious fighter who proved time and again that he was one of the war's most brilliant combat strategists. Mixing an aggressive style with superb battlefield instincts, his attacks on Northern military positions and supply centers became so disruptive that Union general **William T. Sherman** (1820–1891; see entry) warned that "there will never be peace in Tennessee till Forrest is dead."

Forrest's tough reputation and military exploits made him a hero in the South. In the North, however, he emerged as one of the most hated men of the Civil War era. Northerners feared and hated Forrest partly because of his success as a raider and his fearsome reputation. But they also despised him because of his prewar career as a slave trader, his involvement in a wartime massacre of Union soldiers, and his early leadership role in the violent white supremacist group known as the Ku Klux Klan during Reconstruction.

"Forrest simply used his horsemen as a modern general would use motorized infantry. He liked horses because he liked fast movement, and his mounted men could get from here to there much faster than any infantry could. . . ."

Historian Bruce Catton

Nathan Bedford Forrest.
(Reproduced by permission of Archive Photos, Inc.)

Growing up in poverty

Nathan Bedford Forrest was born in a frontier cabin in a remote area of Tennessee on July 13, 1821. The oldest son of nine children, Forrest lost five of his brothers and sisters to typhoid fever. The rest of the family barely survived on the money his father made as a blacksmith. This struggle to put food on the table made education seem like a luxury, so Forrest received only six months of schooling during his childhood. When Forrest was thirteen years old, he moved with his family to northern Mississippi. Three years later, his father died and the teenager became the head of the household.

In 1841, Forrest moved to Hernando, Mississippi, to start a new life. He formed a brief business partnership with one of his uncles, who had been feuding with another family for a long time. Their business relationship ended when they were attacked by members of that family. Forrest's uncle was killed in the assault, but Forrest killed or wounded all four attackers.

In 1842, Forrest married Mary Ann Montgomery, the daughter of a Presbyterian minister. The couple had two children, a boy and a girl. Their son, William, grew up to ride with his father in the Civil War. But their daughter, Frances, died from disease at the age of six.

Becomes a wealthy slave trader

During the 1840s, Forrest worked hard to build a comfortable life for his family. His lack of education sometimes made these efforts more difficult. After all, he had only a very limited capacity to read and write, and he never received any formal training in subjects like business or mathematics. Nonetheless, his intelligence and determination helped him through the tough times.

After working for a time as a real estate agent, Forrest moved his family to Memphis, Tennessee, in 1851. Once in Memphis, he quickly established himself as one of the city's leading traders of black slaves. Under slavery, white slaveholders treated black people as property, forced them to perform hard labor, and controlled every aspect of their lives.

Forrest knew that even in the South, some people looked down on slave traders as members of a disgraceful profession. But Forrest did not feel that there was anything wrong with buying and selling black people, and he recognized that the slave trade was a booming business. During the 1850s, Forrest's skill as a slave trader and real estate investor made him one of the richest men in Tennessee. By 1860, he owned more than three thousand acres of land, including several big cotton plantations in Arkansas and Mississippi. He also personally owned more than forty slaves.

Beginning of the Civil War

As a slaveowner who depended on the continued existence of the slave trade to add to his fortune, Forrest opposed all Northern efforts to restrict or abolish (completely do away with) slavery in the United States. His support of slavery and his background as a Southerner made it easy for him to side with the Confederacy when the American Civil War erupted in the spring of 1861.

The Civil War came about as a result of long-time disagreements between the Northern United States and the Southern United States over a variety of issues. The most important issue dividing these regions was slavery. Many Northerners believed that slavery was wrong and wanted to take steps to end it. But slavery played a vital role in the Southern economy and culture, and Southerners resented Northern efforts to halt or contain the practice. Fearful that the national government might pass laws that would interfere with their traditional way of life, white Southerners argued that each state should decide for itself whether to allow slavery. Finally, America's westward expansion worsened these disputes because both sides wanted to spread their way of life—and their political ideas—into the new territories and states.

By the spring of 1861, several Southern states had seceded from (left) the United States to form a new country that allowed slavery, called the Confederate States of America. But the Federal government declared that it would use force if necessary to make the Confederate states return to the Union. When it became clear that neither side was going to back down, America's North and South began the process of building their armies for war.

Forrest becomes a rebel cavalry leader

Forrest enlisted in the Southern army as a private in June 1861, a week after his native Tennessee voted to secede from the Union and join the Confederacy. But he was discharged (released from service) a short time later so that he could recruit his own battalion of cavalry (a military division that rides on horseback to conduct raids and scout enemy movements). Using his own money to provide his troops with needed supplies, Forrest quickly assembled a cavalry force of about six hundred men. The Confederate Army then promoted him to lieutenant colonel so that he could formally command them.

Forrest first attracted national attention in February 1862 for his actions at Fort Donelson in Tennessee. The fort had been targeted for capture by Union forces led by **Ulysses S. Grant** (1822–1885; see entry). As Grant's troops advanced on the stronghold, Confederate brigadier general Gideon J. Pillow decided to surrender. But Forrest refused to admit defeat. Even as thirteen thousand rebel soldiers surrendered to Grant's troops, Forrest's cavalry escaped from the area by taking an unguarded road that had flooded.

Two months later, Forrest again proved his worth to the Confederate cause at the Battle of Shiloh in April 1862. The clash ended with Confederate forces in full retreat, hounded by pursuing Union troops. But Forrest's cavalry stepped in and slowed the Union pursuit with a series of quick strikes against Federal forces. This brilliant performance brought Forrest even more attention, especially since he had led his cavalry even after suffering a serious bullet wound.

After recovering from his wound, Forrest returned to the field. Forrest's superiors were eager to make use of his aggressive style and strategic abilities, so they decided to grant him a great deal of independence from other Confederate military operations. This decision proved to be a good one, as Forrest used his cavalry to torment Union patrols and supply centers. In mid-July 1862, for example, Forrest completed an extended raid of Union positions in middle Tennessee by bluffing (purposely mislead) the Union commander at Murfreesboro into surrendering. Forrest thus seized more than one thousand Union soldiers and hundreds of thousands of dollars in Union supplies.

Forrest continued to strike against Union forces with great effectiveness for the next eighteen months. Ranging from western Tennessee to the Ohio River, his cavalry moved at a speed that frustrated all Northern pursuers. His most dramatic triumph during this period came in Alabama in the spring of 1863, when he fooled a Union commander into surrendering to him, even though the Union leader had three times as many soldiers. But Forrest also led dozens of other effective raids that did not receive as much publicity. "[Forrest] was probably the best cavalry leader in the entire war," wrote Bruce Catton in *The Civil War*. "Forrest simply used his horsemen as a modern general would use motorized infantry. He liked horses because he liked fast movement, and his mounted men could get from here to there much faster than any infantry could; but when they reached the field they usually tied their horses to trees and fought on foot, and they were as good as the very best infantry."

The Fort Pillow Massacre

Forrest's cavalrymen admired their leader's bravery and leadership. But his reputation as a violent man with a terrible temper made them fear him, too. The most famous example of Forrest's ruthlessness was a controversial clash that took place at Fort Pillow, Tennessee, in April 1864. In this incident, known as the Fort Pillow Massacre, hundreds of Union troops were killed. Many of these Union soldiers, which included both black soldiers and white soldiers from Tennessee, were apparently killed while trying to surrender. The correspondence of some members of Forrest's command indicates that their leader approved of the

 Forrest's Unlucky Horses

During the course of the Civil War, Nathan Bedford Forrest reportedly had twenty-nine horses shot out from under him in battle. In addition, the cavalry leader suffered several serious wounds during the war. The most unusual of Forrest's war injuries came in June 1863, when he was shot by an angry Confederate aide named Andrew W. Gould. Forrest survived the attack by killing Gould with a penknife.

None of Forrest's injuries kept him out of the saddle for very long, however. Fearless and grimly determined to fight for the Southern cause, Forrest hated being away from the action. This attitude made him a deadly foe on the field of battle. By the end of the war, he claimed that he had taken revenge for every horse he lost by personally killing thirty Union soldiers. Some people viewed this boast as yet another sign of his callous (unfeeling) attitude toward human life. But Forrest usually responded to such accusations by saying that "war means fighting and fighting means killing."

massacre. "The slaughter was awful," wrote Confederate cavalryman Achilles V. Clark. "Words cannot describe the scene. . . . I with several others tried to stop the butchery and at one point had partially succeeded—but Gen. Forrest ordered them shot down like dogs and the carnage continued." Today, the Fort Pillow Massacre remains the biggest blemish on Forrest's war record. "Whether Forrest ordered [the massacre] or not, and that is still debated, he certainly watched as the slaughter went on," wrote historian Brian Pohanka.

Raids in the western theater

In the fall of 1863, Forrest was transferred to the war's western theater (the area west of the Appalachian Mountains). He wasted no time in making his presence felt. In the months following his arrival, his cavalry conducted damaging raids on Union positions throughout northern Mississippi and western Tennessee.

Beginning in June 1864, Forrest launched a series of raids against the supply lines of Union general William T. Sherman, who had begun a major invasion of the Confederacy's western region earlier in the year. Sherman responded by ordering a force of eighty-five hundred Northern troops to find Forrest and stop him. Instead, Forrest launched a surprise attack on his pursuers. This clash, which took place at Brices Cross Roads, Mississippi, on June 10, resulted in one of the greatest Confederate cavalry victories of the war. Despite being outnumbered by almost a two-to-one margin, Forrest pushed his foes into a wild retreat. By the end of the day, his cavalry had captured two thousand soldiers, sixteen cannons, and hundreds of supply wagons.

Forrest's cavalry continued to strike against Union troops and supply lines through the rest of 1864 and into early 1865. But the Union Army's growing dominance over its Confederate foes elsewhere in the South made these raids seem less and less important. In addition, Forrest's cavalry operated during this period under the same shortages of food and supplies that were weakening other Confederate armies. On April 2, 1865, Forrest's fading cavalry was disabled once and for all when it absorbed a terrific beating outside Selma,

Alabama, at the hands of Union cavalry forces led by Major General James H. Wilson (1837–1925).

A member of the Ku Klux Klan is shown attacking a black family. *(From* Harper's Weekly, *February 24, 1872.)*

Forrest and the Ku Klux Klan

Forrest and the remnants of his cavalry surrendered to Union troops in May 1865, a few weeks after General **Robert E. Lee** (1807–1870; see entry) and the main Confederate Army surrendered at Appomattox, Virginia. After the war, Forrest expressed a deep desire to put the conflict behind him and return to his business interests. "I did all in my power to break up the government but I found it a useless undertaking and I now resolve to stand by the government as earnestly and honestly as I fought it. I'm also aware that I am at this moment regarded in large communities of the North with abhorrence [hatred] as a detestable monster, ruthless and swift to take life."

After obtaining a pardon (official forgiveness) from President **Andrew Johnson** (1808–1875; see entry) for his wartime activities, Forrest resumed his life as a businessman. As time passed, though, he became very angry about federal Reconstruction policies that gave blacks increased economic and political rights in the South. (Reconstruction refers to the period in American history immediately after the Civil War, when the Southern states were readmitted into the Union.)

Forrest and some other white Southerners who were angry about Reconstruction policies subsequently formed the Ku Klux Klan. This organization of ex-Confederates quickly became known for its white supremacist philosophy and its willingness to use violence against blacks and people who helped them. Forrest was reportedly one of the Klan's early leaders, but some historians contend that he eventually withdrew from the organization because of its heavy use of violence and intimidation. In the 1870s, Forrest's business ventures in farming, insurance, and railroads failed. By the time of his death from illness on October 29, 1877, the former cavalry leader was deeply in debt.

Where to Learn More

Davis, William C., Brian C. Pohanka, and Don Troiani. *Civil War Journal: The Leaders.* Nashville, TN: Rutledge Hill, 1997.

The Forrest Preserve. [Online] http://nbforrest.com/ (accessed on October 9, 1999).

General Nathan Bedford Forrest Historical Society. [Online] http://www.tennessee-scv.org/ForrestHistSociety/ (accessed on October 9, 1999).

Hurst, Jack. *Nathan Bedford Forrest: A Biography.* New York: Knopf, 1993.

Jordan, Thomas, and J. P. Pryor. *The Campaigns of Lieut.-Gen. N. B. Forrest and of Forrest's Cavalry.* New Orleans: Blelock, 1868. Reprint, New York: Da Capo Press, 1996.

Lytle, Andrew Nelson. *Bedford Forrest and His Critter Company.* New York: Minton, Balch and Co., 1931. Reprint, Nashville: J. S. Sanders and Co., 1992.

Wills, Brian S. *A Battle from the Start: The Life of Nathan Bedford Forrest.* New York: HarperCollins, 1992. Reprint, Lawrence: University Press of Kansas, 1998.

Wills, Brian S. *The Confederacy's Greatest Cavalryman: Nathan Bedford Forrest.* Lawrence: University Press of Kansas, 1998.

Wyeth, John A. *Life of General Nathan Bedford Forrest.* New York: Harper, 1899. Reprint, Baton Rouge: Louisiana State University Press, 1989.

John C. Frémont

Born January 21, 1813
Savannah, Georgia
Died July 13, 1890
New York, New York

American West explorer
known as the "Pathfinder"
Removed from his command as a Union general
for issuing his own "emancipation proclamation"
in Missouri

John Frémont "remains a symbol of a younger, untamed, and adventurous America."
Writer Edward D. Harris

John C. Frémont. *(Courtesy of the Library of Congress.)*

J ohn C. Frémont was one of the best-known explorers of the American West in the first half of the nineteenth century. "His scientific and surveying work was crucial in opening America beyond the Mississippi, and his heroic image and legend helped imbue [fill] the West with the romance with which it is still colored," according to Edward D. Harris in *John Charles Frémont and the Great Western Reconnaissance.* "He remains a symbol of a younger, untamed, and adventurous America."

In 1856, Frémont became the antislavery Republican political party's first presidential candidate. When the Civil War began a few years later, he took command of Union forces in Missouri—one of the four "border states" that allowed slavery but remained part of the United States. Instead of using diplomacy to gain the support of those residents who had wanted to join the Confederacy, Frémont used harsh, controversial measures to maintain order. In fact, Frémont declared that he would take away property and free slaves belonging to anyone who supported the Southern cause. He took this step a full year before President **Abraham**

Lincoln (1809–1865; see entry) issued his Emancipation Proclamation freeing the slaves in the South. Because Frémont had exceeded his authority, the president removed him from command a short time later.

Born out of wedlock

John Charles Frémont was born on January 21, 1813, in Savannah, Georgia. His last name was originally Frémon, but he added the *t* in 1836 to make it sound more American. His father, a dashing Frenchman named Jean Charles Frémon, made a living teaching French. His mother, Anne Whiting Pryor, was actually married to a man other than his father at the time of his birth. She had married a wealthy Virginia landowner, much older than herself, at the age of seventeen in order to help her family out of financial problems. But she fell in love with Frémon and ran off to Georgia with him when their affair became public. They were married after her first husband died. Sadly, Jean Frémon died a short time later, when John was five years old.

After the death of her husband, Anne Frémon took her four children to Charleston, South Carolina. She supported the family by taking boarders into their home. John managed to overcome his family's poverty and the circumstances of his birth with his intelligence, charm, and good looks. Several local businessmen took an interest in him as a boy. They helped him attend a local private school and then enter Charleston College. Although Frémont had the potential to be a good student, he did not pay much attention to his schoolwork and left college after a few months. He took a teaching position at a private school and continued his education on his own. He particularly enjoyed studying navigation, and learned how to calculate a geographical position in latitude and longitude using scientific instruments.

Becomes an explorer

In 1834, Frémont got a chance to put his navigational knowledge to work. A prominent Charleston resident, Joel Roberts Poinsett (1779–1851), invited him to serve as a mathematics teacher aboard the American warship *Natchez* during a two-year tour of South America. The trip convinced Frémont that he was destined to lead a life of adventure. Shortly after he returned, he helped survey a railroad route from Charleston to Cincinnati, Ohio. In 1836, he joined a government survey team that mapped the Cherokee Indian territory in North Carolina, Tennessee, and Georgia. The U.S. government wanted a detailed map of the region because they were preparing to force the Cherokee off of their ancestral lands. Frémont did not question the government's policies. In general, he liked and respected the Indians he met on his travels. But he was not overly concerned that his mission—charting areas for future white settlement—would destroy the native cultures.

In 1837, Frémont joined the U.S. Army Bureau of Topographical Engineers. This section of the army produced detailed maps of the natural and man-made features of various regions for the government. For his first assignment, he accompanied the famous explorer and scientist Joseph Nicolas Nicollet (1790–1843) on an expedition to survey the area of the West that had been acquired from France in 1803. Known as the Louisiana Purchase, this territory had not been fully explored until that time. In 1839, Frémont traveled with Nicollet to Washington, D.C., to present their findings to the U.S. Congress.

During his time in Washington, Frémont met Thomas Hart Benton (1782–1858), a powerful U.S. senator from Missouri. Benton was known for his stand against slavery and for his strong support of westward expansion. The senator liked Frémont and encouraged Congress to let him lead his own survey expeditions. But Benton was not pleased when Frémont fell in love with his daughter Jessie. He wanted her to marry someone more stable, wealthy, and politically connected. But the young couple ignored his objections and were married in 1841.

Missouri senator Thomas Hart Benton. Benton's daughter married John Frémont. *(Courtesy of the Library of Congress.)*

Gains reputation across the country as the "Pathfinder"

The following year, Frémont got an opportunity to lead his own expedition. He took a survey team to the Rocky Mountains. When he returned in 1843, he produced a colorful report for Congress with the help of his wife, who was an accomplished writer. The report included detailed maps, a catalog of plants and rocks, latitude and longitude readings of key spots, and advice for settlers, along with exciting stories about Frémont's adventures. It was soon published as a book and became very popular. People across the eastern part of the country hailed Frémont as a hero. Newspapers even gave him a nickname, the "Pathfinder."

In 1844, Frémont led an even bigger expedition to Oregon Country, along the Pacific coast. His team surveyed along the Columbia River and returned by way of the Great Basin region of the Southwest. His 1845 report to Congress about this trip was the most extensive survey of the West yet completed. Once again, copies of his report were snapped up by adventure-loving readers. They did not seem to care whether all of his stories were strictly true. They simply enjoyed his vivid accounts of his travels in the wilderness. "In later years critics and even some of Frémont's companions of the trail would charge that he artfully embellished [improved by adding imaginary details] his accounts to create himself a hero," Harris noted, "but there is no doubt that Frémont's vision of the West captured the imagination of countless Americans."

Trouble in California

In 1845, Frémont led a group of explorers on an expedition to California. At that time, California was a territory that belonged to Mexico. But many Americans had settled in the region, and some of them wanted the United States to claim it. Mexican officials knew that the U.S. government was interested in taking California away from them. So when Frémont and his heavily armed men arrived, the Mexicans viewed them as a threat and ordered them to leave. Instead, Frémont added to the Mexican fears by building a log fort and raising the American flag over it. Frémont finally backed down after a tense standoff with the Mexican army.

By this time, however, many of his men were looking for a fight. As they moved north into the Sacramento Valley, they met American settlers who told them that the Klamath Indians who lived in the region were hostile (unfriendly). Frémont and his men soon confronted the Klamath. Nearly two hundred Indians died in the fight that followed. A short time later, a Klamath leader took revenge for the massacre by killing one of Frémont's men as he slept. Frémont's group responded with more violence, slaughtering many members of peaceful Indian tribes who lived nearby.

In 1846, with the approval of Frémont, a group of American settlers organized a rebellion against the Mexican authorities in California. In what became known as the Bear Flag Rebellion, the Americans ended up gaining control of the region without much difficulty. Then Frémont and several other military leaders in California became engaged in a heated dispute about who was in charge. Without the proper authority to do so, Navy commodore Robert Stockton (1795–1866) named Frémont governor of California. Then word arrived from Washington, D.C., that Army general **Winfield Scott** (1786–1866; see entry) had named another soldier, Stephen Kearney, as governor. Finally, Frémont received orders to return to Washington in June 1847.

When Frémont reached the Missouri River, however, he was arrested for mutiny (refusing to follow the orders of a higher-ranking military officer). As he was transported to Washington to face a court-martial (military trial), thousands of people turned out to show their support for the flamboyant explorer who had helped California gain its independence. His trial became front-page news across the country. Although the court found him guilty, he did not receive any punishment. Nevertheless, Frémont felt insulted by the verdict and resigned from the army.

Winter expedition fails

In 1848, Frémont decided to move his family to California, where he had purchased a forty thousand–acre ranch near Yosemite Valley. His wife and children traveled by boat around the southern coast of the United States. But he decided to make a privately financed winter expedition to the

West. He convinced a group of twenty-two men to accompany him across the San Juan Mountains, along the present-day border of Colorado and New Mexico. By crossing the mountain range in winter, he hoped to prove that it was possible to create a transcontinental railroad linking East and West.

But the trip ended up being a disaster. Frémont and his men encountered blizzard conditions, with ten feet of snow and temperatures reaching twenty degrees below zero. They suffered from altitude sickness, snow blindness, and frostbite. To make matters worse, they ran out of food and ended up eating their pack mules. Finally, the party separated and Frémont's group went for help. But upon reaching safety, Frémont remained behind while one of his men led a rescue party to collect the survivors. In the end, ten of his men had lost their lives. But Frémont still considered the trip a success, and even attempted another winter crossing of the mountains several years later.

Enters politics

Frémont eventually made it to California and settled down with his family. Within a short time, prospectors discovered gold on his property, and he became a wealthy man. In 1849, Frémont was elected to represent California in the U.S. Senate when it became a state. Due to the timing of California's statehood, he ended up serving only three weeks in office. But he introduced eighteen separate pieces of legislation during this brief time. He also emerged as an outspoken opponent of the expansion of slavery.

After leaving office, Frémont spent some time traveling in Europe with his family. He also provided financial backing for the transcontinental railroad. In 1856, he ran for president of the United States as the candidate of the newly formed Republican political party. This party was founded by people who opposed slavery. "For the first time, a purely northern major political party had positioned itself squarely against the supporters of slavery," Kenneth C. Davis explained in *Don't Know Much about the Civil War.* "The distinctly regional division that the country had been moving toward was now firmly established."

At forty-three, Frémont became the youngest presidential candidate in American history. He used the campaign slogan "Free Soil, Free Speech, Free Men, and Frémont." His Democratic opponents launched fierce attacks on his background and his career. People who supported slavery desperately wanted him to be defeated. In fact, some Southern states threatened to secede (withdraw) from the United States if he were elected. Frémont ended up gaining a great deal of support in the North, but losing the overall election to James Buchanan (1791–1868).

Issues premature "Emancipation Proclamation" during the Civil War

In the next election, however, an antislavery candidate did become president. Shortly after Abraham Lincoln was elected, the Southern states made good on their threat to secede from the Union and form their own country that allowed slavery, called the Confederate States of America. But Northern leaders would not allow the Southern states to leave without a fight. In early 1861, the two sides went to war.

President Lincoln asked Frémont to rejoin the Union Army when the Civil War began. Frémont received the rank of major general and took command of the Department of the West. He was stationed in Missouri, a so-called "border state" that allowed slavery but decided to remain in the Union. Many people in Missouri still supported the South. Lincoln wanted Frémont to use diplomacy to gain the support of the state's residents.

Instead, Frémont immediately began instituting harsh measures to control Missourians who favored secession. In August 1861, he declared martial law (law enforced by military rather than civilian authorities) in Missouri and suspended many of the people's rights. He also announced his intention to confiscate (take away) the property of secessionists and free their slaves. At this point, however, the North's stated purpose in fighting the Civil War was to restore the Union. Lincoln worried that any talk about freeing slaves would drive Missouri and the other three border states into the Confederacy. In addition, Frémont did not have the authority to issue and enforce this order. As a result, Lincoln removed Frémont from his command in September.

Frémont received another chance to contribute to the Union war effort in 1862. He took command of the Department of West Virginia, but lost several battles against Confederate general **Thomas "Stonewall" Jackson** (1824–1863; see entry) in the Shenandoah Valley. After being replaced once again, Frémont sat out the rest of the war in New York City.

Loses his fortune and fades from view

After the war ended in a Union victory in 1865, Frémont began to fade from public view. He lost his fortune when one of the railroad companies he had financed went bankrupt. He ended up losing his California property and going into debt. In the 1880s, he spent a great deal of time writing his life story. He hoped that it would be as popular as his earlier books and help him to regain his wealth. But his autobiography, *Memoirs of My Life,* generated little interest when it was published in 1887.

In 1890, the U.S. government recognized Frémont's early contributions as an army officer and granted him a military pension. But he became ill and died a short time later, on July 13, 1890. Frémont was pleased to see that many of the areas he had explored became states before his death, including Minnesota, North and South Dakota, Nebraska, Colorado, Nevada, Oregon, Washington, Idaho, and Wyoming. He brought the West to the attention of the American people and led the way for future settlers. As his wife once proclaimed, "Cities have arisen on the ashes of his lonely campfires."

Where to Learn More

Egan, Ferol. *Frémont: Explorer for a Restless Nation.* Garden City, NY: Doubleday, 1977. Reprint, Reno: University of Nevada Press, 1985.

Frémont, John C. *Memoirs of My Life.* Chicago: Belford, Clarke, 1887.

Harris, Edward D. *John Charles Frémont and the Great Western Reconnaissance.* New York: Chelsea House, 1990.

Viola, Herman J. *Exploring the West.* Washington, D.C.: Smithsonian Books, 1987.

Josiah Gorgas

Born July 1, 1818
Daupin County, Pennsylvania
Died May 18, 1883
Tuscaloosa, Alabama

Chief of Confederate Ordnance Bureau

Supervised production of weapons and ammunition for the Confederate Army

General Josiah Gorgas was one of the Confederacy's most valuable officers during the American Civil War. Born in the North, he sided with the South at the war's outset. For the next four years, he supervised the Southern effort to provide its soldiers with the weapons and ammunition that they needed in the conflict. He faced many obstacles during this period, from shortages of raw materials to the huge Union naval blockade of Confederate ports. Despite these difficulties, however, Gorgas did a remarkable job of producing and delivering weaponry to rebel (Confederate) troops during the Civil War. In numerous cases, rebel armies continued to receive needed rifles and ammunition long after their supplies of food and other materials had evaporated.

Born and raised in the North

Josiah Gorgas was born on July 1, 1818, in Pennsylvania. His parents, Joseph and Sophia Atkinson Gorgas, sometimes struggled to provide for their family on his earnings as a clock maker, mechanic, and innkeeper. They often moved from

"Gorgas proved to be a genius at organization and improvisation. He almost literally turned plowshares into swords."
Historian James M. McPherson

Josiah Gorgas. *(Courtesy of the Library of Congress.)*

151

town to town in an effort to improve their economic situation. These relocations made it difficult for young Josiah to make friends, and he later described his childhood as a lonely one.

At age seventeen, Gorgas left his parents' home and joined an older sister in Lyons, New York. He took a job as an apprentice at a local printing shop and quickly gained a reputation as a hard-working young man. Gorgas also became acquainted with a U.S. congressman named Graham Chapin (1799–1843) around this time. Impressed with Gorgas's intelligence and ambition, Chapin helped the young Pennsylvanian to gain admittance into the U.S. Military Academy at West Point in New York.

When Gorgas entered West Point in 1837, he did not have big dreams of building a military career for himself. He just wanted to gain a good education so that he could be successful in engineering or a related field. Motivated by his strong desire to avoid the economic problems that had dogged his father, Gorgas studied hard and became known as one of the most industrious and disciplined cadets (students in a military academy) in his class. In 1841, he graduated sixth in his class of fifty-two students.

Career advancement and disappointment

After leaving West Point, Gorgas entered the U.S. Army's Ordnance Corps (ordnance is another term for weaponry). The Ordnance Corps was responsible for designing, acquiring, maintaining, and distributing weapons and ammunition to the military. Since Gorgas was knowledgeable about rifle design, gunpowder manufacturing, and other aspects of ordnance, he thought that he would receive promotions fairly quickly. As time passed, however, he became impatient with the progress of his career. In 1845, he even sent a letter to Secretary of State James Buchanan (1791–1868) in which he demanded a promotion. Gorgas's letter angered his superiors and nearly resulted in his dismissal from the service.

In 1846, Gorgas received orders to report to Mexico, where American and Mexican forces were engaged in the Mexican War (1846–48). This conflict was a struggle for ownership of vast expanses of land in the West. It ended in 1848, when the stronger American army forced the Mexican government to give up two-fifths of its total territory—including California and New Mexico—in return for $15 million.

When Gorgas first reached Mexico, he tackled his duties with energy in hopes that his performance would help him gain the promotions that he wanted. Soon after his arrival, however, he became involved in quarrels with other officers. His reputation as a troublemaker continued to grow, and as a result he did not receive any promotions while in Mexico.

After the war ended, Gorgas was stationed in Virginia, where he became acquainted with a wealthy munitions (weapons and ammunition) factory owner named Joseph Anderson (1813–1892). He also continued to study ordnance. As the years passed, he established a reputation as an expert on ammunition, artillery, and firearms while stationed at outposts around the South. Nonetheless, Gorgas continued to express dissatisfaction with the progress of his military career.

In the mid-1850s, Gorgas married Amelia Gayle. She was the daughter of a former Alabama governor named John Gayle, who had become a wealthy plantation owner. Impressed with John Gayle's operation and mindful of his wife's love for her home state of Alabama, Gorgas began to view himself as a Southerner.

Joins the Ordnance Board

In 1858, Gorgas was appointed to help build military facilities in Charleston Harbor. Two years later, Secretary of War John B. Floyd (1806–1863) assigned Gorgas to serve on the prestigious Ordnance Board—a committee charged with monitoring the quality and quantity of the army's rifles, cannons, and other weaponry—as a favor for his longtime friend, John Gayle. Gorgas and his wife promptly relocated to Washington, D.C., where the offices of the Ordnance Board were located.

Gorgas may have received his position on the Ordnance Board because of his father-in-law's influence, but he quickly showed that he was a good selection. Using his expertise in the field of ordnance, he became a leading reviewer of Federal military inventories and a recognized authority on weapons and ammunition. In the spring of 1861, however, the onset of the American Civil War abruptly ended Gorgas's involvement on the Board.

The Civil War came about because of bitter divisions between America's Northern and Southern regions. The main issue dividing the two regions was slavery. Many Northerners believed that slavery was wrong. They wanted to outlaw it throughout America, or at least prevent it from spreading beyond the Southern states where it was already allowed. But slavery played an important role in the South's economy and culture, and white Southerners felt threatened by Northern efforts to contain slavery. They believed that each state should decide for itself whether to allow the practice. In early 1861, relations between the two sections had deteriorated to the point that America's Southern states announced their decision to secede from (leave) the United States and form a country that allowed slavery, called the Confederate States of America. The North responded by declaring its intention to keep the Union together by force if necessary. As both regions began forming armies for the coming war, thousands of soldiers had to decide whether to fight on the side of the Union or the Confederacy.

Chief of ordnance for the Confederacy

Influenced by his wife's Southern background and his own affection for Southern culture, Gorgas resigned from the Federal Army in March 1861 in order to join the Confederate Army. Once he arrived in the South, rebel leaders immediately made use of his knowledge of weaponry. They promoted him to major and made him the army's chief of ordnance. This meant that Gorgas was in charge of acquiring, storing, and distributing all the rifles, artillery, and ammunition that the Confederate Army would need during the war.

As Gorgas investigated the South's existing ordnance supplies during the spring of 1861, he quickly realized that the job of supplying weapons and bullets to Confederate soldiers was going to be extremely difficult. After all, most of America's ordnance-making factories were located in the North. In addition, most existing supplies of weapons could not be used, either because they lay deep in Northern territo-

Stacks of ammunition at Fort Sumter. Josiah Gorgas was in charge of supplying Confederate soldiers with the weapons and ammunition they needed for the war. *(Courtesy of the Library of Congress.)*

ry or because they had been confiscated (seized) by Confederate state governments that refused to share them. Finally, he knew that he had only a limited amount of money that he could spend on arms and ammunition. But rather than despair about the obstacles that he faced, Gorgas used his experience and energy to address each problem.

By the fall of 1861, when he was promoted to lieutenant general, Gorgas had taken several steps to ensure that the Confederate Army would have all the arms and ammunition that it needed. For example, he purchased large amounts of ordnance from foreign nations before the Union Navy could complete its blockade of the Southern coastline. He also began the process of converting mills and factories to the production of gunpowder, rifles, and other weaponry. Finally, Gorgas persuaded the Confederate Congress to provide greater financial and legislative assistance to his arms-building efforts. "When Josiah Gorgas accepted appointment as chief of ordnance in April 1861 he faced an apparently . . .

hopeless task," wrote James M. McPherson in *Battle Cry of Freedom*. "But Gorgas proved to be a genius at organization and improvisation [coming up with new ways of doing things]. He almost literally turned plowshares into swords."

As the war progressed, Confederate armies suffered from shortages of blankets, food, and other provisions (supplies) with increasing frequency. But the Confederate Ordnance Bureau maintained regular shipments of arms and ammunition to rebel armies across the South, thanks to the tireless efforts of Gorgas and trusted lieutenants like George W. Rains. Gorgas used all sorts of schemes to meet the military's ammunition and weaponry needs. For example, he launched an extensive blockade-running operation that provided the Confederate Army with nearly two-thirds of its small arms (blockade runners were small ships that evaded the Union naval blockade of Confederate harbors in order to bring needed supplies to the South). He also expanded production of gunpowder, rifle barrels, and other weaponry by using private homes as small factories. When the South began to experience shortages of raw materials used in the production of ordnance, Gorgas even became an expert at finding substitute materials that could be used.

By 1864, however, shortages of manpower and raw materials were affecting the Ordnance Bureau's abilities to produce and distribute arms and ammunition. Gorgas worked hard to meet the rebel army's needs, but shortages of labor and materials became even worse as Union forces captured large areas of Confederate territory. By the time the Civil War ended in the spring of 1865, Gorgas had sacrificed his health and much of his fortune in his doomed efforts to meet the Confederate Army's ordnance needs.

Postwar career as teacher

After the war, Gorgas struggled as a businessman for several years. In 1869, he abandoned his hopes of regaining the money that he had lost in the last years of the war. Instead, he accepted a teaching position at the University of the South in Sewanee, Tennessee. In 1872, he was named vice-chancellor of the college, but he also continued to work as an instructor. Poor health forced him to resign from the school in 1878. Later that same year, however, friends arranged to have Gorgas named president of the University of Alabama.

Gorgas appreciated the gesture and expressed hope that he might eventually be able to fulfill his presidential responsibilities. His health continued to decline, however, and in 1879, the presidency was given to someone else. Gorgas was appointed university librarian, but his poor health forced his wife to take care of many of his duties. Gorgas died four years later, on May 18, 1883.

Where to Learn More

Goff, Richard D. *Confederate Supply.* Durham, NC: Duke University Press, 1969.

The Gorgas House. [Online] http://www.ua.edu/gorgasmain.html (accessed on October 10, 1999).

Vandiver, Frank E. *Ploughshares into Swords: Josiah Gorgas and Confederate Ordnance.* Austin: University of Texas Press, 1952. Reprint, College Station: Texas A & M University Press, 1994.

Wakelyn, Jon L. "Josiah Gorgas" in *Leaders of the American Civil War.* Edited by Jon L. Wakelyn and Charles F. Ritter. Westwood, CT: Greenwood Press, 1998.

Wiggins, Sarah Woolfolk, ed. *The Journals of Josiah Gorgas, 1857–1878.* Tuscaloosa: University of Alabama Press, 1995.

Ulysses S. Grant

Born April 27, 1822
Point Pleasant, Ohio
Died July 23, 1885
Mount McGregor, New York

Union general who captured Vicksburg and defeated Lee's Army of Northern Virginia, ending the Civil War

Eighteenth president of the United States

Ulysses S. Grant was one of the greatest—and most un-likely—military commanders in American history. Prior to the Civil War, he struggled to provide for his family, first as a soldier and then as a businessman. But when the war began, he quickly showed that he was one of the North's top military leaders. During the first two years of the conflict, his victories at Fort Donelson, Vicksburg, and Chattanooga helped the Union seize control of the Confederacy's western states.

Grant then moved to the war's eastern theater (a large geographic area in which military operations take place), where he was given command of all the Union armies. Beginning in the spring of 1864, he brought the full power of the Union forces against the South. Grant's merciless use of sustained pressure against the weary armies and citizens of the Confederacy eventually forced the South to surrender in 1865. Four years later, Grant became president of the United States. But the North's greatest military hero never really learned how to be a good political leader, and his two terms in the White House were marked by scandal.

"I have but one sentiment now. We have a government and laws and a flag and they must be sustained. There are but two parties now: traitors and patriots."

Ulysses S. Grant. *(Courtesy of Colonial Press.)*

159

Humble beginnings

Ulysses S. Grant was born on April 27, 1822, in Point Pleasant, Ohio. His parents were Hannah Simpson Grant and Jesse Root Grant, who supported his family as a tanner (a converter of animal hides into leather) and farmer. Named Hiram Ulysses by his parents, Grant was a quiet and sensitive child. As a youngster he labored in his father's tannery for a time, but he disliked the tedious work of tanning hides and his father's constant criticism. He later received permission to work on the family's small farm, where he developed a deep love for horses.

When Grant was seventeen, his father pushed him to apply for admittance into the U.S. Military Academy at West Point, America's leading military academy. Grant dutifully took the school's entrance exam and was surprised when he learned that he had passed. He entered the academy a few months later, only to discover that the school had erroneously listed his name as Ulysses Simpson Grant rather than Hiram Ulysses Grant. He tried to have his name corrected, but when his initial efforts failed, he simply accepted his new name and used it for the rest of his life.

Early life in the military

Grant's years at West Point passed quietly. Nicknamed "Sam" by his friends, Grant posted grades that were acceptable but unremarkable. In fact, the only subjects for which he showed any enthusiasm at all were watercolor painting and horsemanship. "A military life held no charms for me," he later admitted. Despite his lack of enthusiasm for the military, Grant became a soldier after graduating from West Point in 1843. He requested assignment to a federal cavalry unit so that he could work with horses, but was instead placed in the infantry.

Grant's first exposure to war came in 1846, when the United States and neighboring Mexico went to war. The Mexican War (1846–48) came about when the United States became interested in acquiring significant sections of Mexican territory in order to expand its own land holdings. In 1845, America annexed (added) Texas to the Union and tried to buy California and New Mexico from Mexico. But Mexico regarded Texas as part of its own territory, and it refused to give up California and New Mexico. America's determination to take possession of these lands did not diminish, however, and the two countries ended up going to war over the territories.

Grant worked as a regimental quartermaster (a military officer responsible for providing food, clothing, ammunition, and other equipment to troops) during the war, serving under both General Zachary Taylor (1784–1850) and General **Winfield Scott** (1786–1866; see entry). As the war unfolded, Grant became an admirer of the decisive military style favored by these two military leaders. In fact, their example has often been credited as an influence in Grant's own generalship during the Civil War.

But while Grant learned some valuable lessons about leading men into combat during the Mexican War, he regarded the war itself as a "wicked" one. Grant took part in the war because "I considered my supreme duty was to my flag." But he and many others believed that America had basically picked a fight with Mexico so that when Mexico struck back against its bullying behavior, the United States could go to war and take the land that it wanted without feeling guilty about it.

This conflict ended in 1848, when American military victories forced Mexico to cede (give up its claims on) Texas, California, New Mexico, and other lands in the West in exchange for $15 million. Everyone knew that the land was worth far more than $15 million, but the Mexican government had no choice but to accept the deal. Years later, Grant called the Mexican War "one of the most unjust ever waged by a stronger against a weaker nation."

A long period of struggle

In 1848, Grant married Julia Dent, the daughter of a slave-owning Missouri planter. They started a family, and eventually had three sons and a daughter. But military assignments along the Pacific coast placed Grant far away from his wife and children for long periods of time, and he proved unable to raise enough funds so that his family could join him. In the summer of 1854, Grant—a captain at the time—abruptly resigned from the army under somewhat mysterious circumstances. Many historians believe that he left the military because of charges of alcoholism, but unhappiness over his long separation from his family might have been a factor, too.

After returning to civilian life in the eastern United States, Grant worked hard to provide for his family. But every career and business scheme that he attempted failed, from bill collecting to real estate. One Christmas, he sold his watch so that he would have a little money to buy presents for his wife and children. As one business venture after another failed, Grant was finally forced to accept a clerk position at an Illinois tannery owned by his father in order to feed his family.

The Civil War begins

Grant left his father's tannery in the spring of 1861, when the American Civil War began. The Civil War came about because of long-standing and bitter disagreements between America's Northern and Southern states over several issues. One of these issues was slavery. Many Northerners believed that slavery was wrong and wanted to abolish (completely do away with) it. But the economy of the South had been built on slavery, and Southerners resented Northern efforts to halt or contain the practice.

The two regions also disagreed about the appropriate balance between state and federal authority. The Northern states favored a strong central government and argued that the Union—the entire country—was more important than any individual state. Southern states, though, supported the concept of states' rights, which held that people in each state could make their own decisions about slavery and other issues. America's westward expansion during this time made these disputes even worse, since both sides wanted to spread their way of life—and their political ideas—into the new territories and states.

By early 1861, hostilities between the two regions had become so strong that several Southern states voted to secede from (leave) the United States and form a new country that allowed slavery, called the Confederate States of America (eleven Southern states eventually seceded).The U.S. government declared that the formation of the Confederacy was treasonous (an illegal betrayal of the country) and warned that it was willing to use force to make the Southern states return to the Union. But the South refused to back down, and in the spring of 1861, the two sides finally went to war.

Return to military service

The Civil War gave Grant a second opportunity to prove himself in the Federal army. But although his choice to rejoin the army was based partly on his desire to revive his military career, he also had a genuine desire to see the Confederacy destroyed and the Union restored. "I have but one sentiment now," Grant stated at the beginning of the war. "We have a government and laws and a flag and they must be sustained. There are but two parties now: traitors and patriots."

When the war started, Union military leaders gave Grant command of a group of Illinois volunteers because of his previous military experience. Promoted to brigadier general, he spent most of 1861 in Kentucky and Missouri. Grant's troops got into a couple minor scrapes during this time. The biggest of these minor battles was a clash at Belmont, Missouri, that ended without a clear winner.

In the spring of 1862, Grant posted his first major triumph of the war when his small army captured a Confederate garrison (military post) of fifteen thousand men at Fort Donelson, Tennessee. This victory came at a time when many other Union generals were suffering terrible defeats, so Northerners naturally embraced Grant as a hero. Their opinion of Grant surged even higher when they heard that he had responded to Confederate requests to negotiate terms of surrender by saying, "The only terms I can offer are immediate and unconditional surrender." Grant's uncompromising stand greatly appealed to Northerners, who started saying that his initials, U.S., stood for "Unconditional Surrender."

The Battle of Shiloh

After his performance at Fort Donelson, Grant was given more important responsibilities. In March 1862, he was ordered to take forty-five thousand troops and track down a Confederate army commanded by General Albert S. Johnston (1803–1862). Grant pursued Johnston all the way to the northern Mississippi town of Corinth, where Johnston received reinforcements that increased the size of his army to about forty-four thousand troops. Grant, meanwhile, stopped his advance outside of Corinth, near a small country church called Shiloh. He set up camp and waited for reinforcements of his own to arrive.

As Grant waited for his reinforcements, however, he established only basic defenses around the camp because he figured that Johnston's exhausted army would not dare to attack him. On April 6, though, Johnston launched a deadly surprise attack on the Union camp just as Grant's soldiers were waking up for breakfast. The Confederate offensive smashed the unprepared Federal troops, and for a time it appeared that the Union Army would be forced to call a full retreat. But Grant furiously rallied his men, and the troops held their ground until nightfall, when he finally received his reinforcements.

Armed with these new troops, Grant ordered a full-scale Union attack the following morning. All day long, Grant delivered terrible punishment to the outnumbered rebel army. The Confederate troops finally had to retreat back to Corinth in order to avoid total defeat. Grant did not give chase, though, because he knew that his own army was exhausted.

The Battle of Shiloh shocked people all across the country because it produced casualty figures that were far higher than had been seen before. When people in the North and South heard that more than twenty-three thousand Union and Confederate soldiers were classified as killed, wounded, or missing at Shiloh, they realized that they had been fooling themselves with their dreams of easy and bloodless victory.

Grant captures Vicksburg

Grant's next major mission took him to Vicksburg, Mississippi, a heavily fortified city located high atop bluffs along the Mississippi River's eastern shoreline. Vicksburg was the last major Confederate stronghold along the Mississippi.

Grant knew that if he could capture the city, Northern control of the river would be complete. The eastern Confederate states would have no way of getting grain, cattle, and other desperately needed supplies from Confederate lands west of the river like Texas, Arkansas, and western Louisiana.

At first, Vicksburg's rebel defenders pushed back every one of Grant's offensives. But in April 1863, the Union general launched a daring and brilliant plan to capture the stronghold. He marched his troops southward down the western banks of the Mississippi, then ferried his army across the river on boats that had earlier dashed past Vicksburg's mighty cannons under cover of darkness.

Grant's strategy worked flawlessly. By the end of April, he had successfully transported his army across the river to the eastern shoreline. Grant's army was now on the same side of the river as Vicksburg itself. Over the next few weeks, he steadily advanced on Vicksburg, destroying rebel supplies and small Confederate armies with ease. By mid-May, Grant had captured the town of Jackson, chased off the main Southern army in the region, and completely encircled Vicksburg.

Shortly after surrounding Vicksburg, Grant tried to take the city by force. When these attempts failed, however, he settled in for a long siege of the city. By stopping all shipments of food and supplies into Vicksburg, Grant planned to starve the city into surrendering. Once again, Grant's strategy worked. On July 4, the Confederate garrison surrendered the city to Grant, and Union troops moved in. A few days later, Grant took control of Port Hudson, Louisiana, a smaller rebel outpost on the Mississippi. Thanks to Grant's brilliant campaign, the entire Mississippi River Valley now belonged to the North.

Victories in the West

By the fall of 1863, Grant's successes and tough style had made him a favorite of President **Abraham Lincoln** (1809–1865; see entry). Writing in *Reflections on the Civil War*, historian Bruce Catton noted that Lincoln viewed Grant as "a man who was completely reliable, who got the job done, who could be trusted, and who always seemed to come out on top." In mid-October 1863, Lincoln's confidence in Grant led him to give the general command over the newly created Division of the Mississippi, which included all Union forces operating between the Mississippi River and the Appalachian Mountains.

Grant immediately proved that the president's confidence in him was well placed. At the time of his promotion, the Union-held cities of Chattanooga and Knoxville were both under siege from Confederate armies. But by the end of the year, Grant had lifted the siege on both cities and forced the Confederate military out of Tennessee.

Lincoln picks a new general

In March 1864, Grant was ordered to Washington to take command of the entire Union Army. Promoted to the rank of lieutenant general—a position last held by George Washington—Grant was given complete freedom to use the military as he saw fit. "After years of searching, Lincoln had found what he wanted," wrote Catton. "A completely reliable General to whom he could turn over the entire conduct of the military part of the war, without needing to look over the General's shoulder, be told what he was doing, and help him plan strategy. Lincoln called Grant in, gave him a free hand, and undertook to support him as vigorously as he could."

Grant immediately made plans to launch a coordinated offensive (attack) against Confederate military targets using the full might of the Union Army. He gave General **William T. Sherman** (1820–1891; see entry) command of the armies in the West and ordered him to march into the South and destroy the main Confederate army there. Meanwhile, Grant took control of the Army of the Potomac—the Union's primary army in the East—and marched southward in search of **Robert E. Lee** (1807–1870; see entry) and the Confederate Army of Northern Virginia.

Grant and Lee

As Grant moved his army into Virginia, he clashed repeatedly with Lee's army. The first of these battles took place in early May 1864 in a region of dense, tangled woods known as the Wilderness. In two horribly bloody days of fighting, Grant lost approximately seventeen thousand men. But unlike earlier Union generals who had always retreated when challenged by Lee, Grant expressed grim determination to continue his campaign. "I'm heartily sick and tired of hearing what Lee is going to do," he snapped at one of his worried officers during the Wilderness battle. "Go back to your command and think about what we're going to do to Lee instead of worrying about what he's going to do to us."

Instead of returning to Washington, Grant pushed deeper into Virginia. Again and again, he tried to maneuver his army around the right flank of Lee's army in order to destroy it and then move on the Confederate capital of Richmond. Grant knew that if he could break Lee's army and capture Richmond, the South would have to give up. But Lee anticipated Grant's strategy and successfully fended off every Union attack. The struggle continued for six long weeks, as the two weary armies met in bloody combat at Spotsylvania, Cold Harbor, and countless other places in the Virginia countryside.

Confederate general Robert E. Lee. *(Painting by John Adams Elder. Courtesy of the Library of Congress.)*

By mid-June, Grant had pushed Lee's army back to Petersburg, where the Confederate general erected a final defensive position to keep the Union forces out of nearby Richmond. By this time Grant's army had lost fifty thousand men, an average of about two thousand casualties a day. These high casualty numbers shocked Union communities, and some Northern critics charged that Grant was a poor general who did not value human life. "Grant is a butcher and not fit to be at the head of an army," First Lady **Mary Todd Lincoln** (1818–1882; see entry) declared at one point. President Lincoln remained loyal to his general, though. He recognized that Grant's campaign had immobilized (brought to a halt) Lee's forces and put the Army of Northern Virginia into a situation where it would have to try and outlast a Union force that was far larger and better supplied.

Grant laid siege to Petersburg for ten long months. During this time, Lee stood by helplessly as other Union armies further west posted a string of major victories. By the spring of 1865, Lee's army remained bottled up in Petersburg and Richmond. Outside of Virginia, meanwhile, Union armies led by Sherman and others had torn the Confederacy apart.

In April, Lee decided to abandon Petersburg. Leaving Petersburg and Richmond to Grant's army, the Confederate general fled south with the hungry and battered remnants of his army in a desperate bid to gain supplies and continue the fight. But Grant chased Lee down. On April 9, 1865, the Civil War came to an end when Lee surrendered at Appomattox, Virginia.

Grant's White House years

The Union's dramatic victory made Grant one of the great heroes of the North. After the war, he joined the Republican political party. In 1868, he was elected president of the United States, defeating Democratic nominee Horatio Seymour (1810–1886) by a slim margin. In 1872, he easily defeated **Horace Greeley** (1811–1872; see entry). Grant entered the White House hoping to help America heal the many deep wounds left by the Civil War. But he struggled with his presidential duties, and his administration became known for scandal and mismanagement of the national economy. "The qualities that served U.S. Grant so well in war—resolution, independence, aversion to [dislike of] politics—deserted him in peacetime," commented Geoffrey C. Ward in *The Civil War*. "He entered the White House pledged to peace, honesty, and civil rights [for blacks]. But corruption tainted [damaged] his two terms—though it did not touch him personally—and the North was already weary of worrying about the status of southern blacks."

Financial troubles return

In 1877, Grant left the White House and became involved in a variety of business ventures. In 1880, he invested heavily in a Wall Street brokerage firm, only to see the company crumble a few years later when another partner stole millions of dollars. The collapse of the brokerage firm nearly bankrupted Grant, who also found out around this time that he was suffering from inoperable cancer of the throat.

In 1885, Grant moved to a cottage in the Adirondack Mountains and began writing his memoirs. He hoped that sales of the book would provide his family with financial security after his death. All summer long, he worked on his memoirs on the front porch of the cottage. After awhile, his throat cancer made it impossible for him to eat or speak, but he remained determined to complete the book. He finished his manuscript on July 16 and died one week later.

Grant's memoirs were published later that year by famed American novelist Mark Twain (1835–1910). Grant's work, which was published in two volumes, proved enormously popular with American book buyers, and his family quickly regained its financial security. Today, Grant's memoirs continue to be regarded as one of the most thoughtful and interesting works ever written about the Civil War era.

Where to Learn More

Archer, Jules. *A House Divided: The Lives of Ulysses S. Grant and Robert E. Lee.* New York: Scholastic, 1995.

Catton, Bruce. *Grant Moves South.* Boston: Little, Brown, 1960.

Catton, Bruce. *Grant Takes Command.* Boston: Little, Brown, 1969.

Grant Cottage. [Online] http://saints.css.edu/mkelsey/cottage.html (accessed on October 10, 1999).

Grant, Ulysses S. *Personal Memoirs of U.S. Grant.* 2 vols. New York: C. L. Webster, 1885. Reprint, New York: Modern Library, 1999.

Kent, Zachary. *Ulysses S. Grant: Eighteenth President of the United States.* Chicago: Children's Press, 1989.

Marrin, Albert. *Unconditional Surrender: U. S. Grant and the Civil War.* New York: Atheneum, 1994.

McFeely, William S. *Grant: A Biography.* New York: Norton, 1981. Newtown, CT: American Political Biography Press, 1996.

National Park Service. *General Grant National Memorial.* [Online] http://www.nps.gov/gegr.index.htm (accessed on October 10, 1999).

National Park Service. *Ulysses S. Grant National Historic Site.* [Online] http://www.nps.gov/ulsg (accessed on October 10, 1999).

O'Brien, Steven. *Ulysses S. Grant.* New York: Chelsea House, 1991.

Rickarby, Laura N. *Ulysses S. Grant and the Strategy of Victory.* Englewood Cliffs, NJ: Silver Burdett Press, 1991.

Simpson, Brooks D. *Let Us Have Peace: Ulysses S. Grant and the Politics of War and Reconstruction, 1861–1868.* Chapel Hill: University of North Carolina Press, 1991.

Ulysses Grant Home Page: Civil War General and President. [Online] http://www.mscomm.com/~ulysses/ (accessed on October 10, 1999).

Ulysses S. Grant Association. [Online] http://www.lib.siu.edu/projects/us-grant/ (accessed on October 10, 1999).

Ulysses S. Grant Network. [Online] http://saints.css.edu/mkelsey/gppg.html (accessed on October 10, 1999).

Horace Greeley

Born February 3, 1811
Amherst, New Hampshire
Died November 29, 1872
New York City, New York

Newspaper publisher and abolitionist

H orace Greeley was America's leading journalist of the Civil War era. He was the founder and editor of the *New York Tribune,* America's most popular newspaper of the mid-nineteenth century. Using his newspaper editorials as a tool to comment on American society and politics, Greeley became known as a crusader for a wide range of social causes, including women's rights and land reform. He became most famous, however, for his fierce opposition to slavery and his strong support of the Union war effort.

Independent at an early age

Horace Greeley was born on February 3, 1811, to a poor farming family in Amherst, New Hampshire. His father, Zaccheus Greeley, uprooted his family on numerous occasions in failed efforts to establish a successful farm. This unsettled existence made it difficult for young Horace to obtain a good education. Nonetheless, he showed considerable abilities as a speller and reader. One classmate even stated that Greeley's spelling skills were known "for miles around." As

"With its brilliant staff, exciting editorials, broad coverage of international and national events, [Greeley's] *Tribune* set a new standard for American journalism."

Author Lewis Leary

Horace Greeley. *(Courtesy of the Library of Congress.)*

Greeley entered his teen years, he began to think of ways in which he might use his spelling and reading talents to escape the family farm.

At age fourteen, Greeley left his parents' home to accept a position as a printer's apprentice in Vermont. This apprenticeship (agreement to work for another person in exchange for instruction in a trade) enabled him to learn a great deal about printing and newspaper production. In 1831, he left Vermont and traveled to New York City in hopes of securing a job with one of the city's many newspapers.

Greeley spent the next three years working for a number of New York newspapers, including the *Morning Post* and the *Spirit of the Times.* These jobs enabled him to continue to develop his knowledge of the newspaper business. As the months passed by, he began to dream of operating his own newspaper. He also started a family around this time. In 1836, he married Mary Cheney. The couple eventually had seven children, but only two survived to adulthood.

Launches the *New York Tribune*

From 1834 to 1840, Greeley served as editor and co-owner of several New York publications. These periodicals, which were devoted to literature and politics, increased Greeley's reputation among the city's publishers and politicians. But he did not become famous until 1841, when he launched the *New York Tribune.*

Guided by Greeley's steady hand, the *Tribune* quickly became one of America's largest and most respected newspapers. "With its brilliant staff, exciting editorials, broad coverage of international and national events, the *Tribune* set a new standard for American journalism," wrote Lewis Leary in *Horace Greeley.*

Greeley's newspaper increased in popularity throughout the 1840s and early 1850s. As the audience for Greeley's wide-ranging newspaper editorials grew, he became powerfully influential in shaping public opinion in the Northern states. "Greeley's positions in his editorials represented some of the most important trends of public, social, and political commentary of the day," wrote Leary. For example, he became a leading advocate of women's rights and a strong defender of temperance, a movement that called for people to quit drinking alcohol. He also emerged as a leading critic of American laws and land distribution that favored rich people over farmers and laborers. As Greeley wrote in 1851, "if democracy be what we believe, it must have a wider and more perfect application [usage]. It must create a new social as well as a new political system. It must reform the relations of labor, of property and of social life, nor stop till all servitude [slavery], all castes [social classes], all inequality of privilege have disappeared to give place to . . . liberty, justice and fraternal [brotherly] cooperative relations."

By the 1850s, Greeley was known across the country for his support of policies that he thought might eliminate poverty and improve opportunities for poor and uneducated people. This concern for the poor led Greeley to become a leading champion of settlement of western territories, even though he thought that much of that land had been unfairly snatched from Mexico during the Mexican War (1846–48). He proclaimed that "I believe in migration—believe that there are thousands in the Eastern and Middle Western states who would improve their circumstances and prospects by migrating to the cheaper lands and broader opportunities of the West and South." In fact, Greeley popularized the slogan "Go West, young man," a famous expression associated with the settlement of the West.

Calls for end to slavery

Greeley's strong interest in eliminating poverty in America was a major factor in his antislavery stands of the 1850s. Slavery had been a part of America since the 1600s, when white people first captured African blacks and brought them to North America. The basic belief behind slavery was that black people were inferior to whites. Under slavery, white slaveholders treated black people as property, forced them to perform hard labor, and controlled every aspect of their lives. States in the Northern section of the United States began outlawing slavery in the late 1700s. But slavery continued to exist in the Southern half of the country, where it became an important part of the region's economy and culture.

Greeley hated the conditions in which many slaves were forced to live, and argued that the continued existence of slavery contradicted the nation's ideals of freedom and liberty. Many of his criticisms were directed at white people of the American South, who continued to defend slavery. But Greeley also criticized Northerners for their racist treatment of free black men and women.

By the mid-1850s, Greeley had become one of the country's most visible abolitionists (people who worked to end slavery in America). In 1854, he helped establish the antislavery Republican Party, and he repeatedly spoke out against Southern efforts to expand the rights of slaveowners and the territories in which slavery would be permitted. "This is not an age of the world in which new domain [territories] can be opened to slavedrivers without an instinctive shudder convulsing the frame of Humanity," he wrote. By 1856, Greeley's editorials against slavery had grown so strong that proslavery Arkansas congressmen Albert Rust (1818?–1870) physically attacked him on the streets of Washington, D.C. Greeley quickly recovered from the assault, however, and resumed his abolitionist activities.

Greeley and the Civil War

By the late 1850s, most Northerners had become convinced that slavery was wrong. They wanted the federal government to take steps to outlaw slavery or at least keep it from spreading beyond the Southern states where it was already allowed. But the Southern economy had become so dependent on slavery that white Southerners worried that their way of life would collapse if slavery was abolished (completely done away with). Arguing that each state should decide for itself whether to allow the practice, Southerners refused to go along with attempts to limit or end slavery. By 1861, Southern dissatisfaction with the North had become so great that several states decided to secede from (leave) the Union and form a country that accepted slavery, called the Confederate States of America. The Northern states, however, were unwilling to see the United States split in two. They vowed to force the South back into the Union.

As America's Northern and Southern sections prepared to go to war to settle their differences, Greeley initially counseled the federal government to let the secessionist states leave in peace. Doubtful about the ability of President **Abraham Lincoln** (1809–1865; see entry) to guide the nation, Greeley desperately wanted to avoid a bloody war. He also argued that the departure of the Confederate states would finally eliminate slavery from the United States.

After the war erupted in April, however, Greeley became a key supporter of the Northern war effort. He knew that if the Union forces could stomp out the Confederate rebellion, the federal government would be able to institute laws ending slavery across all of North America. With this in mind, Greeley churned out a series of editorials urging Northerners to rally behind the Union flag.

Greeley's "Prayer of Twenty Millions"

Lincoln recognized that Greeley's views helped increase Northern support for the war, especially during the first two years of the conflict. Nonetheless, Greeley's editorials in the *Tribune* sometimes angered the president. The publisher sometimes criticized Lincoln for his military leadership, and he repeatedly called on Lincoln to free all blacks who were enslaved in the Southern states. Lincoln, though, worried that such a declaration would erode support for the war among Northerners, whose main concern was restoring the Union.

On August 19, 1862, Greeley issued his most famous demand for immediate emancipation (freeing) of slaves. Claiming that he spoke for twenty million disappointed Northerners, the abolitionist published an open letter to Lincoln in which he harshly criticized the president's "timid" policies toward slavery and the South. Lincoln responded three days later with his own note. "My paramount [most important] object is to save the Union and not either to save or destroy slavery," Lincoln stated.

Lincoln's response to Greeley seemed to indicate that he had no intention of tackling the slavery issue any time soon. In reality, though, the president's views on the

Greeley's War of Words with President Lincoln

In August 1862, Horace Greeley and President Abraham Lincoln exchanged strongly worded letters concerning the continued existence of slavery in the Confederacy. Greeley wanted Lincoln to officially outlaw slavery in the South, even though the Federal government did not have any power to enforce such a law at the time. Lincoln, though, responded by saying that he would not take any action that might hurt his ability to eventually restore the divided Union.

Excerpt from Greeley's "Prayer of Twenty Millions":

To Abraham Lincoln, President of the United States:

Dear Sir: I do not intrude to tell you—for you must know already—that a great proportion of those who triumphed in your election, and of all who desire the unqualified suppression [complete crushing] of the rebellion now desolating [destroying] our country, are sorely disappointed and deeply pained by the policy you seem to be pursuing with regard to the slaves of rebels. . . .

We complain that you, Mr. President, elected as a Republican, knowing well what an abomination [great evil] Slavery is, and how emphatically [clearly]

it is the core and essence of this atrocious [terrible] rebellion, seem never to interfere with these atrocities, and never give a direction to your military subordinates, which does not appear to have been conceived in the interest of Slavery rather than of Freedom. . . .

On the face of this wide earth, Mr. President, there is not one disinterested [impartial], determined, intelligent champion of the Union cause who does not feel that all attempts to put down the rebellion and at the same time uphold its inciting cause [the issue that triggered it] are preposterous [absurd] and futile—that the rebellion, if crushed out to-morrow, would be renewed within a year if Slavery were left in full vigor. . . .

I close as I began with the statement that what an immense majority of the loyal millions of your countrymen require of you is a frank, declared, unqualified, ungrudging execution of the laws of the land, more especially of the Confiscation Act [an 1862 law that declared all property—including slaves—owned by rebels to be "contraband of war"; since slaves were considered property in the South, escaped slaves were allowed to remain in the North under this law]. . . . As one of the millions who would gladly have avoided the struggle at any sacrifice but that of principle and honor, but who now feel that the triumph of the Union is indis-

issue changed dramatically during 1862. By the time that Greeley delivered his August 19 letter, Lincoln had come to believe that Northern support for the war might actually increase if he called for an end to slavery. After all, most Northerners felt that slavery was an immoral practice. In addition, many Northerners believed that restoration of the

Abraham Lincoln. *(Courtesy of the Library of Congress.)*

pensable [absolutely necessary] not only to the existence of our country but to the well-being of mankind, I entreat [beg] you to render a hearty and unequivocal [clear] obedience to the law of the land.

Yours, Horace Greeley

Excerpt from President Lincoln's response:

The sooner the national authority can be restored, the nearer the Union will be the Union it was.

If there be those who would not save the Union unless they could at the same time save slavery, I do not agree with them.

If there be those who would not save the Union unless they could at the same time destroy slavery, I do not agree with them.

My paramount object [main goal] is to save the Union and not either to save or destroy slavery.

If I could save the Union without freeing any slave, I would do it—If I could save it by freeing all the slaves, I would do it—and if I could do it by freeing some and leaving others alone, I would also do that.

What I do about slavery and the colored race I do because I believe it helps to save this Union; and what I forbear [decide not to do], I forbear because I do not believe it would help to save the Union. . . .

. . . I have stated my purpose according to my views of official duty; and I intend no modification [change] of my oft-expressed personal wish that all men everywhere could be free.

Union would never be possible if slavery were allowed to continue. By the fall of 1862, Lincoln had decided that "slavery must die [so] that the nation might live!" On January 1, 1863, Lincoln issued his famous Emancipation Proclamation, which freed all slaves in the Confederate states. This announcement delighted Greeley, who immediately published an editorial praising both Lincoln and his Proclamation.

War weariness sets in

In the months immediately following Lincoln's Emancipation Proclamation, Greeley's support for the war effort remained strong. From the summer of 1863 to the summer of 1864, however, the publisher's feelings about the Civil War changed dramatically. Horrified at the steadily rising casualty lists, he became convinced that the conflict had disintegrated into a bloody stalemate (deadlock). By the summer of 1864, Greeley was imploring Lincoln to make peace with the South, even if it meant giving up Northern dreams of a restored Union. "Our bleeding, bankrupt, almost dying" country cannot withstand "new rivers of human blood," wrote Greeley.

Greeley's disillusionment with the war became so strong that he made a failed attempt to negotiate an end to the conflict with Confederate officials. He also considered joining other Republicans who wanted to replace Lincoln with someone else for the fall 1864 presidential elections. In the weeks leading up to the election, however, Union forces won a series of dramatic victories in the South. These triumphs enabled Lincoln to win reelection and signaled the impending collapse of the Confederacy.

Postwar activities

The period in American history immediately after the war, from 1865 to 1877, was known as Reconstruction. During this time the federal government supervised the rebuilding of the Southern states. Greeley became personally involved in this effort. He devoted his time and energy to building a brighter future for Southern whites and blacks alike. For example, he opposed some Northern leaders who wanted to further punish Confederate soldiers and political leaders for their wartime activities. He felt that white Southerners should instead be encouraged to put the war behind them and rebuild their lives peacefully. Greeley also urged whites across the nation to treat free blacks and former slaves with fairness. "The Blacks are a portion not merely of the Southern but of the American people," wrote Greeley. He added that the North must protect blacks "no matter what the cost." In accordance with these beliefs, he strongly supported amendments to the U.S. Constitution that made blacks American citizens (the Fourteenth Amendment, ratified, or officially approved, in 1868) and gave them the right to vote (the Fifteenth Amendment, ratified in 1870).

In 1872, Greeley ran for president as the nominee of both the Democratic Party and the Liberal Republicans, a group of Republicans that did not like the policies of Republican president **Ulysses S. Grant** (1822–1885; see entry). The presidential campaign became a nightmarish one for Greeley, however. Grant's allies ridiculed Greeley's frantic peacemaking efforts during the Civil War. They convinced many Americans that the publisher was too eccentric (odd or unconventional) to be president. To make this difficult time worse, Greeley's wife died less than a week before the election.

Grant easily defeated Greeley in the election, winning 56 percent of the popular vote. The crushing defeat, combined with his wife's death, plummeted Greeley into deep despair. Within a matter of weeks, his mental and physical health declined greatly. He died in New York City on November 29, 1872, less than a month after the election.

Where to Learn More

Cross, Coy F. *Go West Young Man!: Horace Greeley's Vision for America*. Albuquerque: University of New Mexico Press, 1995.

Hale, William Harlan. *Horace Greeley: Voice of the People*. New York: Harper, 1950.

Horace Greeley (1811–1872), Editor of the New York Tribune. [Online] http://www.honors.unr.edu/~fenimore/greeley.html (accessed on October 10, 1999).

Lunde, Erik S. *Horace Greeley*. Boston: Twayne, 1981.

Maihafer, Harry J. *The General and the Journalists: Ulysses S. Grant, Horace Greeley, and Charles Dana*. Washington, D.C.: Brasseys, 1998.

Van Deusen, Glyndon G. *Horace Greeley: Nineteenth-Century Crusader*. Philadelphia: University of Pennsylvania Press, 1953. Reprint, New York: Hill and Wang, 1964.

Rose O'Neal Greenhow

Born 1815 or 1817
Port Tobacco, Maryland
Died October 1, 1864
Wilmington, North Carolina

Washington socialite and Confederate spy

Provided information that allowed Confederate forces to win the First Battle of Bull Run

Rose O'Neal Greenhow was one of the most successful female Confederate spies of the Civil War. A prominent hostess in Washington society, she learned about Union military plans from her wide circle of important friends and passed that information along to Confederate leaders. In July 1861, she provided key information that helped Confederate forces win the First Battle of Bull Run in Virginia. "I employed every capacity with which God has endowed [provided] me," she once said, "and the result was far more successful than my hopes could have flattered me to expect."

Becomes a popular hostess in Washington social circles

Rose O'Neal Greenhow was born to a wealthy slaveholding family in southern Maryland in 1817. When she was a young girl, one of the family's slaves murdered her father. From that point on, Greenhow strongly opposed the movement to abolish (put an end to) slavery and grant equal rights to black Americans.

Spying "was far more successful than my hopes could have flattered me to expect."

Rose O'Neal Greenhow.
(Reproduced by permission of Duke University, Special Collections Library.)

As a young woman, Greenhow married a wealthy Southern gentleman and moved to Washington, D.C. She loved to entertain, so she and her husband threw frequent dinner parties. The guests at these social events often included members of the U.S. Congress and foreign diplomats. Over time, Greenhow developed a wide circle of friends that included many important political figures, such as former President James Buchanan (1791–1868). She remained a popular hostess even after her husband died in the mid-1800s.

Washington was the site of heated political debate during this time. The Northern and Southern regions of the country had been arguing about a number of issues, including slavery, for many years. By 1861, this ongoing dispute had convinced several Southern states to secede from (leave) the United States and attempt to form a new country that allowed slavery, called the Confederate States of America. Greenhow considered herself a Southerner and supported the Confederate states' decision to secede. But Northern political leaders were determined to keep the Southern states in the Union. Before long, the two sides went to war.

Leads a spy network

As the Civil War began, Greenhow made no secret of her pro-Southern feelings. One day, Captain Thomas Jordan approached her about serving as a spy for the Confederacy. Jordan was a member of the Union Army and the U.S. War Department, but he secretly recruited spies for the South. Greenhow agreed to act as a spy and also to serve as the center of a Confederate spy ring in Washington. Her spy network included other prominent Washington residents, clerks in several government departments, and a number of female couriers. Greenhow collected information about the Union's war plans from the network, as well as from her friends and admirers in Washington. She then passed the information along to Confederate leaders in Richmond, Virginia.

Helps Confederates win the First Battle of Bull Run

When the war began, people in both the North and the South were confident that it would end quickly in a victory for their side. Spurred by such confidence, Northerners pressured President **Abraham Lincoln** (1809–1865; see entry) to make an early offensive advance into Confederate territory. After consulting with his advisors, Lincoln decided to attack a large Confederate encampment at Manassas Junction, Virginia. Since this rebel stronghold was located about thirty miles from Washington, Union leaders viewed it as a threat to the Federal capital. It also blocked the path that Union troops would take to reach Richmond, the capital of the Confederacy.

On July 16, 1861, thirty-five thousand Union troops under General Irvin McDowell (1818–1885) marched out of Washington toward Manassas. They intended to fight twenty thousand Confederate troops camped on the banks of nearby Bull Run Creek, under the command of General **Pierre G. T. Beauregard** (1818–1893; see entry). In the meantime, fifteen thousand Union troops under General Robert Patterson traveled separately. They intended to meet eleven thousand Confederate troops camped at Harpers Ferry, Virginia, under the command of General **Joseph E. Johnston** (1807–1891; see entry). The idea was for Patterson to keep Johnston busy while McDowell pushed Beauregard out of Manassas.

Unfortunately for the Union, Greenhow obtained a copy of McDowell's orders. She told the Confederate leaders when the Union forces would leave Washington, how many troops would be involved, what route they would take toward Manassas, and what strategy they planned to use in the battle. The First Battle of Bull Run (also known as the First Battle of Manassas) began on July 21. Just as McDowell began to gain ground against Beauregard's outnumbered forces, thousands of Johnston's troops arrived to save the day. Johnston had fooled Patterson into thinking that his Confederate forces were preparing an offensive attack, then snuck his men away to help Beauregard.

The Union forces made a panicky retreat, joined by thousands of spectators who had come down from Washington to watch the battle. People in the North were shocked that the rebels (Confederates) had won the first major battle of the Civil War. But people in the South were thrilled. Confederate president **Jefferson Davis** (1808–1889; see entry) thanked Greenhow personally for her part in the victory. "But for you there would have been no Battle of Bull Run," he told her.

Rose O'Neal Greenhow sometimes involved her daughter when carrying out her spying operations.
(Reproduced by permission of Corbis Corporation.)

Keeps spying after her arrest

This early success encouraged Greenhow to become even bolder in her spying activities. Union authorities finally caught on and arrested her in August 1861. But they made the mistake of arresting her outside of her home, in front of witnesses. Greenhow managed to warn one of her agents of the danger by signaling with a handkerchief. Once the Union officials brought her inside, she faked an attack of heat stroke and was allowed to rest in her room alone. While the unsuspecting authorities waited for her to recover, she had enough time to destroy much of the evidence of her activities.

Union authorities placed Greenhow under house arrest, meaning that she became a prisoner in her own home. But she continued to send messages to Richmond. After awhile, Union detectives broke the code she used for her messages, so at least they knew what information she had leaked to the Confederates.

In January 1862, Greenhow was transferred to Old Capitol Prison in Washington, along with her daughter and her maid. During her five months there under tight security, she still managed to send messages South. Sometimes she involved her daughter in her schemes. The guards often brought the young girl rubber balls to play with. Greenhow would wrap a message around a rubber ball and toss it out the window at a certain time. A fellow Confederate spy would catch the ball and carry the information to Confederate officials.

Tries to gain support of France and England

Greenhow was finally released from prison in May 1862. Unable to keep her from spying, Union officials forced her to leave the North. She traveled to Richmond, where she was greeted warmly by Confederate leaders. In August 1863, President Jefferson Davis sent Greenhow to Europe. Her mission was to convince the leaders of England and France to support the Confederates in their fight for independence.

Greenhow proved to be just as popular in Europe as she had been in Washington. She published a book about her spy activities, *My Imprisonment and the First Year of Abolition Rule at Washington,* which became a bestseller. She was also entertained by royalty. Although she failed to convince European leaders to provide official support to the Confederacy, she did get some wealthy Europeans to donate money to the cause.

Dies for the Confederate cause

In the summer of 1864, Greenhow decided to return to the United States. She made the final leg of her journey aboard a Confederate ship called the *Condor.* On October 1, the ship ran aground in a raging storm just off the coast of Wilmington, North Carolina. Before long, a Union ship approached. Fearing that she would be arrested, Greenhow asked to be rowed ashore in a small boat. Unfortunately, the boat capsized in the waves. Although the other people on board were saved, Greenhow drowned. It turned out that she had sewn the gold she had received from European supporters into the fabric of her dress. The gold in her clothing was so heavy that it pulled her to the bottom of the ocean.

Confederate officials later recovered both Greenhow's body and the gold she had carried. They recognized her contributions to the cause with a military funeral in Richmond. Every year since then, the Daughters of the Confederacy have honored the anniversary of her death by placing a wreath on her grave.

Where to Learn More

Burger, Nash K. *Confederate Spy: Rose O'Neal Greenhow.* New York: Franklin Watts, 1967.

Duke University, Special Collections Library. *Rose O'Neal Greenhow Papers. An On-line Archival Collection.* http://scriptorium.lib.duke.edu/greenhow (accessed on October 8, 1999).

Faber, Doris. *Rose Greenhow, Spy for the Confederacy.* New York: Putnam, 1967.

Greenhow, Rose O'Neal. *My Imprisonment and the First Year of Abolition Rule at Washington.* London: Richard Bently, 1863.

Markle, Donald E. *Spies and Spymasters of the Civil War.* New York: Hippocrene Books, 1994.

Nolan, Jeannette Covert. *Spy for the Confederacy: Rose O'Neal Greenhow.* New York: J. Covert, 1960.

Ross, Ishbel. *Rebel Rose: Life of Rose O'Neal Greenhow, Confederate Spy.* New York: Harper, 1954.

Winfield Scott Hancock

Born February 4, 1824
Montgomery Square, Pennsylvania
Died February 9, 1886
Governors Island, New York

Union general known as "the Superb"
Became a hero during the Battle of Gettysburg

Winfield Scott Hancock was one of the most efficient and successful corps commanders in the Union Army. His bravery, intelligence, quick decision-making, and professional attitude earned the respect of his troops and helped make him a war hero. Although he fought in many of the most important battles of the Civil War, Hancock is best known for his performance at the Battle of Gettysburg in Pennsylvania in July 1863. He selected the site of this historic battle, set up the Union defenses, and helped turn back the full-scale Confederate attack on the final day of fighting. A career military man, Hancock served as a military district commander during Reconstruction. He ran for president in 1880 and lost by one of the closest margins in history.

Named after a war hero

Winfield Scott Hancock was born on February 4, 1824, in southeastern Pennsylvania. He was named after General **Winfield Scott** (1786–1866; see entry), a brilliant military man who had been a hero during the War of 1812 (a

"Hancock was superb!"

Union general George McClellan

Winfield Scott Hancock.
(Courtesy of the Brady National Photographic Art Gallery, Library of Congress.)

struggle from 1812 to 1815 between the United States and Great Britain for possession of lands in the West). Hancock's father, Benjamin, was a teacher and later became a lawyer. His mother, Elizabeth, operated a ladies' hat shop out of the family home. Hancock also had a twin brother, Hilary.

The Hancock family moved to Norristown, Pennsylvania, when the boys were two years old. Hancock attended school there and proved himself to be a good student with a quick mind. In 1840, he was admitted to the U.S. Military Academy at West Point in New York. This prestigious school served as the training ground for many top army officers. Hancock was a well-respected and popular student, but he ranked in the lower third of his class upon graduation in 1844.

Hancock then entered the U.S. Army and served in the Mexican War (1846–48), a conflict between the United States and Mexico over huge sections of land in the West. Led by Hancock's namesake, General Scott, U.S. forces claimed a series of dramatic victories that forced Mexico to give up its claims on California and other western lands in exchange for $15 million.

Fights for the Union during the Civil War

Shortly after the Mexican War ended, Hancock married Almira Russell and had two children. He remained in the army and eventually was posted in California, where he lived when the Civil War began in 1861. The Northern and Southern sections of the country had been arguing over several issues, including slavery, for many years. Growing numbers of Northerners believed that slavery was wrong. Some people wanted to outlaw it, while others wanted to prevent it from spreading beyond the Southern states where it was already allowed. But slavery played a big role in the Southern economy and culture. As a result, many Southerners felt threatened by Northern efforts to contain slavery. They believed that each state should decide for itself whether to allow slavery. They did not want the national government to pass laws that would interfere with their traditional way of life.

America's westward expansion only increased the tension between the North and South. Both sides wanted to spread their political views and way of life into the new states and territories. Finally, the ongoing dispute convinced a group of Southern states to secede (withdraw) from the United States and form a new country that allowed slavery, called the Confederate States of America. Some residents of California wanted to join the Confederacy. But Hancock was determined to fight to preserve the Union. He used his troops to break up meetings of secessionists and help keep California as part of the United States.

As fighting began in the East, Hancock longed to join the action. He went to Washington in September 1861 and received the rank of brigadier general in the Union's main army, the Army of the Potomac. This promotion meant that he commanded a brigade of over three thousand soldiers, including infantry (foot soldiers), artillery (heavy guns), and cavalry (soldiers on horseback) units. His brigade took part in the first major Union offensive, known as the Peninsula Campaign. Union general **George McClellan** (1826–1885; see entry) transported the Army of the Potomac to the Virginia peninsula by water, hoping to catch Southern forces by surprise and capture the Confederate capital of Richmond. Although Confederate general **Robert E. Lee** (1807–1870; see entry) managed to hold off the Union assault, Hancock performed well while leading a critical attack. Afterward, McClellan reported back to President **Abraham Lincoln** (1809–1865; see entry) that "Hancock was superb!" Northern newspapers picked up the report and often referred to Hancock as "The Superb" from that time on.

In September 1862, Hancock was promoted to the rank of major general and took over command of the First Division in the Second Corps of the Army of the Potomac. He fought well that month at the Battle of Antietam in Maryland, and then received another promotion to commander of the Second Corps. As a corps commander, Hancock led his troops into battle in December at Fredericksburg and the following May at Chancellorsville in Virginia. The Union Army suffered a defeat at Chancellorsville, but Hancock's corps protected the rear so that their battered forces could escape.

Becomes a hero during the Battle of Gettysburg

Although Hancock saw action in many of the most important battles of the Civil War, he is probably best known for his performance during the Battle of Gettysburg in Pennsylvania in July 1863. General **George Meade** (1815–1872; see entry) had taken command of the Army of the Potomac a few days before the battle took place. He had so much faith in Hancock's judgment that he sent the young officer ahead to decide whether or not the Union forces should fight there. Hancock arrived at Cemetery Ridge, a large hill on the outskirts of Gettysburg, on July 1. He immediately announced, "I select this as the battlefield." Hancock then calmly began preparing the Union forces for battle. His professional attitude helped restore confidence and order to the troops. He organized them into a long defensive line across the hilltops, ready for a Confederate attack.

Meade finally arrived with reinforcements just before the battle began. Hancock took command of his Second Corps, which was charged with holding the center section of the Union position. During heavy fighting on July 2, Hancock noticed that Confederate forces were about to break through the left flank. He led a group of his men in an assault that protected the position, near a strategic hill called Little Round Top.

On July 3, Confederate general **Robert E. Lee** (1807–1870; see entry) launched a full-scale attack on the middle of the Union defenses. Lee began the assault by firing heavy artillery into the Union lines. The first artillery shell blew up the table where Hancock had just finished eating lunch. But rather than taking cover, Hancock rode along the ridge—in range of enemy fire—in order to inspire his troops. When a fellow officer warned that he risked being killed, Hancock replied, "There are times when a corps commander's life does not matter."

After the artillery attack ended, Lee sent fifteen thousand Confederate troops toward Hancock's position. The Union commander directed his troops in a spirited counterattack. At one point, as Hancock rode along the lines surveying his troops, an enemy bullet smashed through his saddle and drove bits of wood and a nail into his thigh. He was seriously wounded, but he waited until the Confederate forces turned back before he allowed his troops to remove him from the battlefield. The Union ended up claiming a significant victory at Gettysburg, and the U.S. Congress officially thanked Hancock for his role in it.

Enters politics after the war

Hancock's wound from Gettysburg kept him on the sidelines for the next six months. After that, though, he regained his command and fought bravely in the Battle of the Wilderness in Virginia (May 5–7, 1864). In August 1864, he was promoted to the rank of major general after leading his troops through the Confederate lines in the Battle of Spotsylvania (May 8–19, 1864). In November 1864, Hancock's war wound began acting up again. He returned to Washington, D.C., and recruited veterans to serve as cooks, nurses, and sentries (military guards) for the fighting forces.

After the war ended in a Union victory in 1865, Hancock remained in the army. For the next two years, he served in military campaigns against Indian tribes in the West. In 1867, however, he was appointed commander of the Fifth Military District in the South during Reconstruction (1865–77). The United States continued to struggle with important and complicated issues after the Civil War ended. For example, government officials had to decide whether to punish the Confederate leaders, what process to use to readmit the Southern states to the Union, and how much assistance to provide in securing equal rights for the freed slaves. This difficult period in American history was known as Reconstruction.

President **Andrew Johnson** (1808–1875; see entry), who took office after Abraham Lincoln was assassinated, controlled the earliest Reconstruction efforts. He pardoned (officially forgave) many former Confederates and set lenient (easy) conditions for the Southern states to return to the Union. But many Northerners, and especially Republican leaders in the U.S. Congress, worried that Johnson's Reconstruction policies would allow Confederate leaders to return to power and continue to discriminate against blacks. As a result, Congress took over the Reconstruction process in 1867 and sent federal troops into the South to enforce its policies.

As commander of some of these federal troops, Hancock was expected to follow Congress's orders. But he felt that Congress's policies were too harsh toward the South, and he was reluctant to use the military to enforce them. Instead, he attempted to restore civilian (nonmilitary) rule in Texas and Louisiana. His actions angered Congress. President **Ulysses S. Grant** (1822–1885; see entry), who took office after Johnson's term ended in 1868, transferred Hancock out of the South.

Hancock continued to serve in the U.S. Army for his remaining years. In 1880, the Democratic political party selected him as their candidate for president. The Democrats chose Hancock because he was a war hero. But since he had spent his entire career in the military, he had very little political experience. The press criticized his lack of experience and claimed that he did not even understand tariffs (a type of tax on goods that are imported into the country). Nevertheless, Hancock ended up losing a very close race to James Garfield (1831–1881). Hancock received only 7,023 fewer popular votes than his opponent, out of nearly nine million total votes cast. Over the next few years, Hancock developed diabetes (a disease in which the body cannot produce the hormone insulin, which enables it to digest sugars). He died on Governors Island, New York, on February 9, 1886.

Where to Learn More

Gambone, A. M. *Hancock at Gettysburg . . . and Beyond.* Baltimore: Butternut & Blue, 1997.

Green, Carl R., and William R. Sanford. *Union Generals of the Civil War.* Springfield, NJ: Enslow, 1998.

Hancock, Almira Russell. *Reminiscences of Winfield Scott Hancock.* New York: C. L. Webster, 1887. Reprint, Scituate, MA: Digital Scanning, 1999.

Jordan, David M. *Winfield Scott Hancock: A Soldier's Life.* Bloomington: Indiana University Press, 1988.

Tucker, Glenn. *Hancock the Superb.* Indianapolis: Bobbs-Merrill, 1960.

W. S. Hancock Society. [Online] http://www.achiever.com/freehmpg/civil-war/ (accessed on October 10, 1999).

Winslow Homer

Born February 24, 1836
Boston, Massachusetts
Died September 29, 1910
Prout's Neck, Maine

American painter who received critical acclaim for his portrayals of Civil War scenes

Winslow Homer was one of the most famous and respected American artists of the nineteenth century. He is best known for the dramatic paintings that he created from the 1880s until his death in 1910. These works emphasized mankind's relationship with a natural world that could be both beautiful and violent. But the first works composed by Homer to receive critical acclaim were actually created many years earlier, during the American Civil War. His drawings and paintings of that period showed the harsh life of Civil War soldiers in an honest and sympathetic way. Today, Homer's wartime paintings and drawings continue to provide a powerful representation of the Civil War experience.

A Massachusetts childhood

Winslow Homer was born in Boston, Massachusetts, in February 1836 to a middle-class family. Six years later, the family moved to nearby Cambridge, where Winslow and his two brothers attended school. Winslow's father was a jolly businessman who tried many different schemes to get rich

"[Homer] came home [from the war front] so changed that his best friends did not know him." *Homer's mother*

Winslow Homer. *(Reproduced by permission of Corbis-Bettmann.)*

over the years. His mother was a gentle woman who introduced Winslow to the world of art at a young age. Before long, he was spending a great deal of his free time drawing pictures of the world around him.

As a youngster, Winslow spent long hours roaming through the countryside around his family's house. He sometimes took pencils and paper with him on his hikes so that he could draw farmhouses, lakes, trees, and other outdoor subjects. When he was nineteen, he reluctantly accepted a job as an assistant at a local lithography or print-making shop called Bufford's. As he feared, the job proved to be a very boring one with little opportunity for him to be creative. But he continued to work at the shop until he was twenty-one, as he had earlier agreed.

After leaving the print shop, Homer resolved to become a freelance artist. A freelancer is a person—usually an artist or writer—who sells his services to various businesses or individuals without making a long-term commitment to any of them. Homer quickly taught himself a new method of illustration known as woodblock engraving and started selling his services to a number of American publishers.

Moves to New York

In the fall of 1859, Homer moved from Boston to New York, where many of America's leading publishers kept their offices. He soon began taking classes at the National Academy of Design, a leading art school in the city. He also continued with his freelance drawing. Within weeks of his arrival in New York, the editors of a leading newspaper called *Harper's Weekly* offered him a permanent position on their staff. Homer liked the independent life of freelancing, though, so he turned down their offer. "I declined because I had had a taste of freedom," he stated. "The slavery at Bufford's was too fresh in my recollection. . . . From the time that I took my nose off that lithographic stone, I have had no master, and never shall have any [again]."

Still, he continued to sell many of his drawings to *Harper's,* which was quickly emerging as one of America's leading publications. "Homer's modest . . . renditions [interpretations] of [America at mid-century] made him one of the most popular illustrators in the era's greatest news magazine," wrote James Thomas Flexner in *The World of Winslow Homer.* "He depicted those aspects of local life that appealed to him. He showed America at play, sometimes children but more often young men and women of the right age for flirtation and courting [dating]. . . . So Winslow Homer fiddled in historic sunshine, ignoring storm clouds that were mounting on the horizon. The storm was to break as the greatest tragedy in American history: the Civil War."

Homer and the Civil War

The American Civil War, which began in April 1861, pitted the nation's Northern and Southern states against one another. These two regions had been arguing with one another for years over a range of social, economic, and political issues. The main issue dividing the two sides, however, was slavery. The Northern states wanted to abolish (eliminate) slavery, convinced that it was an immoral practice. The South, however, refused to consider taking such a step. White Southerners argued that their economy and social institutions could not survive without slavery. As Northern calls to end slavery persisted, Southerners became increasingly resentful and defensive. America's westward expansion during this time made this dispute even worse, since both sides wanted to spread their way of life—and their political ideas—into the new territories and states. The two sides finally went to war when the Southern states tried to secede from (leave) the Union and form a new country that allowed slavery, called the Confederate States of America.

At first, the Civil War did not seem to have much of an impact on Homer's work. He spent the summer of 1861 in New York and Massachusetts, where he continued to draw peaceful scenes of America. He also started painting around this time. But as the months passed and the war produced its first significant casualties, Homer decided to investigate the conflict firsthand.

In the fall of 1861, Homer arranged to travel with Union general **George B. McClellan** (1826–1885; see entry) and his Army of the Potomac. In March 1862, McClellan and his army launched a major offensive into Virginia in an effort to capture the Confederate capital of Richmond. Homer accompanied McClellan's army on this offensive, which came to be known as the Peninsula Campaign.

Over the next several months, Homer witnessed repeated clashes between Union and Confederate troops as McClellan fought rebel (Confederate) general **Robert E. Lee** (1807–1870; see entry) for control of the Virginia peninsula. He also studied ordinary scenes of camp life, watching lonely and battered soldiers as they ate, slept, underwent training, and took care of camp chores. According to Homer's mother, her artist son "suffered much" during these months at the front (the area where enemy armies meet and fight). Homer was "without food 3 days at a time & all in camp either died or were carried away with typhoid fever," wrote his mother in a letter. "He came home so changed that his best friends did not know him."

Homer eventually recovered from his grim experiences during the Peninsula Campaign. As the war continued, he even returned to the front on a few other occasions. He spent most of the rest of the war, however, in his New York studio, where he composed paintings and drawings based on sketches that he had made in the field.

Many of Homer's drawings appeared in *Harper's Weekly* while the war was still raging. They helped the newspaper gain a reputation as one of the leading chroniclers (recorders) of the war in America. As time passed, however, the artist became better known for his Civil War paintings. As with his drawings, Homer concentrated on scenes of camp life or individual portraits in these works. Rather than create heroic battlefield scenes, he painted images that showed the impact of war on individual soldiers.

In *Home, Sweet Home* (produced in 1863), for example, Homer showed two men thinking about their families after receiving letters from home. In *Trooper Meditating beside a Grave* (1865), Homer shows a lone soldier mourning over the gravestone of a comrade. In *The Veteran in a New Field* (1865), he offers an image of a solitary army veteran who has returned home to tend to his wheat field. And in *Prisoners from the Front* (1866), Homer shows three weary Confederate soldiers as they surrender to a solemn Union officer.

Altogether, Homer produced more than fifty paintings on the American Civil War during the mid-1860s. Today, these works continue to stand as some of the most powerful representations of that chapter in the nation's history.

A life of travel

After the war ended, Homer's reputation as one of the country's most promising painters continued to grow. Many of his early postwar paintings depicted American rural scenes, but as time passed he turned to other subjects. In the late 1870s, he traveled to the American South, where he produced a series of colorful paintings on black life. His dignified portraits of black families and workers made some white Southerners angry, but he ignored their complaints. When one white Southern woman asked him, "Why don't you paint our lovely girls instead of these dreadful creatures?" he replied that he preferred painting black females because they were prettier.

Winslow Homer in 1867.
(Reproduced by permission of Corbis-Corporation [Bellevue].)

During the 1880s and 1890s, Homer spent long periods of time in England, the West Indies, and Canada. All of these locations became subjects for his paintings, which by this time were well-known around the world. His base of operations, however, became a cottage at Prout's Neck, Maine, along the Atlantic Ocean. The rugged seascapes of this region became an inspiration for a series of bold paintings showing the power of the sea and man's relationship to the natural world. These dramatic works—*Fog Warning* (produced in 1885), *Eight Bells* (1886), *The Wreck* (1897), *Right and Left* (1909), and many others—became the most famous paintings of Homer's entire career. Homer died at Prout's Neck in 1910, leaving behind a long and distinguished body of work that continues to earn praise today.

Where to Learn More

Cikovsky, Nicolai Jr., and Franklin Kelly. *Winslow Homer*. Washington, D.C.: National Gallery of Art, 1995.

Cooper, Helen A. *Winslow Homer Watercolors*. New Haven, CT: Yale University Press, 1987.

Flexner, James Thomas. *The World of Winslow Homer, 1836–1910*. New York: Time Inc., 1966.

Gardner, Albert Ten Eyck. *Winslow Homer, American Artist: His World and His Work*. New York: C. N. Potter, 1961.

Grossman, Julian. *Echo of a Distant Drum: Winslow Homer and the Civil War*. New York: Abrams, 1974.

Little, Carl. *Winslow Homer: His Art, His Light, His Landscapes*. First Glance Books, 1997.

National Gallery of Art: The Collection. *Winslow Homer Watercolors*. [Online] http://www.nga/gov/collection/gallery/homerwc/homerwc-main3.html (accessed on October 10, 1999).

Simpson, Marc, ed. *Winslow Homer: Paintings of the Civil War*. San Francisco: Fine Arts Museums of San Francisco, 1988.

Winslow Homer 1836–1910. [Online] http://web.syr.edu/~ribond/homer.html (accessed on October 10, 1999).

Winslow Homer: The Obtuse Bard. [Online] http://pages.prodigy.net/bueschen/homer/ (accessed on October 10, 1999).

John Bell Hood

Born June 1, 1831
Owingsville, Kentucky
Died August 30, 1879
New Orleans, Louisiana

Confederate general
Led failed Southern effort to keep Union forces
from capturing Atlanta in 1864

John Bell Hood was a Confederate general of unquestioned bravery and dedication. As a division commander he displayed great courage at many of the Civil War's most violent battles. These skirmishes included Second Bull Run (August 1862) and Fredericksburg (December 1862) in Virginia; Antietam (September 1862) in Maryland; Gettysburg (July 1863) in Pennsylvania; and Chickamauga (September 1863) in Georgia. Hood's devotion to the Southern cause was so great that he remained on active military duty even after suffering wounds that crippled one arm and required the amputation of one of his legs. But Hood's performance as commander of the Confederate Army of Tennessee from July 1864 to January 1865 has tarnished his reputation. During that period he not only failed to stop Union forces from capturing Atlanta, Georgia, but also made a series of disastrous battlefield decisions that virtually destroyed his army.

Adopts Texas as home state

John Bell Hood was born in Bath County, Kentucky, in 1831. His father was a prosperous planter (plantation

"An aggressive, ferocious fighter, Hood came to be considered one of Lee's better brigade commanders. . . ."

Writer Steven E. Woodworth

John B. Hood. *(Reproduced by permission of the National Portrait Gallery.)*

owner) who also ran a rural medical practice. Hood's childhood environment became even more comfortable in the mid-1830s, when his maternal grandfather died and left the family more than 225,000 acres of land.

As a youngster, Hood was a troublemaker who got in fistfights with other boys on a regular basis. He managed to gain admission into the prestigious U.S. Military Academy at West Point in 1849, however, thanks to his father's wealth and the assistance of an uncle who was a U.S. congressman. During his time at West Point, his poor grades and taste for mischief nearly resulted in his expulsion. As a senior, however, he developed a deep admiration for **Robert E. Lee** (1807–1870; see entry), who took over as the academy's superintendent during that year. This admiration may have helped Hood reduce some of his bad behavior. In any event, he managed to perform just well enough to graduate from the school in 1853 (he ranked forty-fourth out of fifty-two graduates).

After leaving West Point, Hood was made a second lieutenant in an infantry company. He served in the U.S. Army in both New York and California until 1855, when he became a second lieutenant in the Second U.S. Cavalry in Texas. Hood developed a deep love for Texas's rugged frontier country over the next several years. He liked the rough beauty of the land and identified with the independent pioneer spirit of its settlers.

Hood's career in the U.S. Army came to an end in early 1861, after years of growing hostility between America's Northern and Southern states finally boiled over into war. The main issue dividing the two regions was slavery. Northern states wanted to abolish slavery because many of their citizens became convinced that it was a cruel and evil institution. Southern states resisted efforts to end slavery, though. The Southern economy had become dependent on slavery over the years, and white Southerners worried that their way of life would collapse if slavery was abolished (eliminated). America's westward expansion during this time made this dispute even worse, since both sides wanted to spread their way of life—and their political ideas—into the new territories and states. The two sides finally went to war in early 1861 when the Southern states tried to secede from (leave) the Union and form a new country that allowed slavery, called the Confederate States of America.

Hood's Texas Brigade

Early in John Bell Hood's Civil War career, he commanded a famous brigade (military unit consisting of two or more regiments) of Confederate troops that came to be known as Hood's Texas Brigade. This brigade was first organized in November 1861 from thirty-two volunteer infantry companies recruited in Texas. Its three regiments of Texas soldiers—the First, Fourth, and Fifth Texas Infantry—were the only units from that state who served in General Robert E. Lee's Army of Northern Virginia (the brigade also included the Eighteenth Georgia Infantry and the Third Arkansas Infantry at various points during the war).

This brigade was originally commanded by Louis T. Wigfall. But when he left in early 1862 to take a seat in the Confederate Senate, Hood took his place. He quickly established the brigade as one of the fiercest fighting units in the entire war. By mid-1862, when Hood left for a new command assignment, his Texas Brigade was known across the country as a fearless and ferocious unit. Even after Hood departed, the members of the unit continued to refer to themselves by their old leader's name in order to honor him. In fact, their regard for Hood was so great that when he lost his leg after the Battle of Chickamauga, the members of the brigade collected $3,100 in contributions in a single day in order to buy him a good artificial leg.

The fighting spirit shown by Hood's Texas Brigade made it one of the war's most respected units. The brigade's fearless style, however, did take a heavy toll on its members. In fact, the brigade suffered record casualty rates during the war. It is estimated that approximately forty-five hundred men served in its ranks at one time or another, either as original members, later recruits, or replacements. Of those soldiers, fewer than 480 remained to see the Confederacy surrender in the spring of 1865.

Hood resigned from the U.S. Army on April 17, 1861, after the Texas legislature voted to secede from the Union and join the Confederacy. Disgusted by Kentucky's decision to stay with the Union, he subsequently adopted Texas as his new home state and enlisted in the Confederate Army from there.

A fighting general

Once the Civil War started, Hood quickly gained a reputation as a tough and brave officer. He joined the Confederate military as a captain, but he rose rapidly through the ranks as word of his bravery and no-nonsense leadership spread. In March 1862, he was promoted to brigadier general and given command of the tough Texas Brigade, which was part of General Robert E. Lee's Army of Northern Virginia.

Lee's force was the Confederacy's largest army, and as the war progressed it engaged in many of the conflict's biggest battles. Hood participated in most of these clashes, impressing friend and foe alike with his fearless approach to war. "Hood turned out to be an excellent combat commander," wrote Steven E. Woodworth in *Jefferson Davis and His Generals*. "An aggressive, ferocious fighter, Hood came to be considered one of Lee's better brigade commanders and was soon promoted to major general."

Hood's bold approach to combat made him one of the Confederacy's best-known officers and helped Lee secure several big battlefield victories. As the war progressed, however, Hood's hard-charging style earned him a number of serious war injuries. The most serious of these injuries took place at the battles of Gettysburg and Chickamauga. At Gettysburg (fought July 1–3, 1863, in Pennsylvania), Hood received a wound that permanently crippled his left arm. A few months later at Chickamauga (fought September 19–20, 1863, in Georgia), Hood was shot in the right leg while leading a charge. Soldiers quickly transported him to Richmond, where doctors were forced to amputate his leg at mid-thigh in order to save his life.

Hood spent the next several months in Richmond. As he worked to regain his strength, he struck up a pleasurable friendship with Confederate president **Jefferson Davis** (1808–1889; see entry) and his family. Hood's stay in the Confederacy's capital city also brought him sorrow, though. As a man who had always been physically active and strong, he found it very difficult to adjust to his new physical limitations. In addition, he waged a desperate campaign to win the heart of an attractive Southern woman named Sally Buchanan Preston during this time. When she rejected him over the Christmas holidays, Hood was emotionally crushed.

Battling against Sherman

In February 1864, Hood returned to active military service despite his injuries. Assigned to command a corps of troops in the Army of Tennessee, Hood reached its camp in Georgia at the end of the month. Once Hood arrived, he tackled his new responsibilities with great eagerness. He routinely rode twenty miles a day, even though he had to be strapped on to his horse because of his war injuries. He also encouraged Army of Tennessee commander **Joseph E. Johnston** (1807–1891; see entry) to adopt a plan advanced by Davis to launch an invasion into Union-held Tennessee. Davis believed that one or two more big Southern victories might convince the Northern states to end their efforts to break the Confederacy and restore the Union.

Johnston, however, resisted calls for a major offensive. More cautious than Hood, he hesitated to attack unless he was sure that he could win. In addition, he believed that the Confederacy's best chance of gaining independence was to avoid major losses and hope that Northern voters replaced President Abraham Lincoln in the fall 1864 elections with someone who would agree to Confederate independence in exchange for peace.

Davis and Johnston argued over strategy throughout the first few months of 1864. Then, in May 1864, Union general **William T. Sherman** (1820–1891; see entry) launched a full-scale invasion of Georgia in hopes of destroying the Army of Tennessee. Johnston used a variety of skillful maneuvers to avoid a full-scale battle with Sherman's much-larger army. But while Johnston's evasive tactics frustrated Sherman, the Union general kept moving his army deeper into Georgia. By early summer, the Army of Tennessee had been pushed all the way from northern Georgia to the outskirts of Atlanta, one of the most important cities still controlled by the Confederacy.

Hood takes command in the West

As Davis received reports detailing Sherman's advance on Atlanta, he became convinced that Johnston's reluctance to attack the invading Northern army would eventually result in the loss of the city. Hood contributed to Davis's mounting anxiety by sending a series of letters that were highly critical of Johnston's defensive strategy. The Confederate president thus decided to replace Johnston with Hood, even though General Lee thought that appointing Hood was a bad idea. "Hood is a bold fighter," stated Lee. "I am doubtful as to [whether he possesses] other qualities necessary [to lead the army effectively]."

Hood assumed his new position as commander of the Confederate Army of Tennessee on July 17, 1864. One day later he was made a full general with temporary rank. Hood understood that he had been promoted because of his aggressiveness and willingness to fight. With this in mind, he immediately made plans to attack Sherman's forces. He ignored the advice of many other officers, engaging Sherman's larger force in a series of battles around the outskirts of Atlanta. Delighted with the dramatic change in the South's strategy, Sherman battered Hood in each of these engagements.

By August, Hood's tired army was trapped in the city of Atlanta, and Sherman had seized control of most of the surrounding countryside. Rather than order a bloody assault on the city's defenses, though, Sherman placed the city under siege (a military blockade designed to prevent the city from receiving food and other supplies from outside). Hood's defense of Atlanta ended on September 1, when his forces lost control of the last railway lines providing supplies to Atlanta at the Battle of Jonesboro. Aware that he could no longer keep Atlanta out of Union hands, Hood hurriedly withdrew his army out of the city. Sherman's Army of the Mississippi moved in to take possession of the town one day later, on September 2.

Hood's desperate gamble

In the weeks following Sherman's capture of Atlanta, the Union Army engaged in a series of skirmishes (minor fights) with Hood's force, which continued to lurk in the region. In November 1864, Sherman's army set fire to Atlanta and marched eastward out of the city. Sherman planned to march through the heart of the Confederacy, seizing supplies and destroying croplands along the way. "If we can march a well-appointed [prepared] army right through [Jefferson

Davis's] territory, it is a demonstration to the world . . . that we have a power which Davis cannot resist," said Sherman. "I can make the march, and make Georgia howl!"

Hood knew that his battered army did not have the muscle to stop Sherman's superior force as it began its fearsome "March to the Sea." Instead, the Confederate commander moved his army into Tennessee in a desperate attempt to catch Sherman's attention. He hoped to lure Sherman out of Georgia by threatening both his supply lines and the Union-held city of Nashville. Hood's strategy, wrote historian James M. McPherson in *Battle Cry of Freedom,* created "the odd spectacle of two contending armies turning their backs on each other and marching off in opposite directions. As it turned out, there was more method in Sherman's madness than in Hood's."

Sherman ignored Hood's offensive. The Union general knew that his army could supply itself by taking what it needed from Southern towns and farms as it made its way across the Confederate heartland. In addition, he knew that sixty thousand federal troops under the command of General **George H. Thomas** (1816–1870; see entry) would be awaiting Hood in Tennessee. Sherman thus continued his methodical march across the South, destroying Confederate property and morale with each passing mile.

Hood, meanwhile, continued to move deeper into Tennessee with his weary forty thousand–man army. Worried that the Confederacy was on the verge of total collapse, he came up with another desperate plan to reverse the war's momentum. He decided to use his army in a bid to regain control of Tennessee and Kentucky and eventually move against Union forces gathered in Virginia. This plan was doomed to fail, but as historian Bruce Catton wrote in *The Civil War,* "the plain fact of the matter was that Hood had no good choice to make."

On November 30, 1864, Hood's dreams of somehow reversing the South's fortunes were crushed once and for all. On that day he launched a full-scale assault on Union forces at Franklin, Tennessee, about twenty-five miles south of Nashville. The well-entrenched Union Army, commanded by Major General John M. Schofield (1831–1906), easily turned back every rebel charge. By the time Hood called off the disastrous attack, he had lost more than sixty-two hundred men and the respect of many of his troops. "I have never seen an

Covered guns can be seen on the steps of the state capitol in Nashville, Tennessee, on a rainy day prior to the Battle of Nashville. *(Photograph by George N. Barnard. Courtesy of the Library of Congress.)*

army so confused and demoralized," confessed one member of the Army of Tennessee who took part in the battle. "The whole thing seemed to be tottering and trembling."

Two weeks later, Thomas finished off Hood's exhausted and demoralized army at the Battle of Nashville. This battle, fought on December 15 and 16, virtually destroyed the Army of Tennessee, as wave after wave of Union troops battered Hood's defenses. Remnants of the courageous rebel army managed to escape, but Confederate authorities never managed to put the pieces back together again. The Army of Tennessee remained sidelined for the remainder of the war.

Hood survived the Battle of Nashville, but the destruction of his army depressed him terribly. Wracked with guilt and grief at his failures, he resigned his command on January 13, 1865. Four months later he surrendered to Union troops in Natchez, Mississippi, as the war drew to a close.

Settles in New Orleans

After the Civil War ended, Hood started a cotton business in New Orleans. He married Anna Marie Henen, with whom he had eleven children. He also wrote a book about his wartime experiences called *Advance and Retreat.* Before he could find a publisher for his memoirs, however, a yellow fever epidemic swept through New Orleans. The epidemic disrupted businesses throughout the city and bankrupted several prominent businessmen, including Hood.

In August 1879, the epidemic claimed the lives of Hood, his wife, and one of his daughters. At first, it appeared that Hood's ten orphaned children might be cast into poverty by the deaths of their parents. But family friends found a publisher for Hood's memoirs and arranged to have the profits distributed to his children.

Where to Learn More

Coffey, David A. *John Bell Hood and the Struggle for Atlanta.* Abilene, TX: McWhiney Foundation Press, McMurray University, 1998.

Hood, John Bell. *Advance and Retreat: Personal Experiences in the United States & Confederate States Armies.* New Orleans: Hood Orphan Memorial Fund, 1880. Reprint, Lincoln: University of Nebraska Press, 1996.

McMurry, Richard M. *John Bell Hood and the War for Southern Independence.* Lexington: University Press of Kentucky, 1982. Reprint, Lincoln: University of Nebraska Press, 1992.

Warner, Ezra J. *Generals in Gray: Lives of the Confederate Commanders.* Baton Rouge: Louisiana State University Press, 1959.

Woodworth, Steven E. *Jefferson Davis and His Generals.* Lawrence: University Press of Kansas, 1990.

Julia Ward Howe

Born May 27, 1819
New York, New York
Died October 1910
Portsmouth, New Hampshire

Author and social reformer
Wrote the words to "Battle Hymn of the Republic," which became the Union anthem during the Civil War

Julia Ward Howe accomplished many things as a writer, lecturer, abolitionist, and promoter of women's rights. But she is best remembered as the author of the words to "Battle Hymn of the Republic," the stirring song that became the Union anthem during the Civil War. The song's popularity, combined with her active support of various social causes, made her one of the most famous and respected women of her time.

Sheltered girlhood in New York City

Julia Ward Howe was born on May 27, 1819, in New York City. She was the third of six children born to Samuel Ward, a wealthy banker, and his wife Julia Cutler Ward. Howe was a bright and strong-willed child with a lively wit. She loved both music and drama from an early age. But young girls were relatively sheltered in those days. They did not receive the same level of education or personal freedom given to boys. Instead, they were trained to be well-mannered ladies who could run a household and care for children.

"Mine eyes have seen the glory of the coming of the Lord . . ."

Julia Ward Howe.
(Photograph by Alice Boughton. Courtesy of the Library of Congress.)

When Howe's mother died in 1824, her father became even more restrictive with his daughters. He did not allow them to attend parties, see plays, or read popular books because he wanted to protect them from harmful outside influences. But Howe loved to read and dreamed of becoming a writer. She often rebelled against her father's rules, especially when she spent time with less-strict relatives on the Atlantic coast each summer. Her oldest brother and several other family members encouraged her to pursue her writing.

Samuel Ward died in 1839, leaving a fortune estimated at six million dollars. Within a short time, Howe's beloved brother Henry Ward died as well. She became deeply depressed and spent the next two years recovering her spirits. After her period of mourning ended, however, she began to enjoy her newfound freedom. She socialized with all kinds of important people in New York. Along with her sisters, she became known as an excellent hostess in the city's literary and cultural circles.

Joins the fight against slavery

Julia Ward married a prominent older man, Samuel Gridley Howe, in 1843. He was a medical doctor who ran a hospital for the deaf and blind in Boston, Massachusetts. He was also a social reformer who worked to improve conditions and treatment methods for his patients. Although Samuel Howe respected his wife's intelligence, he still believed that women's primary role should be as homemakers and mothers. For this reason, he was not particularly supportive of Howe's efforts as a writer. Partly as a way to please her husband, Howe had six children over the next fifteen years.

Shortly after their marriage, the Howes traveled to the South. They visited a plantation there and saw the effects of slavery. Black people were taken from Africa and brought to North America to serve as slaves for white people beginning in the 1600s. The basic belief behind slavery was that black people were inferior to whites. Under slavery, white slaveholders treated black people as property, forced them to perform hard labor, and controlled every aspect of their lives. States in the Northern half of the United States began outlawing slavery in the late 1700s. But slavery continued to exist in the Southern half of the country because it played an important role in the South's economy and culture.

Following their trip to the South, the Howes joined a growing number of Northerners who believed that slavery was wrong. They became active in the movement to abolish (put an end to) slavery in the United States. Their anger over slavery increased in 1850, when Southerners in the U.S. Congress passed the Fugitive Slave Act. This measure granted slaveowners sweeping new powers to capture and reclaim escaped slaves. It also required people in the North to assist the slaveowners in retrieving their property. Many Northerners resented the Fugitive Slave Act. They were able to ignore slavery when it was confined to the South, but not when they saw black people being captured and carried off in chains within their own cities. The Fugitive Slave Act ended up increasing the antislavery and anti-Southern feelings of many people in the North.

In 1852, the Howes took over management of an abolitionist magazine, the *Commonwealth,* for a year. In 1859, Samuel Howe was one of six prominent Northern abolitionists who provided financial backing for John Brown's Raid. **John Brown** (1800–1859; see entry) was a radical abolitionist who believed that violence was a necessary part of the fight against slavery. He came up with an ambitious plan to raid a federal armory (a storage facility for weapons and ammunition) in Harpers Ferry, Virginia, and use the captured weapons to arm slaves and start a violent uprising throughout the South. Brown's plan failed, however, and he was captured and executed. But his actions added to the bitter feelings between the North and the South that led to the Civil War.

Despite the lack of support from her husband, Howe wrote several poems and plays during the 1850s. Her first book of poetry, *Passion Flowers,* was published in 1853. Her husband refused to speak to her for several weeks after the book came out. He was angry about one poem that seemed to discuss their relationship and her struggles to express her independent spirit. In 1857, Howe published a travel journal called *A Trip to Cuba.* At that time, Cuba was the source of many new slaves that were brought into the United States illegally (although slavery was still legal, importing new slaves had been outlawed in 1808). She discussed the issue of slavery in the book and pointed out its negative effects on society. But she still made it clear that—like many Northerners—she believed that black people were inferior to whites.

"Battle Hymn of the Republic"

In 1861, the long-standing dispute between the North and South over slavery and other issues finally erupted into war. The Southern states seceded (withdrew) from the Union and formed a new country that allowed slavery, called the Confederate States of America. But Northern politicians would not allow the South to leave the Union without a fight. In the fall of that year, Howe made a trip to Washington, D.C. Along the way, her train passed a number of military camps where soldiers were stationed to protect the capital. Once there, she joined a large group of Union supporters who went to watch General **George B. McClellan** (1826–1885; see entry) review his troops at nearby Munson's Hill, Virginia. As the spectators watched the troops parade by, however, Confederate forces launched a surprise attack.

As both the Union soldiers and the spectators tried to flee to the safety of Washington, the roads became jammed. Howe and her friends were stuck in their carriage for several hours. They passed the time by singing popular army songs, including one called "John Brown's Body" that featured the chorus "Glory, Glory, Hallelujah!" Some of the soldiers who heard this song stopped to compliment Howe. Then one of her friends suggested that she could write better words to the tune.

Howe returned to her Washington hotel room and went to sleep. In the middle of the night, she awoke with new words to the song filling her head. "As I lay waiting for the dawn, the long lines of the desired poem began to twine themselves in my mind," she recalled. "Having thought out all the stanzas, I said to myself, 'I must get up and write these verses down, lest I fall asleep again and forget them.' So, with a sudden effort, I sprang out of bed, and . . . scrawled the verses almost without looking at the paper."

The new lyrics said that God was on the side of the North, and that He would help them destroy their enemies. Howe's version began: "Mine eyes have seen the glory of the

An engraving shows Julia Ward Howe waving the American flag as she rides her horse. Her "Battle Hymn of the Republic" became a rallying song for the Union troops. *(Reproduced by permission of EPD Photos.)*

coming of the Lord / He is trampling out the vintage where the grapes of wrath are stored / He has loosed the fateful lightning of his terrible swift sword / His truth is marching on." Howe's poem was published in the literary magazine *Atlantic Monthly* in early 1862, and she received five dollars for it. Before long, people all across the North were singing her words to the tune of "John Brown's Body." In 1863, shortly after the Union's July victory in the bloody Battle of Gettys-

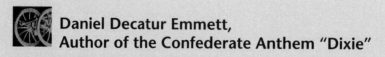

Daniel Decatur Emmett, Author of the Confederate Anthem "Dixie"

Musician Daniel Decatur Emmett was born in 1815 in Ohio. He remained in the North throughout his life and supported the Union during the Civil War. For this reason, it seems strange that a song he composed about the South, "Dixie," became the most popular patriotic song among Confederate troops.

Emmett had no formal music education but was blessed with great natural talent. As a teenager, he wrote a manual that was used by drum students for many years, *Emmett's Standard Drummer.* He later used his skills as a songwriter and performer to form one of the first minstrel shows. In this form of entertainment—which was popular in the mid-1800s—white performers painted their faces and did impersonations of black music and dance.

Around 1860, Emmett wrote a song called "I Wish I Was in Dixie's Land." Dixie was a nickname for the South that probably came from the term Mason-Dixon line. This line originally marked the border between Maryland and Pennsylvania, but came to mean the line dividing North from South during the debate over slavery. The song began, "I wish I was in the land of cotton /

Old times there are not forgotten / Look away! Look away! Look away! Dixie Land!"

The rousing song "Dixie" soon became very popular around the country. In 1861, the Southern states seceded (withdrew) from the Union and formed a new country that allowed slavery, called the Confederate States of America. A band played "Dixie" when **Jefferson Davis** (1808–1889; see entry) was inaugurated (sworn in) as the president of the Confederacy. Before long, Emmett's tune had become the most popular marching song for Southern troops as they went to fight in the Civil War.

Since Emmett supported the North, the popularity of "Dixie" among Southerners embarrassed him. He spent the next few years struggling to prove his loyalty to the Union. When the war ended in a Northern victory in 1865, however, U.S. president Abraham Lincoln admitted that "Dixie" was one of his favorite songs. Lincoln declared that the North had captured the song along with the South, and that it now belonged to the whole nation. Emmett continued to work as songwriter, conductor, and theater manager during and after the war. He retired in 1888 and died in 1904.

burg, Army Chaplain Charles Caldwell McCabe (1836–1906) sang it at an official function with President **Abraham Lincoln** (1809–1865; see entry) in the audience. With tears in his eyes, Lincoln stood up and asked McCabe to sing it again. It soon became the unofficial anthem of the Union war effort.

Joins the women's rights movement

With the success of "Battle Hymn of the Republic," Howe became one of the most famous women of her time. After the war ended in a Union victory in 1865, she continued to write and began lecturing on a variety of social issues, including women's rights. In 1868, Howe helped organize the New England Woman's Club. She acted as its president for the next forty years. This group focused on educating women so that they could speak in public, make formal reports, and influence people's opinions about social issues.

Howe also became a strong supporter of efforts to grant women the right to vote. "All that I had felt regarding the sacredness and importance of the woman's part in private life now appeared to me equally applicable to the part which she should bear in public life," she stated. She came to believe that women were equal to men. She saw the right to vote as key to women's advancement, as well as the advancement of American society. She did not want to change the traditional role of women as wives and mothers, but believed that political activity would make women better companions for their husbands and better instructors for their children.

Howe continued to write and lecture on literary and cultural topics for the rest of her long life. In recognition of her achievements, she was the first woman elected to the prestigious American Academy of Arts and Letters. In 1873, she held the first Mother's Peace Day celebration in Boston. This holiday was intended to show women's support for world peace. Some historians claim that it provided the original source for today's Mother's Day holiday. Howe died in October 1910, at the age of ninety-one.

Where to Learn More

Clifford, Deborah Pickman. *Mine Eyes Have Seen the Glory: A Biography of Julia Ward Howe*. Boston: Little, Brown, 1979.

Currie, Stephen. *Music in the Civil War*. Cincinnati: Betterway Books, 1992.

Grant, Mary H. *Private Woman, Public Person: An Account of the Life of Julia Ward Howe from 1819 to 1868*. Brooklyn, NY: Carlson Publishers, 1994.

Richards, Laura E., and Maud Howe Elliott. *Julia Ward Howe, 1819–1910*. Boston: Houghton Mifflin, 1915. Reprint, Atlanta: Cherokee, 1990.

Williams, Gary. *Hungry Heart: The Literary Emergence of Julia Ward Howe.* Amherst: University of Massachusetts Press, 1999.

Thomas "Stonewall" Jackson

Born January 21, 1824
Clarksburg, Virginia (now West Virginia)
Died May 10, 1863
Guiney Station, Virginia

Confederate general whose successful 1862
Shenandoah campaign and other military exploits
made him beloved throughout the South

Thomas "Stonewall" Jackson is one of the legendary military heroes of the American Civil War. The Virginia native first attracted national attention in 1862, when his brilliant Shenandoah Valley campaign demoralized much larger Union forces. As the most trusted lieutenant of General **Robert E. Lee** (1807–1870; see entry), Jackson then helped guide the Confederate Army of Northern Virginia to its greatest battlefield victories. In May 1863, however, Stonewall Jackson's spectacular military career was cut short when he was accidentally shot and fatally wounded by his own troops. His death was a serious blow to the Confederacy. In fact, many Southerners insisted after the war that the conflict might have ended differently if Jackson had not been killed.

A solitary childhood

Thomas Jonathan Jackson was born in a small town called Clarksburg in what is now West Virginia (it was part of Virginia at the time of his birth). The son of poor farmers, he was orphaned at the age of seven. Jackson subsequently went

"Look, men! There stands Jackson like a stone wall! Rally behind the Virginians!"

Confederate general Barnard E. Bee

Thomas "Stonewall" Jackson.

to live on an estate called Jackson's Mill, owned by a wealthy uncle named Cummings Jackson. Young Thomas Jackson spent his next eleven years at Jackson's Mill, where he learned a great deal about its agricultural, sawmill, and racetrack operations. But although he was accepted by his relatives, Jackson apparently felt very lonely as a child. "In his [later] years," his second wife wrote, "he was not disposed [inclined] to talk much of his childhood and youth, for the reason that it was the saddest period of his life."

In 1842, Jackson enrolled in the U.S. Military Academy at West Point in New York. Jackson was eager to make his mark at the academy, which was the leading military and engineering school in the nation. During his first year, he struggled with homework and had difficulty making friends. As time passed, however, the cadet's determination to succeed helped him rise through the school's academic ranks. Using the saying "You may be whatever you resolve to be" for inspiration, he devoted nearly all of his energies to study. His years at West Point remained solitary ones, but by the time he graduated in 1846, this discipline and desire had lifted him into the upper ranks of his class.

Serves in Mexican War

Jackson graduated from West Point just as the Mexican War (1846–48) was beginning. This clash between America and its southern neighbor came about when the United States became interested in acquiring significant sections of Mexican territory in order to expand its own land holdings. When Mexico refused to give up these lands, the two countries ended up going to war in 1846. The conflict finally ended in 1848, when American military victories forced Mexico to cede (give up) its claims on Texas, California, New Mexico, and other lands in the West in exchange for $15 million. Everyone knew that the land was worth far more than $15 million, but the Mexican government had no choice but to accept the deal.

Eager to test himself in combat, Jackson joined the U.S. Army immediately after graduation. He was named a second lieutenant of artillery and sent to Mexico, where he distinguished himself as a brave and tough officer. By the time the war ended in 1848, Jackson had participated in several of the war's biggest battles, earned three awards for gallantry (heroic courage) in combat, and risen to the brevet (honorary) rank of major.

Jackson returned to the United States after the war concluded. He remained with the army for a few years, serving at posts in New York and Florida. In 1851, however, he resigned from the military to become an instructor in artillery and natural philosophy at the prestigious Virginia Military Institute (VMI) in Lexington, Virginia.

Professor Jackson's struggles

Jackson spent the next ten years of his life at VMI, where he developed a reputation as one of the institute's least effective instructors. He was skilled at teaching artillery, but his natural philosophy classes called for him to teach physics, astronomy, and other subjects that he had never studied. Relying on memorized lectures and strict discipline to disguise his unfamiliarity with the subjects he taught, Jackson was strongly disliked by many cadets. In fact, he was challenged to duels (formal fights with deadly weapons between two people) by cadets on at least two occasions. "[Jackson] had not the qualifications needed for so important a chair," admitted the superintendent of VMI after his departure from the school. "He was no teacher, and he lacked the tact [sensitivity] required in getting along with his classes. Every officer and every cadet respected him for his many sterling [excellent] qualities. He was a brave man, a conscientious man, and a good man, but he was no professor."

Jackson's unusual habits, known as eccentricities, also led some cadets to make fun of their instructor behind his back. For example, Jackson usually ate food that he did not like because he thought that it was probably better for him. He also was a terrible hypochondriac (someone who falsely imagines disease or illness). For instance, he often kept one arm raised up in the air because he thought that the limbs on one side of his body were larger than the other. He believed that by raising his arm, he could drain extra blood out of it and into his other limbs.

Jackson's strange ways and stern teaching style sometimes made it difficult for him to fulfill his duties at VMI. Despite his classroom struggles, however, he enjoyed his years in Lexington. In 1853, he married Elinor Junkin, the daughter of a local minister. Their marriage lasted only fourteen months before she died while trying to give birth to their first child. The death of his wife and child deeply depressed Jackson. In 1857, however, he married another minister's daughter, Mary Anna Morrison. Their marriage was by all accounts a deeply loving one.

Jackson also enjoyed a respected position in the Lexington community. Known for his honesty and devotion to duty, he particularly impressed fellow townspeople with his deep religious faith. "Jackson's faith permeated every action of his adult life," confirmed James I. Robertson Jr. in *Stonewall Jackson*. "He began each task by offering a blessing, and he completed every duty by returning thanks to God. To say merely that he kept the Sabbath holy would be an understatement. In the prewar years, he would not read a newspaper or discuss secular [non-religious] subjects on Sunday." Jackson's strong religious beliefs eventually led him to organize and teach a Sunday School class for slaves and free blacks, openly defying a state law that prohibited blacks from gathering together in public.

Jackson joins the Confederacy

Jackson's years at VMI ended in 1861, when long-simmering disputes between America's Northern and Southern states finally boiled over into war. For years, the two regions had been arguing over slavery. Many Northerners believed that slavery was wrong and wanted to abolish it. But the economy of the South had been built on slavery, and Southerners resented Northern efforts to halt or contain the practice. In early 1861, these differences over slavery and other issues convinced several Southern states to secede from (leave) the United States. They announced their intention to form a new country that allowed slavery, called the Confederate States of America. But Northern political leaders were determined to keep the Southern states in the Union. In April 1861, the two sides finally went to war over their differences.

Jackson had hoped that his home state of Virginia would choose not to secede. "I am strong for the Union at present, and if things become no worse, I hope to continue so," he stated during the first wave of secession. In April 1861, however, Virginia's state legislature voted to join the Confederacy. When Jackson heard the news, he decided that his loyalty to his home state was greater than his loyalty to the United States.

Upon joining the Confederate Army in April, Jackson was made a colonel of infantry. Within a matter of weeks, however, he was promoted to brigadier general as part of the army of General **Joseph E. Johnston** (1807–1891; see entry). In July 1861, Johnston's army joined with a Confederate force led by General **Pierre G. T. Beauregard** (1818–1893; see entry) to defeat Union forces at Manassas Junction, Virginia, in the first major battle of the Civil War. It was during this clash—known as the First Battle of Bull Run or the First Battle of Manassas—that Jackson acquired the most famous nickname in American military history.

On July 21, Union troops nearly broke through Confederate defenses at a place called Henry House Hill. But Jackson and his brigade (military unit consisting of two or more regiments) rushed to stop the advance. As they held their position against several waves of Union attacks, Confederate general Barnard E. Bee (1824–1861) encouraged his men by pointing to Jackson's brave example. "Look, men! There stands Jackson like a stone wall! Rally behind the Virginians!" Jackson's courageous stand at Henry House Hill thus earned him the nickname "Stonewall" and his brigade the title of the "Stonewall Brigade." For the remainder of the war, Jackson's brigade was the only Confederate brigade to have its nickname become its official designation.

Jackson's Shenandoah Valley campaign

In October 1861, the Confederate War Department promoted Stonewall Jackson to major general and gave him command of the entire Shenandoah Valley. This forested region of western Virginia was regarded as strategically important to both sides, because it could be used by either Union or Confederate forces as a natural invasion route. The following

March, Jackson entered the Shenandoah Valley with an army of about eight thousand men (reinforcements eventually increased the size of his army to about fifteen thousand men). Jackson's orders were to prevent Union forces from seizing control of the region and keep Union troops operating in the valley so busy that they could not provide assistance to Northern armies that were invading eastern Virginia.

Jackson's mission was an enormously difficult one. After all, he faced Union forces that totaled almost eighty thousand troops. Over the next three months, however, Stonewall conducted a dazzling campaign that thoroughly baffled and frustrated the enemy. On several occasions, Jackson's Confederate troops won big victories over Union armies of much greater size. At other times, Stonewall and his troops seemed to melt into the woodlands of the Shenandoah region, repeatedly escaping Union traps.

By May, Jackson's maneuvers had thrown the North's military leaders into such complete confusion that they became worried about a Jackson-led attack on Washington, D.C. This perceived threat to the U.S. capital convinced President **Abraham Lincoln** (1809–1865; see entry) to keep an additional forty thousand troops around Washington rather than let them join the Union offensive in eastern Virginia. Lincoln also ordered additional Union troops into the Shenandoah Valley to neutralize Jackson. But Jackson continued to strike against his enemies, avoiding all Union efforts to stop him. Eventually, even his Union opponents expressed admiration for his brilliant tactics and fearlessness. "[Jackson's] chief characteristics as a military leader were his quick perceptions of the weak points of the enemy, his ever readiness, the astounding rapidity of his movements, his sudden and unexpected onslaughts [intense attacks], and the persistency with which he followed them up," said one Union officer. "His ruling maxim [saying] was that war meant fighting, and fighting meant killing, and right loyally did he live up to it."

Jackson and his army remained in the Shenandoah Valley until mid-June. The legendary general then slipped away to eastern Virginia, where Union armies were trying to reach the Confederate capital of Richmond. Upon arriving in the region, he helped General Robert E. Lee's Army of Northern Virginia stop the Union invasion and force the Yankee (Union) Army to return to the North.

Lee's greatest lieutenant

Stonewall Jackson's spectacular Shenandoah Valley campaign made him famous across the country. In Southern communities, tales of his bold deeds instantly made him the first great Confederate military hero. Even more importantly, however, Jackson's performance in the valley made his troops extremely devoted to him. "There was a charm about General Jackson which inspired all private soldiers under his command with a sublime [perfect], unquestioned confidence in his leadership," said one rebel officer. "An indescribable something amounting almost to fascination on the part of his soldiers that induced [caused] them to do uncomplainingly whatever he would order." The only troops that Jackson did not get along with were his officers. He often refused to discuss military strategy with them, and punished them severely for even minor violations.

After joining Lee in June 1862, Jackson remained with the Army of Northern Virginia. Recognizing Jackson's bravery and tactical knowledge, Lee decided that he wanted to keep him in Virginia, where much of the war's heaviest fighting was taking place. Over the next several months, Jackson and his troops emerged as Lee's deadliest weapon. In battle after battle—including the Second Battle of Bull Run (August 1862), the Battle of Sharpsburg (also known as the Battle of Antietam; September 1862), and the Battle of Fredericksburg (December 1862)—Jackson and his troops delivered devastating blows against their Union enemies. These blows lifted Lee's Army of Northern Virginia to many of their greatest victories.

These triumphs increased Stonewall's legendary reputation in the South. But he refused to take any credit for these victories, even after his October 1862 promotion to lieutenant general gave him command of half of Lee's army. Instead, the deeply religious Jackson claimed that his successes were the will of God. Jackson saw the war "as a trial ordained [ordered] by God to test the faith of man," explained historian James I. Robertson Jr. "[According to Jackson], the Civil

The Strange Tale of Stonewall's Arm

When Stonewall Jackson was accidentally shot by his own troops at the Battle of Chancellorsville in May 1863, one of the bullets that struck him shattered the bone in his left arm below the shoulder. Doctors amputated the arm in an effort to save him, then rushed Jackson off to a safe spot so that he could recover. Their efforts failed, however, when pneumonia claimed the soldier's life a few days later. Jackson's body was then taken to Richmond, where more than twenty thousand mourners paid their respects to him before his burial in a Lexington cemetery.

Stonewall's amputated arm, meanwhile, remained at Chancellorsville. An aide bundled up the arm and carried it to a nearby graveyard, where it was buried on May 3. A short time later, a stone with an inscription that read "Arm of Stonewall Jackson May 3 1863" was placed on the burial spot. The arm lay undisturbed until 1921, when Marine Corps general Smedley D. Butler (1881–1940) expressed disbelief that Jackson's arm was really buried there. He dug up the spot, only to find the arm nestled in a box. Stunned and regretful of his actions, Butler reburied the arm and erected a bronze plaque honoring the spot. The plaque was eventually stolen, but the original stone marker continues to stand watch over the final resting place of Stonewall's arm.

War was a religious crusade [holy mission] to regain the Almighty's favor. Christian faith and the Confederate cause were, for Jackson, one and the same."

Battle of Chancellorsville

The greatest victory of the Lee-Jackson partnership came in early May 1863, when their sixty thousand–troop army whipped a Union force of 130,000 men at the Battle of Chancellorsville in Virginia. This dramatic rebel (Confederate) triumph against overwhelming odds was Lee's finest moment. He used his strong defensive position effectively, and devised clever troop movements that thoroughly confused his Union counterparts. The key to Lee's victory, however, was his decision to send Jackson on a deadly attack against the enemy's exposed flanks on May 2. This brutal assault struck a crushing blow against the Union Army, which retreated to the North a few days later.

Nonetheless, Stonewall's successful attack ended in tragedy for the South. As evening fell over the battlefield, a group of Confederate soldiers accidentally shot Jackson, who had been returning to camp after scouting out the enemy's position. At first, it appeared that he might recover from his three bullet wounds, even though doctors had to amputate his left arm. But Jackson developed pneumonia, which doctors could not treat at that time. His condition quickly worsened and he died on May 10, 1863.

The Stonewall Jackson Monument in Richmond, Virginia. *(Courtesy of the Library of Congress.)*

A Confederate legend

When Stonewall Jackson died, the entire South went into mourning. "The affections of every household in the [Confederate] nation were twined about this great and unselfish warrior," stated the *Richmond Daily Dispatch*. "He has fallen, and a nation weeps." Historian James I. Robertson called Jackson's death "the greatest personal loss [the Confederacy] would ever know. . . . The effect on the civilian population could only be called paralyzing."

Stonewall's death stunned his fellow rebel soldiers as well. "A greater sense of loss and deeper grief never followed the death of mortal man," wrote one veteran of the Stonewall Brigade. "Under him we had never suffered defeat. . . . We were the machine he needed to thresh [process] his grain, and the machine must be in order. We knew he would not needlessly risk our lives, and we knew that when needful to accomplish an object, our lives were as nothing, success was all that counted. We had a confidence in him that knew no bounds, and he knew and appreciated it. He was a soldier, and a great one, to our cause; his loss was irreparable."

Where to Learn More

Alexander, Bevin. *Lost Victories: The Military Genius of Stonewall Jackson.* New York: Holt, 1992.

Bennett, Barbara J. *Stonewall Jackson: Lee's Greatest Lieutenant.* Englewood Cliffs, NJ: Silver Burdett Press, 1991.

Farwell, Bryon. *Stonewall: A Biography of General Thomas J. Jackson.* New York: Norton, 1992.

Pflueger, Lynda. *Stonewall Jackson: Confederate General.* Springfield, NJ: Enslow, 1997.

Robertson, James I., Jr. *Stonewall Jackson: The Man, the Soldier, the Legend.* New York: Macmillan, 1997.

Royster, Charles. *The Destructive War: William Tecumseh Sherman, Stonewall Jackson, and the Americans.* New York: Knopf, 1991.

Southern California Stonewall Jackson Society. *Stonewall Jackson Homepage.* [Online] http://home.san.rr.com/stonewall/ (accessed on October 10, 1999).

Stonewall Jackson House. [Online] http://www.stonewalljackson.org/ (accessed on October 10, 1999).

Andrew Johnson

Born December 29, 1808
Raleigh, North Carolina
Died July 31, 1875
Greeneville, Tennessee

Seventeenth president of the United States

Became the first president to face impeachment when Congress disagreed with his Reconstruction policies

ndrew Johnson became president of the United States in
April 1865, when **Abraham Lincoln** (1809–1865; see entry) was assassinated. He took charge of the country just as the Civil War ended and presided over the difficult period in American history known as Reconstruction (1865–1877). A Southerner by birth, Johnson soon pardoned (officially forgave) Confederate officials and established lenient (easy) conditions for the Southern states to return to the Union. Many Northerners, and especially Republican leaders in the U.S. Congress, worried that Johnson's Reconstruction policies would allow Confederate leaders to return to power and continue to discriminate against blacks. Congress ended up putting its own policies into effect, while Johnson fought them every step of the way. In 1868, Congressional leaders impeached the president (brought him up on legal charges in an attempt to remove him from office), but Johnson kept his job by a single vote.

"I am unwilling, of my own volition, to walk outside of the Union which has been the result of a Constitution made by the patriots of the Revolution."

Andrew Johnson. *(Courtesy of the National Archives and Records Administration.)*

A poor Southern boy

Andrew Johnson was born on December 29, 1808, in a log cabin in the small town of Raleigh, North Carolina. He was the third child born to Jacob Johnson, who worked at various odd jobs, and Mary McDonough ("Polly") Johnson, who worked as a seamstress and laundress. His family was very poor, and the situation only got worse after Jacob Johnson died when Andrew was three years old.

Johnson resented the fact that the wealthy residents of Raleigh looked down upon him. But that did not prevent him from looking down upon black people. "As a poor white boy in a small Southern town, he could not help but realize his lowly position," Hans L. Trefousse wrote in *Andrew Johnson: A Biography*. "Yet, poor though he was, Andrew must also have realized that he was not at the very bottom of the social scale. After all, he was white, a fact that gave him a standing immeasurably higher than that of Raleigh's numerous blacks. . . . Exposed to these attitudes at an early age, Johnson was never able to shake them off."

Johnson's mother could not afford to send him to school, so instead she arranged for him to become an apprentice to the town's tailor. The tailor would provide Johnson with food, clothing, and a place to live, and would teach him the trade of tailoring. In exchange, Johnson would work without pay until he was twenty-one years old. The only thing Johnson liked about this arrangement was that wealthy and educated people often came into the tailor shop. He listened carefully when they argued about politics or read aloud to the tailors as they worked. He was very eager to learn to read and write. But for the most part his apprenticeship was a negative experience. The tailor was very strict with him and made the restless young boy work twelve hours per day. In 1824, Johnson ran away.

On his own at the age of sixteen, Johnson made it as far as Laurens, South Carolina. He lived there for two years and worked in a local tailor shop. In his free time, he read constantly in order to educate himself. He returned to Raleigh briefly and tried to pay his old boss to release him from the apprenticeship contract, but the tailor refused. Then Johnson decided to leave North Carolina for good. With his family in tow, he moved to Greeneville, Tennessee. He soon fell in love with Eliza McCardle, daughter of the local shoemaker, and the two were married on May 17, 1827. They eventually had five children together, three sons and two daughters.

A self-made man

Johnson continued working as a tailor in Greeneville and soon earned a good reputation. Before long, he was able to open his own tailor shop and hire other tailors to work for him. Over time, he earned enough money to buy some property and make other investments. Johnson also continued his education during this time with the help of his wife, who had attended school. He gradually grew more confident about voicing his opinion on issues. One day, a customer in the tailor shop who disagreed with Johnson's opinions challenged him to a public debate. Johnson discovered that he excelled at public speaking and won the debate. He soon joined a debating society to improve his skills further.

In 1834, Johnson launched his political career as mayor of Greeneville. He was proud of the fact that he had raised himself from poverty to claim a position of importance in society. Like many other wealthy Southerners, he bought slaves to act as servants in his home. The following year, he went to Nashville, Tennessee, to represent Greeneville in the state legislature. Over the next few years, Johnson gained a reputation as a defender of the interests of the poor whites against wealthy landowners.

In 1843, the popular and ambitious young Democrat was elected to the U.S. Congress. He ended up serving five terms in the House of Representatives. He was best known for his support of the Homestead Act, which would grant 160 acres of public land in the West to any family that wanted to settle it. Many wealthy Southerners and fellow Democrats opposed this idea. Some of them wanted the Western lands for themselves, while others wanted the government to sell the land rather than giving it away. But Johnson felt it was important for poor people to have access to land of their own so that they would be able to improve their lives, as he had done. He continued pushing the bill until it finally passed many years later.

In 1853, Johnson ran for the office of governor of Tennessee. He promoted himself as a self-made man and a model for poor youths to follow. During his election campaign, he declared his belief that "Democracy is a ladder . . . one up which all, in proportion to their merit, may ascend." Johnson won the election that year and was reelected to a second term two years later. One of his main acts as governor was to pass tax legislation that advanced public education in the state.

An unlikely Union supporter

In 1857, Johnson returned to Washington, D.C., to represent Tennessee in the U.S. Senate. This was a time of great political tension in the United States. For years, the Northern and Southern sections of the country had been arguing over several issues, including slavery. Growing numbers of Northerners believed that slavery was wrong. Some people wanted to outlaw it, while others wanted to prevent it from spreading beyond the Southern states where it was already allowed. But slavery played a big role in the Southern economy and culture. As a result, many Southerners felt threatened by Northern efforts to contain slavery. They believed that each state should decide for itself whether to allow slavery. They did not want the national government to pass laws that would interfere with their traditional way of life.

Johnson did not support the efforts of Northerners to abolish (put an end to) slavery. Like many Southerners, he believed that black people were inferior to white people. He thought that individual states should decide the issue for themselves. But Johnson also resented the power held by wealthy landowners in the South, and he knew that these landowners used slave labor to maintain their power. By 1861, the ongoing dispute over slavery had convinced several Southern states to secede from (leave) the United States and form a new country that allowed slavery, called the Confederate States of America. Tennessee was one of the Southern states that joined the Confederacy. Johnson opposed his state's decision to secede. In fact, he became the only Southern senator to retain his seat in Congress following the secession of his state.

"I am unwilling, of my own volition [will], to walk outside of the Union which has been the result of a Constitution made by the patriots of the Revolution," he stated. "I entreat [urgently request] every man throughout the nation who is a patriot . . . to come forward . . . and rally around the altar of our common country, and swear by our God, and all that is sacred and holy, that the Constitution shall be saved, and the Union preserved."

Northern politicians refused to let the Southern states leave the Union without a fight. As a result, the two sides went to war in April 1861. Within a year, the Union forces had taken control of large sections of territory in Tennessee. President Abraham Lincoln rewarded Johnson's loyalty to the Union by making him a brigadier general and appointing him military governor of Tennessee. His job involved setting up a pro-Union government and rewriting the state's constitution so that Tennessee could be restored to the Union.

Johnson's views on slavery began to change during this time. Although he still believed that whites were superior to blacks, his desire to preserve the United States as a democratic country became more important to him than his desire to preserve slavery. "I am for my Government with or without slavery," he stated in 1863, "but if either the Government or slavery must perish [die], I say give me the Government and let the negroes go." People in the South reacted to Johnson's change of heart by calling him a traitor. But it only increased his popularity in the North.

President of the United States during Reconstruction

In 1864, President Lincoln faced a difficult race for reelection. He and his advisors decided that he could improve his chances by choosing a vice presidential candidate who would balance the ticket. They decided that Johnson, as a Southerner and a Democrat, would appeal to many voters who did not support Lincoln, a Northerner and a Republican. Johnson eagerly accepted the nomination. After Lincoln won the election that November, Johnson was sworn in as vice president on March 4, 1865. Unfortunately, he had been ill for several weeks before this time, and he drank several

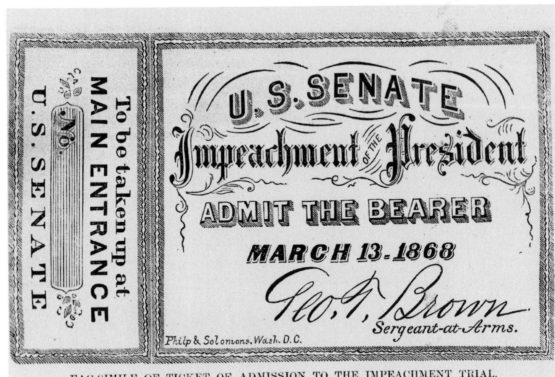

FAC-SIMILE OF TICKET OF ADMISSION TO THE IMPEACHMENT TRIAL.

A facsimile of a ticket to Andrew Johnson's impeachment trial in 1868. *(Reproduced by permission of AP/Wide World Photos.)*

glasses of whiskey to steady his nerves before he appeared at the inauguration (swearing-in) ceremony. He then proceeded to give a rambling speech that many observers found disgraceful and offensive. But Lincoln defended his vice president, saying "I have known Andy Johnson for many years; he made a bad slip the other day, but you need not be scared; Andy ain't a drunkard."

The Civil War ended a few weeks later, when the Confederate Army surrendered to Union forces. For a brief time, people across the North celebrated their victory and looked forward to beginning the process of healing the nation. But on April 14, a deranged (insane) Confederate supporter shot Lincoln as he attended a play in Washington. The president died the next day, and the mood in the North quickly changed from relief and happiness to grief and anger. Johnson took charge of the country as it entered the difficult period of American history called Reconstruction.

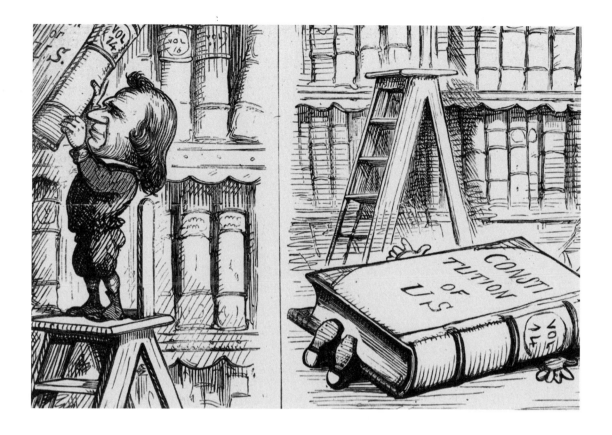

The United States continued to struggle with important and complicated issues after the Civil War ended. For example, government officials had to decide whether to punish the Confederate leaders, what process to use to readmit the Southern states to the Union, and how much assistance to provide in securing equal rights for the freed slaves. From the beginning of his term of office, Johnson made it clear that he intended to control the process of Reconstruction. He believed that restoring the Union was his job rather than the U.S. Congress's. He began implementing his own Reconstruction programs during the summer of 1865, while Congress was in recess (Congress often adjourns to let its members take time off between legislative sessions).

Johnson started out by following the course he believed Lincoln had planned to take. He pardoned many Confederate leaders and set lenient conditions for the Southern states to return to the Union. The former Confederate states

A political cartoon shows Andrew Johnson being crushed by the U.S. Constitution, which allows for removal of federal officals in certain instances. *(Reproduced by permission of Archive Photos.)*

Rutherford B. Hayes, the President Who Ended Reconstruction

When Rutherford B. Hayes became president in 1877, it marked the end of the difficult period in American history known as Reconstruction. The United States continued to deal with complicated issues after the Civil War ended. For example, Northern officials had to decide whether to punish Confederate leaders, how much assistance to provide in securing equal rights for freed slaves, and what process to use to readmit the Southern states to the Union.

Beginning in 1866, Republican members of the U.S. Congress put harsh policies in place to reduce the power of Southern landowners and give black men an opportunity to vote and hold public office. They sent federal troops into the South to enforce their policies. But white Southerners reacted strongly against these Reconstruction measures. In many cases, they used violence to intimidate blacks and prevent them from exercising their rights. This was the political climate when Hayes became president in a hotly contested election.

Rutherford Birchard Hayes was born in Delaware, Ohio, in 1822. His career began as an attorney in 1845. By the mid-1850s, Hayes became caught up in the national debate over slavery, adopting a moderate antislavery position. He hoped that the North and South could reach a compromise on the issue, but this soon proved impossible. When the Civil War began in 1861, Hayes joined the Union Army. As an officer in the Twenty-Third Ohio Volunteer Infantry, he earned the respect of his men

and was wounded in combat several times. Toward the end of the war, members of Ohio's Republican Party nominated him to represent Cincinnati in the U.S. Congress. Hayes accepted the nomination, but refused to leave the army to come home and campaign. "An officer fit for duty who at this crisis would abandon his post to electioneer for a seat in Congress ought to be scalped," he stated. He won anyway.

When the war ended in 1865, Hayes resigned from the army with the rank of major general. He took his seat in Congress that December, just as radical members of the Republican Party began fighting to take control of the Reconstruction process from Democratic president Andrew Johnson. Immediately after taking office, Johnson had pardoned (officially forgiven) many former Confederates and established lenient (easy) conditions for the Southern states to return to the Union. But Hayes and the Republicans worried that the president's policies would allow Confederates to return to power in the South and continue to discriminate against black people. As a result, Congress took charge of Reconstruction and sent federal troops into the South to enforce its policies.

In 1868, Hayes was elected governor of Ohio. In an age of widespread political corruption, his administration was known for its freedom from scandal. During his two terms in office, he reformed the state's prison system and helped found Ohio State University. In 1871, he declined

Rutherford B. Hayes. *(Courtesy of the Library of Congress.)*

to run for a third term and instead attempted to regain his seat in Congress. He lost, but in 1875, he ran for governor again. Upon winning the election, he immediately became one of the leading candidates for his party's presidential nomination.

Hayes won the Republican nomination for president in the election of 1876. His opponent in the general election was the Democratic governor of New York, Samuel J. Tilden (1814–1886). Most Northerners voted for Hayes, and most Southerners voted for Tilden. The election ended up being the closest in history. Tilden won the popular vote—4,284,020 people voted for him, compared to 4,036,572 for Hayes. But the actual winner of presidential elections is determined by an institution known as the electoral college. Each state receives a certain number of electoral votes depending on its population. When the electoral votes were counted, Tilden had 184 and Hayes had 165, and 20 votes were in dispute. A candidate needed 185 electoral votes to win the presidency, so neither man could be declared the winner.

The controversy came down to three Southern states that still had mixed-race Reconstruction governments intact—South Carolina, Florida, and Louisiana. Hayes needed the electoral votes of all three states in order to become president. Congress set up a special committee to examine the election results in these states. But it was difficult to tell for certain which candidate had won because of widespread violence during the elections.

Eventually, the parties arranged a compromise. The Democrats would allow Hayes to become president if he agreed to remove federal troops from the South. This meant that Republicans would lose control of the last three Southern states to white supremacists (people who believe that whites are superior to blacks). The arrangement became known as the Compromise of 1877. When Hayes removed federal troops from the South, this marked the end of Reconstruction.

Hayes served only one term as president. He died in 1893 after suffering a heart attack.

had to prepare new state constitutions that abolished slavery and met a number of other conditions. Then they could elect representatives to the federal government and be readmitted to the Union. But black people were not allowed to vote or to serve as representatives under the president's plan. Johnson was reluctant to impose the power of the federal government on the South in order to guarantee equality for blacks.

By the time Congress came back in session, Johnson's Reconstruction policies had been in effect for nearly six months. Many Republican members of Congress felt that the president was too lenient toward the South. They worried that his policies would allow Confederate leaders to return to power and continue to discriminate against black people. Congress set up a Committee on Reconstruction to study the effects of Johnson's policies. The committee heard numerous stories of discrimination and violence against blacks in the South. As a result, the U.S. Congress took control of the Reconstruction process in 1866 and sent federal troops into the Southern states to enforce their policies.

Faces impeachment over disputes with Congress

As Congress began implementing its Reconstruction program, some members were willing to compromise with President Johnson. But Johnson refused to accept any changes to his lenient policies toward the South. He believed that some of his Republican opponents were engaged in a conspiracy to overthrow him, and he grew more and more determined to resist. Johnson vetoed (rejected) many bills passed by Congress, although Congress was usually able to gather enough votes (two-thirds of its members) to pass the bills over the president's veto. As the struggle for power continued, even the more moderate members of Congress began to believe that the president would do anything to destroy their plans. In 1868, Republican leaders started a movement to remove Johnson from office.

The Constitution says that all federal officials can be impeached (brought up on legal charges) and removed from elected office if they are found guilty of "treason, bribery, or other high crimes and misdemeanors." All of the branches of the federal government have roles in an impeachment trial.

The House of Representatives brings the charges and acts as prosecutors. The chief justice of the Supreme Court presides over the trial as a judge. The Senate hears the case and votes as a jury. Two-thirds of the senators present must vote to convict in order to remove the impeached official from office.

Congress began the process of impeachment on February 22, 1868. It marked the first time in history that an American president had been impeached. Even though the charges against him did not really meet the conditions for impeachment, Johnson was so unpopular by this time that the outcome of the trial was uncertain. The trial before the Senate continued for more than two months and captured the attention of the entire country. Finally, the senators voted on the charges on May 16. Johnson was found not guilty by one vote and remained in office.

The remainder of Johnson's term in office was uneventful. Famed Union general **Ulysses S. Grant** (1822–1885; see entry) was elected to replace him as president later in 1868. Grant took charge of Reconstruction during his two terms in office. In 1877, Rutherford B. Hayes (1822–1893) became president and removed federal troops from the South to end Reconstruction. Meanwhile, Johnson returned to Tennessee but soon grew restless. He became determined to continue his career in politics. He ran unsuccessfully for the U.S. Congress in 1871 and 1873. He finally won his old Senate seat back in 1875, but he suffered a stroke shortly after taking office and died on July 31, 1875. Across the country, the reaction to his death was mixed. Northern newspapers praised his loyalty to the Union during the Civil War, while Southern newspapers praised his service to the South during Reconstruction. "For generations after his death, his reputation has alternately suffered and flourished," Trefousse explained. "After all is said and done, however, it is clear that although the seventeenth president unquestionably undermined the Reconstruction process and left a legacy of racism, he was an able politician."

Where to Learn More

HarpWeek. *The Impeachment of Andrew Johnson.* [Online] http://www.impeach-andrewjohnson.com/ (accessed on October 10, 1999).

Malone, Mary. *Andrew Johnson.* Berkeley Heights, NJ: Enslow, 1999.

McKitrick, Eric L. *Andrew Johnson and Reconstruction.* Chicago: University of Chicago Press, 1960. Reprint, New York: Oxford University Press, 1988.

National Park Foundation. *Andrew Johnson National Historic Site.* [Online] http://www.nationalparks.org/guide/parks/andrew-johns-1928.htm (accessed on October 10, 1999).

President Andrew Johnson Museum and Library. [Online] http://www.inusa.com/tour/tn/knoxvill/johnson.htm (accessed on October 10, 1999).

Simpson, Brooks D. *The Reconstruction Presidents.* Lawrence: University Press of Kansas, 1998.

Trefousse, Hans L. *Andrew Johnson: A Biography.* New York: W. W. Norton, 1989. Reprint, Newtown, CT: American Political Biography Press, 1998.

Trefousse, Hans L. *Impeachment of a President: Andrew Johnson, the Blacks, and Reconstruction.* Knoxville: University of Tennessee Press, 1975. Reprint, New York: Fordham University Press, 1999.

Joseph E. Johnston

Born February 3, 1807
Cherry Grove, Virginia
Died March 21, 1891
District of Columbia

Confederate general
Led Army of Tennessee against Union
general William T. Sherman's forces during
Atlanta campaign

J oseph Johnston's reputation as a Civil War general is a mixed one. On the one hand, he became known as one of the Confederacy's most sensible and intelligent military leaders. Careful and crafty, he never sent his troops into battle rashly. This reluctance to commit troops to battle without good cause understandably made Johnston very popular with many of the soldiers under his command. But critics of Johnston argued that he avoided conflict on too many occasions, such as during the 1863 Vicksburg Campaign and the 1864 Atlanta Campaign. This criticism, coupled with his bitter feud with Confederate president **Jefferson Davis** (1808–1889; see entry) has made Johnston's Civil War performance a subject of continued debate among students and historians.

Born and raised in Virginia

Joseph Eggleston Johnston was born in Virginia in 1807 into a powerful and respected family. His father was Peter Johnston, a judge and congressman who had fought in the Revolutionary War on behalf of the rebellious American

Johnston "was loved, respected, admired; yea, almost worshiped by his troops. I do not believe there was a soldier in his army but would gladly have died for him."

One of Johnston's soldiers

Joseph E. Johnston.
(Reproduced by permission of the National Portrait Gallery.)

241

colonies. The Revolutionary War—also known as the War for Independence—was waged from 1776 to 1783 and eventually resulted in American independence from British rule. Joseph Johnston's mother, meanwhile, was the niece of Patrick Henry (1736–1799), one of the most famous American heroes of the Revolutionary War.

Johnston grew up in Abingdon County, Virginia, attending classes in the state's finest schools. In 1825, he left home for the U.S. Military Academy at West Point in New York. Johnston excelled at his studies at the prestigious military school. He also became friends with a group of fellow cadets (military students) that included a young **Robert E. Lee** (1807–1870; see entry) during his stay at West Point.

Early military experiences

In 1829, Johnston graduated from the academy and joined the U.S. Army. He spent most of the next decade at frontier outposts and in Florida. During his time in Florida, he took part in the expedition through the state of explorer John Wesley Powell (1834–1902) and participated in the so-called Seminole Wars (1835–42). This war between the U.S. military and the Seminole Indians eventually forced the Indians off of their ancestral homelands and onto reservations in Oklahoma.

In 1845, Johnston married Lydia McLane, a member of a prominent Delaware family. A year later he traveled west to fight on behalf of the United States in the Mexican War (1846–48). This war was a struggle between Mexico and the United States for ownership of vast expanses of land in the West. Wounded twice during the conflict, Johnston impressed his commanding officers with his coolness and bravery. The Mexican War ended in 1848 when America forced its southern neighbor to give up its claims on California, New Mexico, and other western lands in exchange for $15 million.

With the conclusion of the Mexican War, Johnston returned to the army's topographical engineering branch. This division was responsible for exploring and surveying the geography of the growing nation (topography is the practice of creating maps that show exact geographic features of a region). In 1855, however, Johnston received a promotion to lieutenant colonel in order to command a newly created army cavalry unit known as the First Cavalry. Five years later he successfully pushed to be appointed as the army's quartermaster general when that position became vacant. Johnston thus became responsible for supervising all efforts to provide soldiers with food, clothing, and equipment. He also was promoted to brigadier general around this time.

In the spring of 1861, though, Johnston abruptly left the ranks of the U.S. Army when the nation's Northern and Southern regions took up arms against one another. The arrival of war did not really surprise Johnston. After all, relations between the two sides had become tattered by years of bitter arguments and threats over a number of issues, especially slavery. Northern states wanted to abolish slavery because many of their citizens thought that it was a cruel and evil institution. The agriculture-based Southern economy had become extremely dependent on slavery over the years, though, and white Southerners worried that their way of life would collapse if slavery was abolished (eliminated). America's westward expansion during this time made this dispute even worse, since both sides wanted to spread their way of life—and their political views—into the new territories and states. The two sides finally went to war in early 1861, after the Southern states tried to secede from (leave) the Union and form a new country where slavery was allowed, called the Confederate States of America.

Early Civil War success

Johnston viewed the South's attempt to secede from the United States as a terrible mistake. Ignoring early offers of generalship in the Confederate Army, he did not join the rebel (Confederate) military until April 1861, when his home state of Virginia announced its intention to secede. But Johnston left the U.S. Army with a heavy heart. As he submitted his resignation to Union secretary of war Simon Cameron (1799–1889), he confessed his belief that secession "was ruin in every sense of the word." Upon arriving in Richmond a few days later, he was made a brigadier general in the Confederate Army.

Initially assigned to defend Harpers Ferry, Virginia, from Union invaders, Johnston played a major role in helping the South win the first major battle of the Civil War in July 1861. Using clever maneuvers to escape from an advancing Federal army, he quickly transported thousands of soldiers by railroad to Manassas Junction, Virginia, where rebel troops under the command of General **Pierre G. T. Beauregard** (1818–1893; see entry) were being challenged by a larger Union force led by General Irvin McDowell (1818–1885). Johnston's troops arrived just in time to turn the battle in favor of the South. Combining their two armies, Johnston and Beauregard produced a sloppy but decisive victory over McDowell's troops. This triumph at the First Battle of Manassas (known as the First Battle of Bull Run in the North) gave Southerners confidence that they could fend off Northern attempts to restore the Union.

The Johnston-Davis feud

The victory at Manassas made Johnston one of the Confederacy's first military heroes. Six weeks later, he and four other Confederate officers were promoted to the newly created rank of full general. Johnston, however, expressed great anger with the details of these promotions. As he understood Confederate law, the seniority of Confederate military officers of the same rank was supposed to be based on the relative position they held back in the federal army. According to Johnston, this meant that he should be "top-ranked" of all the new Confederate generals. But Confederate president Jefferson Davis ranked Johnston fourth in seniority, ahead of only one other general.

Johnston responded to news of the promotions by writing Davis a furious letter. He claimed that the president's rankings had been made "in violation of my rights as an officer, of the plighted [promised] faith of the Confederacy and of the Constitution and laws of the land." Johnston concluded his note by stating that "I now and here declare my claim that . . . I still rightfully hold the rank of first general in the armies of the Southern Confederacy." But Davis refused to reconsider his decision. In fact, he sent Johnston an insulting reply in which he called the general's arguments and statements "one-sided" and "as unfounded [without a factual base] as they are unbecoming [unattractive]."

Prior to the promotion controversy, relations between the two men had been cool and mildly distrustful. But the uproar over Johnston's ranking dramatically worsened tensions between the two men. In fact, it created a cloud of animosity between Davis and Johnston that remained in place for years to come. Stubborn and proud, the two men spent the rest of the war believing the worst about each other.

Service in the West

Johnston's next major engagement took place in the spring of 1862, when Union general **George B. McClellan** (1826–1885; see entry) launched his so-called Peninsula Campaign to capture the Confederate capital of Richmond. By late May, McClellan's army had advanced to Fair Oaks, only a few miles outside of Richmond. But a large Confederate force under Johnston's command awaited the Federal army there. On May 31, the two armies clashed together in a bloody struggle for control of the Virginia peninsula. The two-day battle (known as the Battle of Seven Pines in the South) ended in a virtual stalemate (deadlock), with neither side able to gain an advantage. Johnston, though, was seriously wounded in the clash and had to turn command of his Army of Northern Virginia over to General Robert E. Lee. One month later, Lee forced McClellan to end his offensive campaign by defeating the Union general in a series of fierce clashes that came to be known as the Seven Days' Battles. Lee then followed up that victory with a series of other triumphs. Lee's performance convinced Davis to give him command of the Army of Northern Virginia for the rest of the war.

Johnston spent the last months of 1862 recovering from the wounds he suffered at Fair Oaks. When Johnston returned to active duty in November, Davis sent him to the war's western theater (the area of the country between the Mississippi River and the Appalachian Mountains). Despite growing doubts about Johnston's abilities, Davis wanted him to take general command of the two main Confederate armies in the region. The president hoped that Johnston would be able to increase the effectiveness of the two armies by coordinating their actions. Johnston, though, complained about his new assignment. He told Davis that his command was "useless. . . . The great distance between the [Confederate] Armies of Mississippi and Tennessee, and the fact that they had different objects and adversaries [enemies], made it impossible to combine their action."

Johnston, Davis, and other Confederate officials continued to argue and debate about strategy, military authority, and other issues throughout the first few months of 1863. Union general **Ulysses S. Grant** (1822–1885; see entry), meanwhile, launched a major offensive against Vicksburg, Mississippi, a strategically important Confederate stronghold. Grant knew that if he could seize the city from the Confederacy, the North would control the entire length of the Mississippi River.

By May 1863, Johnston was certain that he did not have enough troops to save Vicksburg from Grant's advancing army. He told Lieutenant General John C. Pemberton (1814–1881), the commander of the Confederate garrison (military post) within the city, to evacuate his army before it was lost to Grant. But Pemberton remained in Vicksburg after receiving orders from Davis to hold the city at all costs.

The struggle for Vicksburg ended in disaster for the Confederacy. In late May, Grant ordered his army to surround the city and stop all shipments of food and other supplies. This strategy, known as a siege, was intended to starve Pemberton's army into surrendering the city. Within a matter of weeks, Grant's siege had created great hunger and misery within Vicksburg. Johnston tried to come up with a plan to lift the siege, but the small size of his army prevented him from posing any significant threat to Grant's much larger force. Pemberton finally surrendered on July 4, giving the North control of both the city and the Mississippi River.

When Davis learned that Vicksburg had fallen into Union hands, he placed the blame squarely on the shoulders of Johnston. The Confederate president and many other people believed that Johnston should have offered more resistance to Grant. They charged that Johnston had been too cautious and timid in his actions. Johnston and his supporters, meanwhile, blamed flawed strategies devised by Davis and other Confederate officials for the loss of the city. They also claimed that Johnston's decision to avoid an all-out fight with Grant had kept the South from losing thousands of men in a hopeless cause. Not surprisingly, the debate over who was to blame for the loss of Vicksburg increased the level of hostility (ill will) and distrust that existed between Davis and Johnston. In fact, one acquaintance of Johnston's commented that from this time forward, Johnston's "hatred of Jeff Davis became a religion with him."

Johnston replaces Bragg

During the fall of 1863, Davis relieved Johnston of many of his command responsibilities. He felt that Johnston's tendency to retreat and avoid combat unless certain of victory was hurting the Southern cause. In November 1863, though, Davis reluctantly appointed Johnston to command the Confederate Army of Tennessee, the South's last major army in the western theater.

The Army of Tennessee was a tough and battle-hardened force. Over the course of 1863, however, it had been badly led by Confederate general **Braxton Bragg** (1817–1876; see entry). By the time Davis finally replaced Bragg, morale among the troops had plummeted to a very low level.

Upon arriving in Dalton, Georgia, to take command of the Army of Tennessee in December 1863, Johnston immediately addressed the lingering morale problem. During the long winter months, he took steps to improve his troops' food rations and living conditions. He also worked hard to reassure the soldiers that his command style would be different than the stern one adopted by Bragg. "[Johnston] passed through the ranks of the common soldiers, shaking hands with every one he met," recalled one soldier. "He restored the soldier's pride; he brought the manhood back to the private's bosom. . . . He was loved, respected, admired; yea, almost worshiped by his troops. I do not believe there was a soldier in his army but would gladly have died for him."

Sherman's Atlanta Campaign

In May 1864, Johnston faced his first major test as commander of the Confederacy's Army of Tennessee. At that

A view of Peachtree Street in Atlanta, Georgia, in 1864, the year before Union general William Sherman marched into that region. *(Photograph by George N. Barnard. Reproduced by permission of the National Portrait Gallery.)*

time, a major Union army under the command of General **William T. Sherman** (1820–1891; see entry) marched into Georgia in order to destroy Johnston's sixty thousand-man army. The North believed that if the Confederate Army of Tennessee could be wiped out, Union control of the West would be complete, and weakening Southern support for the war might collapse altogether.

As Sherman's force of one hundred thousand troops began its pursuit of Johnston, Davis and Johnston once again quarreled about Confederate strategy. Davis and other officials wanted Johnston to strike against Sherman and recapture the state of Tennessee in an offensive campaign. Johnston, however, felt that his best course of action was to engage in a series of strategic retreats against his more powerful opponent. The general thought that if Sherman used up some of his troops in failed attacks, he might eventually be able to launch a counterattack. In addition, Johnston believed that if Sherman failed to gain a major victory during the summer of 1864, Northern voters might replace U.S. president **Abraham Lincoln** (1809–1865; see entry) in the fall elections with a member of the antiwar Democratic Party who would grant independence to the Confederacy in exchange for peace.

Throughout the months of May and June, Sherman moved his army southward in an attempt to smash the Confederate Army of Tennessee. The two armies engaged in countless bloody skirmishes during this period, but Johnston quickly and skillfully avoided all efforts to trap him. Instead, he steadily retreated deeper into Georgia, even as President Davis and other Confederate officials urged him to turn and attack the Yankee (Union) invaders.

By mid-July, Sherman had seized large sections of Georgia. Johnston's Army of Tennessee had been pushed backward to the outskirts of Atlanta, one of the Confederacy's last remaining major cities. Johnston's defensive maneuvers had enabled him to keep most of his army intact, but Davis and many other Confederate officials were very unhappy with his performance. They openly worried that Johnston might give up Atlanta without a fight, and became very frustrated when the general stubbornly refused to tell them about his plans.

On July 17, Davis finally removed Johnston from command and replaced him with **John Bell Hood** (1831–1879; see entry), an officer with the Army of Tennessee who had a reputation as a fierce and aggressive fighter. The switch delighted Sherman, who had grown weary of pursuing Johnston. "I confess I was pleased at the change [in the Confederate command]," he wrote in a letter to his wife.

Hood promptly ordered a series of attacks on the Union Army, but Sherman and his troops smashed all of these attacks. Within a few months, Sherman had captured Atlanta and launched a devastating campaign deep into the heart of the South. Hood, meanwhile, took his army into Tennessee, where it was torn to shreds by Union forces.

End of the war

After being removed from command, Johnston spent the last part of 1864 traveling around the South with his wife.

In February 1865, General Lee convinced Davis to recall Johnston to active service in the disintegrating Confederate Army. Johnston was ordered to assume command of rebel troops in the Carolinas and halt Sherman's advance on Richmond. By this point, however, no Southern army was capable of stopping Union forces as they rolled across the Confederacy. Lee surrendered his Army of Northern Virginia to Union forces on April 9, 1865. Eighteen days later, Johnston signed final surrender terms in a meeting with Sherman. Johnston's surrender marked the end of his military career.

In the years following the Civil War, Johnston became involved in the insurance and railroad industries. He also served his home state of Virginia as a member of the U.S. House of Representatives from 1879 to 1881. In addition, he continued his long-running feud with Davis in a series of articles and memoirs. He died in the District of Columbia in 1891.

Where to Learn More

Connelly, Thomas L. *Autumn of Glory: The Army of Tennessee, 1862–1865*. Baton Rouge: Louisiana State University Press, 1971.

Johnston, Joseph E. *Narrative of Military Operations During the Civil War*. New York: D. Appleton & Co., 1874. Reprint, New York: Da Capo Press, 1990.

Newton, Steven H. *Joseph E. Johnston and the Defense of Richmond*. Lawrence: University Press of Kansas, 1998.

Symonds, Craig L. *Joseph E. Johnston: A Civil War Biography*. New York: Norton, 1992.

Woodworth, Steven E. *Jefferson Davis and His Generals*. Lawrence: University Press of Kansas, 1990.

Where to Learn More

The following list of resources focuses on material appropriate for middle school or high school students. Please note that the web site addresses were verified prior to publication, but are subject to change.

Books

Anders, Curt. *Hearts in Conflict: A One-Volume History of the Civil War.* Secaucus, NJ: Carol Pub. Group, 1994.

Anderson, Nancy Scott, and Dwight Anderson. *The Generals—Ulysses S. Grant and Robert E. Lee.* New York: Knopf, 1988.

Aptheker, Herbert. *Abolitionism: A Revolutionary Movement.* Boston: Twayne, 1989.

Basler, Roy P., ed. *The Collected Works of Abraham Lincoln.* New Brunswick, NJ: Rutgers University Press, 1953.

Berlin, Ira, Joseph P. Reidy, and Leslie S. Rowland, eds. *Freedom's Soldiers: The Black Military Experience in the Civil War.* New York: Cambridge University Press, 1998.

Blight, David W. *Frederick Douglass's Civil War: Keeping Faith in Jubilee.* Baton Rouge: Louisiana State University Press, 1989.

Bradford, Ned, ed. *Battles and Leaders of the Civil War.* New York: New American Library, 1984.

Buell, Thomas B. *The Warrior Generals: Combat Leadership in the Civil War.* New York: Crown, 1997.

Carter, Alden R. *The Civil War: American Tragedy.* New York: Franklin Watts, 1992.

Carter, Samuel. *The Last Cavaliers: Confederate and Union Cavalry in the Civil War.* St. Martin's Press, 1980.

Catton, Bruce. *The Centennial History of the Civil War.* 3 vols. Garden City, NY: Doubleday, 1961–65.

Catton, Bruce. *The Civil War.* Boston: Houghton Mifflin, 1960.

Chadwick, Bruce. *The Two American Presidents: A Dual Biography of Abraham Lincoln and Jefferson Davis.* Secaucus, NJ: Carol, 1999.

Chang, Ina. *A Separate Battle: Women and the Civil War.* New York: Scholastic, 1994.

Civil War Generals: An Illustrated Encyclopedia. New York: Gramercy, 1999.

Commager, Henry Steele. *The Blue and the Gray.* Indianapolis: Bobbs-Merrill, 1950.

Davis, William C. *The Commanders of the Civil War.* San Diego: Thunder Bay Press, 1999.

Davis, William C. *Jefferson Davis: The Man and His Hour.* New York: HarperCollins, 1991.

Donald, David Herbert. *Lincoln.* New York: Simon & Schuster, 1995.

Dowdey, Clifford. *Lee's Last Campaign: The Story of Lee and His Men against Grant.* Lincoln: University of Nebraska Press, 1993.

Foote, Shelby. *The Civil War: A Narrative.* 3 vols. New York: Random House, 1958–74.

Freeman, Douglas S. *Lee's Lieutenants.* 3 vols. New York: Scribner's, 1942–44.

Goen, C. C. *Broken Churches, Broken Nation.* Macon, GA: Mercer University Press, 1985.

Grant, Ulysses S. *Personal Memoirs of U. S. Grant.* New York: Library of America, 1990.

Green, Carl R., and William R. Sanford. *Confederate Generals of the Civil War.* Springfield, NJ: Enslow, 1998.

Green, Carl R., and William R. Sanford. *Union Generals of the Civil War.* Springfield, NJ: Enslow, 1998.

Grimsley, Mark. *The Hard Hand of War, Union Military Policy Toward Southern Civilians, 1861–1865.* New York: Cambridge University Press, 1995.

Gutman, Herbert G. *The Black Family in Slavery and Freedom.* New York: Pantheon, 1976.

Hargrove, Hondon B. *Black Union Soldiers in the Civil War.* Jefferson, NC: McFarland, 1988.

Harmon, Dan. *Civil War Generals.* Philadelphia: Chelsea House, 1997.

Harrell, Carolyn L. *When the Bells Tolled for Lincoln*. Macon, GA: Mercer University Press, 1997.

Haskins, J. *The Day Fort Sumter Was Fired On: A Photo History of the Civil War*. New York: Scholastic, 1995.

Hattaway, Herman. *Shades of Blue and Gray: An Introductory Military History of the Civil War*. Columbia: University of Missouri Press, 1997.

Hendrickson, Robert. *The Road to Appomattox*. New York: John Wiley & Sons, 1998.

Hennessey, John. *Return to Bull Run: The Campaign and Battle of Second Manassas*. New York: Simon & Schuster, 1992.

Holt, Michael F. *The Political Crisis of the 1850s*. New York: John Wiley & Sons, 1978.

Kunhardt, Philip B., Jr. *A New Birth of Freedom: Lincoln at Gettysburg*. Boston: Little, Brown, 1983.

Leonard, Elizabeth D. *All the Daring of the Soldier: Women of the Civil War Armies*. New York: W. W. Norton, 1999.

Lincoln, Abraham. *Abraham Lincoln: Speeches and Writings*. 2 vols. New York: Library of America, 1989.

Linderman, Gerald. *Embattled Courage: The Experience of Combat in the American Civil War*. New York: Free Press, 1987.

Litwack, Leon. *Been in the Storm So Long: The Aftermath of Slavery*. New York: Alfred A. Knopf, 1979.

Macdonald, John. *Great Battles of the Civil War*. New York: Macmillan, 1988.

Macmillan Encylopedia of the Confederacy. New York: Macmillan, 1998.

Massey, Mary Elizabeth. *Women in the Civil War*. Lincoln: University of Nebraska Press, 1966.

McFeely, William S. *Grant: A Biography*. New York: Norton, 1981.

McPherson, James M. *Battle Cry of Freedom*. New York: Oxford University Press, 1988.

McPherson, James M. *For Cause and Comrades: Why Men Fought in the Civil War*. New York: Oxford University Press, 1997.

McPherson, James M. *Ordeal by Fire: The Civil War and Reconstruction*. New York: Alfred A. Knopf, 1982.

McPherson, James M., ed. *Encyclopedia of Civil War Biographies*. Armonk, NY: Sharpe Reference, 2000.

Mitchell, Joseph B. *Military Leaders in the Civil War*. New York: Putnam, 1972.

Mitchell, Reid. *Civil War Soldiers: Their Expectations and Their Experiences*. New York: Viking, 1988.

Morris, Roy, Jr. *Sheridan: The Life and Wars of General Phil Sheridan*. New York: Crown, 1992.

Murphy, Jim. *The Long Road to Gettysburg*. New York: Scholastic, 1995.

Nolan, Alan T. *Lee Considered: General Robert E. Lee and Civil War History.* Chapel Hill: University of North Carolina Press, 1991.

Oates, Stephen B. *With Malice Toward None: The Life of Abraham Lincoln.* New York: Harper & Row, 1977.

Paludan, Phillip S. *The Presidency of Abraham Lincoln.* Lawrence: University Press of Kansas, 1994.

Potter, David M. *The Impending Crisis, 1848–1861.* New York: Harper & Row, 1976.

Ritter, Charles F., and Jon L. Wakelyn. *Leaders of the American Civil War.* Westport, CT: Greenwood Press, 1998.

Royster, Charles. *The Destructive War: William Tecumseh Sherman, Stonewall Jackson, and the Americans.* New York: Alfred A. Knopf, 1991.

Sandburg, Carl. *Abraham Lincoln: The War Years.* 4 vols. New York: Harcourt Brace, 1939.

Sifakis, Stewart. *Who Was Who in the Civil War.* New York: Facts on File, 1988.

Stewart, James Brewer. *Holy Warriors: The Abolitionists and American Slavery.* New York: Hill & Wang, 1976.

Stokesbury, James L. *A Short History of the Civil War.* New York: William Morrow, 1995.

Thomas, Emory. *The Confederate Nation, 1861–1865.* New York: Harper & Row, 1979.

Tracey, Patrick Austin. *Military Leaders of the Civil War.* New York: Facts on File, 1993.

Trelease, Allen W. *Reconstruction: The Great Experiment.* New York: Harper & Row, 1971.

Trudeau, Noah Andre. *Like Men of War: Black Troops in the Civil War, 1862–1865.* Boston: Little, Brown, 1998.

Venet, Wendy Hamand. *Neither Ballots Nor Bullets: Women Abolitionists and the Civil War.* Charlottesville: University Press of Virginia, 1991.

Ward, Geoffrey C. *The Civil War: An Illustrated History.* New York: Alfred A. Knopf, 1990.

Woodworth, Steven E. *Jefferson Davis and His Generals.* Lawrence: University Press of Kansas, 1990.

World Wide Web

American Civil War/Conflict Between the States. http://americanhistory. miningco.com/education/history/americanhistory/msub13.htm (accessed on October 20, 1999).

American Civil War Homepage. http://sunsite.utk.edu/civil-war (accessed on October 20, 1999).

American Civil War Resources on the Internet. http://www.janke.washcoll. edu/civilwar/civilwar.htm (accessed on October 20, 1999).

Civil War Music and Poetry and Music of the War Between the States. http://users.erols.com/kfraser/ (accessed on October 20, 1999).

Library of Congress. *Gettysburg Address Exhibit.* www.lcweb.loc.gov/ex-hibits/gadd (accessed on October 20, 1999).

Library of Congress, American Memory. *Selected Civil War Photographs.* lcweb2.loc.gov/ammem/cwphome.html (accessed on October 20, 1999).

Rutgers University Libraries. *Civil War Resources on the Internet.* http://www.libraries.rutgers.edu/rulib/socsci/hist/civwar-2.html (accessed on October 20, 1999).

Index

Note: *Italic* type indicates volume number; **boldface** indicates main entries and their page numbers; (ill.) indicates photos and illustrations.

M